C-3830 CAREER EXAMINATION SERIES

This is your
PASSBOOK for...

Associate Bookkeeper

Test Preparation Study Guide
Questions & Answers

COPYRIGHT NOTICE

This book is SOLELY intended for, is sold ONLY to, and its use is RESTRICTED to individual, bona fide applicants or candidates who qualify by virtue of having seriously filed applications for appropriate license, certificate, professional and/or promotional advancement, higher school matriculation, scholarship, or other legitimate requirements of education and/or governmental authorities.

This book is NOT intended for use, class instruction, tutoring, training, duplication, copying, reprinting, excerption, or adaptation, etc., by:

1) Other publishers
2) Proprietors and/or Instructors of "Coaching" and/or Preparatory Courses
3) Personnel and/or Training Divisions of commercial, industrial, and governmental organizations
4) Schools, colleges, or universities and/or their departments and staffs, including teachers and other personnel
5) Testing Agencies or Bureaus
6) Study groups which seek by the purchase of a single volume to copy and/or duplicate and/or adapt this material for use by the group as a whole without having purchased individual volumes for each of the members of the group
7) Et al.

Such persons would be in violation of appropriate Federal and State statutes.

PROVISION OF LICENSING AGREEMENTS – Recognized educational, commercial, industrial, and governmental institutions and organizations, and others legitimately engaged in educational pursuits, including training, testing, and measurement activities, may address request for a licensing agreement to the copyright owners, who will determine whether, and under what conditions, including fees and charges, the materials in this book may be used them. In other words, a licensing facility exists for the legitimate use of the material in this book on other than an individual basis. However, it is asseverated and affirmed here that the material in this book CANNOT be used without the receipt of the express permission of such a licensing agreement from the Publishers. Inquiries re licensing should be addressed to the company, attention rights and permissions department.

All rights reserved, including the right of reproduction in whole or in part, in any form or by any means, electronic or mechanical, including photocopying, recording, or by any information storage and retrieval system, without permission in writing from the Publisher.

Copyright © 2025 by
National Learning Corporation

212 Michael Drive, Syosset, NY 11791
(516) 921-8888 • www.passbooks.com
E-mail: info@passbooks.com

PASSBOOK® SERIES

THE *PASSBOOK® SERIES* has been created to prepare applicants and candidates for the ultimate academic battlefield – the examination room.

At some time in our lives, each and every one of us may be required to take an examination – for validation, matriculation, admission, qualification, registration, certification, or licensure.

Based on the assumption that every applicant or candidate has met the basic formal educational standards, has taken the required number of courses, and read the necessary texts, the *PASSBOOK® SERIES* furnishes the one special preparation which may assure passing with confidence, instead of failing with insecurity. Examination questions – together with answers – are furnished as the basic vehicle for study so that the mysteries of the examination and its compounding difficulties may be eliminated or diminished by a sure method.

This book is meant to help you pass your examination provided that you qualify and are serious in your objective.

The entire field is reviewed through the huge store of content information which is succinctly presented through a provocative and challenging approach – the question-and-answer method.

A climate of success is established by furnishing the correct answers at the end of each test.

You soon learn to recognize types of questions, forms of questions, and patterns of questioning. You may even begin to anticipate expected outcomes.

You perceive that many questions are repeated or adapted so that you can gain acute insights, which may enable you to score many sure points.

You learn how to confront new questions, or types of questions, and to attack them confidently and work out the correct answers.

You note objectives and emphases, and recognize pitfalls and dangers, so that you may make positive educational adjustments.

Moreover, you are kept fully informed in relation to new concepts, methods, practices, and directions in the field.

You discover that you are actually taking the examination all the time: you are preparing for the examination by "taking" an examination, not by reading extraneous and/or supererogatory textbooks.

In short, this PASSBOOK®, used directedly, should be an important factor in helping you to pass your test.

ASSOCIATE BOOKKEEPER

DUTIES
Associate Bookkeepers, under general supervision, with some latitude for independent initiative and judgment, perform responsible supervisory bookkeeping functions; and perform related work.

TEST
The multiple-choice test may include questions on examining, preparing and reviewing payment and revenue documentation; classifying accounting transactions; maintaining accounts; reconciling accounts; adjusting, reversing and closing account entries; summarizing and accumulating accounting data; preparing reports and forms; verification of data; payroll; concepts of employee supervision; standards of proper employee ethical conduct.

HOW TO TAKE A TEST

I. YOU MUST PASS AN EXAMINATION

A. *WHAT EVERY CANDIDATE SHOULD KNOW*

Examination applicants often ask us for help in preparing for the written test. What can I study in advance? What kinds of questions will be asked? How will the test be given? How will the papers be graded?

As an applicant for a civil service examination, you may be wondering about some of these things. Our purpose here is to suggest effective methods of advance study and to describe civil service examinations.

Your chances for success on this examination can be increased if you know how to prepare. Those "pre-examination jitters" can be reduced if you know what to expect. You can even experience an adventure in good citizenship if you know why civil service exams are given.

B. *WHY ARE CIVIL SERVICE EXAMINATIONS GIVEN?*

Civil service examinations are important to you in two ways. As a citizen, you want public jobs filled by employees who know how to do their work. As a job seeker, you want a fair chance to compete for that job on an equal footing with other candidates. The best-known means of accomplishing this two-fold goal is the competitive examination.

Exams are widely publicized throughout the nation. They may be administered for jobs in federal, state, city, municipal, town or village governments or agencies.

Any citizen may apply, with some limitations, such as the age or residence of applicants. Your experience and education may be reviewed to see whether you meet the requirements for the particular examination. When these requirements exist, they are reasonable and applied consistently to all applicants. Thus, a competitive examination may cause you some uneasiness now, but it is your privilege and safeguard.

C. *HOW ARE CIVIL SERVICE EXAMS DEVELOPED?*

Examinations are carefully written by trained technicians who are specialists in the field known as "psychological measurement," in consultation with recognized authorities in the field of work that the test will cover. These experts recommend the subject matter areas or skills to be tested; only those knowledges or skills important to your success on the job are included. The most reliable books and source materials available are used as references. Together, the experts and technicians judge the difficulty level of the questions.

Test technicians know how to phrase questions so that the problem is clearly stated. Their ethics do not permit "trick" or "catch" questions. Questions may have been tried out on sample groups, or subjected to statistical analysis, to determine their usefulness.

Written tests are often used in combination with performance tests, ratings of training and experience, and oral interviews. All of these measures combine to form the best-known means of finding the right person for the right job.

II. HOW TO PASS THE WRITTEN TEST

A. NATURE OF THE EXAMINATION

To prepare intelligently for civil service examinations, you should know how they differ from school examinations you have taken. In school you were assigned certain definite pages to read or subjects to cover. The examination questions were quite detailed and usually emphasized memory. Civil service exams, on the other hand, try to discover your present ability to perform the duties of a position, plus your potentiality to learn these duties. In other words, a civil service exam attempts to predict how successful you will be. Questions cover such a broad area that they cannot be as minute and detailed as school exam questions.

In the public service similar kinds of work, or positions, are grouped together in one "class." This process is known as *position-classification*. All the positions in a class are paid according to the salary range for that class. One class title covers all of these positions, and they are all tested by the same examination.

B. FOUR BASIC STEPS

1) Study the announcement

How, then, can you know what subjects to study? Our best answer is: "Learn as much as possible about the class of positions for which you've applied." The exam will test the knowledge, skills and abilities needed to do the work.

Your most valuable source of information about the position you want is the official exam announcement. This announcement lists the training and experience qualifications. Check these standards and apply only if you come reasonably close to meeting them.

The brief description of the position in the examination announcement offers some clues to the subjects which will be tested. Think about the job itself. Review the duties in your mind. Can you perform them, or are there some in which you are rusty? Fill in the blank spots in your preparation.

Many jurisdictions preview the written test in the exam announcement by including a section called "Knowledge and Abilities Required," "Scope of the Examination," or some similar heading. Here you will find out specifically what fields will be tested.

2) Review your own background

Once you learn in general what the position is all about, and what you need to know to do the work, ask yourself which subjects you already know fairly well and which need improvement. You may wonder whether to concentrate on improving your strong areas or on building some background in your fields of weakness. When the announcement has specified "some knowledge" or "considerable knowledge," or has used adjectives like "beginning principles of…" or "advanced … methods," you can get a clue as to the number and difficulty of questions to be asked in any given field. More questions, and hence broader coverage, would be included for those subjects which are more important in the work. Now weigh your strengths and weaknesses against the job requirements and prepare accordingly.

3) Determine the level of the position

Another way to tell how intensively you should prepare is to understand the level of the job for which you are applying. Is it the entering level? In other words, is this the position in which beginners in a field of work are hired? Or is it an intermediate or advanced level? Sometimes this is indicated by such words as "Junior" or "Senior" in the class title. Other jurisdictions use Roman numerals to designate the level – Clerk I, Clerk II, for example. The word "Supervisor" sometimes appears in the title. If the level is not indicated by the title, check the description of duties. Will you be working under very close supervision, or will you have responsibility for independent decisions in this work?

4) Choose appropriate study materials

Now that you know the subjects to be examined and the relative amount of each subject to be covered, you can choose suitable study materials. For beginning level jobs, or even advanced ones, if you have a pronounced weakness in some aspect of your training, read a modern, standard textbook in that field. Be sure it is up to date and has general coverage. Such books are normally available at your library, and the librarian will be glad to help you locate one. For entry-level positions, questions of appropriate difficulty are chosen — neither highly advanced questions, nor those too simple. Such questions require careful thought but not advanced training.

If the position for which you are applying is technical or advanced, you will read more advanced, specialized material. If you are already familiar with the basic principles of your field, elementary textbooks would waste your time. Concentrate on advanced textbooks and technical periodicals. Think through the concepts and review difficult problems in your field.

These are all general sources. You can get more ideas on your own initiative, following these leads. For example, training manuals and publications of the government agency which employs workers in your field can be useful, particularly for technical and professional positions. A letter or visit to the government department involved may result in more specific study suggestions, and certainly will provide you with a more definite idea of the exact nature of the position you are seeking.

III. KINDS OF TESTS

Tests are used for purposes other than measuring knowledge and ability to perform specified duties. For some positions, it is equally important to test ability to make adjustments to new situations or to profit from training. In others, basic mental abilities not dependent on information are essential. Questions which test these things may not appear as pertinent to the duties of the position as those which test for knowledge and information. Yet they are often highly important parts of a fair examination. For very general questions, it is almost impossible to help you direct your study efforts. What we can do is to point out some of the more common of these general abilities needed in public service positions and describe some typical questions.

1) General information

Broad, general information has been found useful for predicting job success in some kinds of work. This is tested in a variety of ways, from vocabulary lists to questions about current events. Basic background in some field of work, such as sociology or economics, may be sampled in a group of questions. Often these are principles which have become familiar to most persons through exposure rather than through formal training. It is difficult to advise you how to study for these questions; being alert to the world around you is our best suggestion.

2) Verbal ability

An example of an ability needed in many positions is verbal or language ability. Verbal ability is, in brief, the ability to use and understand words. Vocabulary and grammar tests are typical measures of this ability. Reading comprehension or paragraph interpretation questions are common in many kinds of civil service tests. You are given a paragraph of written material and asked to find its central meaning.

3) Numerical ability

Number skills can be tested by the familiar arithmetic problem, by checking paired lists of numbers to see which are alike and which are different, or by interpreting charts and graphs. In the latter test, a graph may be printed in the test booklet which you are asked to use as the basis for answering questions.

4) Observation

A popular test for law-enforcement positions is the observation test. A picture is shown to you for several minutes, then taken away. Questions about the picture test your ability to observe both details and larger elements.

5) Following directions

In many positions in the public service, the employee must be able to carry out written instructions dependably and accurately. You may be given a chart with several columns, each column listing a variety of information. The questions require you to carry out directions involving the information given in the chart.

6) Skills and aptitudes

Performance tests effectively measure some manual skills and aptitudes. When the skill is one in which you are trained, such as typing or shorthand, you can practice. These tests are often very much like those given in business school or high school courses. For many of the other skills and aptitudes, however, no short-time preparation can be made. Skills and abilities natural to you or that you have developed throughout your lifetime are being tested.

Many of the general questions just described provide all the data needed to answer the questions and ask you to use your reasoning ability to find the answers. Your best preparation for these tests, as well as for tests of facts and ideas, is to be at your physical and mental best. You, no doubt, have your own methods of getting into an exam-taking mood and keeping "in shape." The next section lists some ideas on this subject.

IV. KINDS OF QUESTIONS

Only rarely is the "essay" question, which you answer in narrative form, used in civil service tests. Civil service tests are usually of the short-answer type. Full instructions for answering these questions will be given to you at the examination. But in case this is your first experience with short-answer questions and separate answer sheets, here is what you need to know:

1) Multiple-choice Questions

Most popular of the short-answer questions is the "multiple choice" or "best answer" question. It can be used, for example, to test for factual knowledge, ability to solve problems or judgment in meeting situations found at work.

A multiple-choice question is normally one of three types—
- It can begin with an incomplete statement followed by several possible endings. You are to find the one ending which *best* completes the statement, although some of the others may not be entirely wrong.
- It can also be a complete statement in the form of a question which is answered by choosing one of the statements listed.

- It can be in the form of a problem – again you select the best answer.

Here is an example of a multiple-choice question with a discussion which should give you some clues as to the method for choosing the right answer:

When an employee has a complaint about his assignment, the action which will *best* help him overcome his difficulty is to
   A. discuss his difficulty with his coworkers
   B. take the problem to the head of the organization
   C. take the problem to the person who gave him the assignment
   D. say nothing to anyone about his complaint

In answering this question, you should study each of the choices to find which is best. Consider choice "A" – Certainly an employee may discuss his complaint with fellow employees, but no change or improvement can result, and the complaint remains unresolved. Choice "B" is a poor choice since the head of the organization probably does not know what assignment you have been given, and taking your problem to him is known as "going over the head" of the supervisor. The supervisor, or person who made the assignment, is the person who can clarify it or correct any injustice. Choice "C" is, therefore, correct. To say nothing, as in choice "D," is unwise. Supervisors have and interest in knowing the problems employees are facing, and the employee is seeking a solution to his problem.

2) True/False Questions

The "true/false" or "right/wrong" form of question is sometimes used. Here a complete statement is given. Your job is to decide whether the statement is right or wrong.

SAMPLE: A roaming cell-phone call to a nearby city costs less than a non-roaming call to a distant city.

This statement is wrong, or false, since roaming calls are more expensive.

This is not a complete list of all possible question forms, although most of the others are variations of these common types. You will always get complete directions for answering questions. Be sure you understand *how* to mark your answers – ask questions until you do.

V. RECORDING YOUR ANSWERS

Computer terminals are used more and more today for many different kinds of exams.
For an examination with very few applicants, you may be told to record your answers in the test booklet itself. Separate answer sheets are much more common. If this separate answer sheet is to be scored by machine – and this is often the case – it is highly important that you mark your answers correctly in order to get credit.
An electronic scoring machine is often used in civil service offices because of the speed with which papers can be scored. Machine-scored answer sheets must be marked with a pencil, which will be given to you. This pencil has a high graphite content which responds to the electronic scoring machine. As a matter of fact, stray dots may register as answers, so do not let your pencil rest on the answer sheet while you are pondering the correct answer. Also, if your pencil lead breaks or is otherwise defective, ask for another.

Since the answer sheet will be dropped in a slot in the scoring machine, be careful not to bend the corners or get the paper crumpled.

The answer sheet normally has five vertical columns of numbers, with 30 numbers to a column. These numbers correspond to the question numbers in your test booklet. After each number, going across the page are four or five pairs of dotted lines. These short dotted lines have small letters or numbers above them. The first two pairs may also have a "T" or "F" above the letters. This indicates that the first two pairs only are to be used if the questions are of the true-false type. If the questions are multiple choice, disregard the "T" and "F" and pay attention only to the small letters or numbers.

Answer your questions in the manner of the sample that follows:

32. The largest city in the United States is
   A. Washington, D.C.
   B. New York City
   C. Chicago
   D. Detroit
   E. San Francisco

1) Choose the answer you think is best. (New York City is the largest, so "B" is correct.)
2) Find the row of dotted lines numbered the same as the question you are answering. (Find row number 32)
3) Find the pair of dotted lines corresponding to the answer. (Find the pair of lines under the mark "B.")
4) Make a solid black mark between the dotted lines.

VI. BEFORE THE TEST

Common sense will help you find procedures to follow to get ready for an examination. Too many of us, however, overlook these sensible measures. Indeed, nervousness and fatigue have been found to be the most serious reasons why applicants fail to do their best on civil service tests. Here is a list of reminders:

- Begin your preparation early – Don't wait until the last minute to go scurrying around for books and materials or to find out what the position is all about.
- Prepare continuously – An hour a night for a week is better than an all-night cram session. This has been definitely established. What is more, a night a week for a month will return better dividends than crowding your study into a shorter period of time.
- Locate the place of the exam – You have been sent a notice telling you when and where to report for the examination. If the location is in a different town or otherwise unfamiliar to you, it would be well to inquire the best route and learn something about the building.
- Relax the night before the test – Allow your mind to rest. Do not study at all that night. Plan some mild recreation or diversion; then go to bed early and get a good night's sleep.
- Get up early enough to make a leisurely trip to the place for the test – This way unforeseen events, traffic snarls, unfamiliar buildings, etc. will not upset you.
- Dress comfortably – A written test is not a fashion show. You will be known by number and not by name, so wear something comfortable.

- Leave excess paraphernalia at home – Shopping bags and odd bundles will get in your way. You need bring only the items mentioned in the official notice you received; usually everything you need is provided. Do not bring reference books to the exam. They will only confuse those last minutes and be taken away from you when in the test room.
- Arrive somewhat ahead of time – If because of transportation schedules you must get there very early, bring a newspaper or magazine to take your mind off yourself while waiting.
- Locate the examination room – When you have found the proper room, you will be directed to the seat or part of the room where you will sit. Sometimes you are given a sheet of instructions to read while you are waiting. Do not fill out any forms until you are told to do so; just read them and be prepared.
- Relax and prepare to listen to the instructions
- If you have any physical problem that may keep you from doing your best, be sure to tell the test administrator. If you are sick or in poor health, you really cannot do your best on the exam. You can come back and take the test some other time.

VII. AT THE TEST

The day of the test is here and you have the test booklet in your hand. The temptation to get going is very strong. Caution! There is more to success than knowing the right answers. You must know how to identify your papers and understand variations in the type of short-answer question used in this particular examination. Follow these suggestions for maximum results from your efforts:

1) Cooperate with the monitor

The test administrator has a duty to create a situation in which you can be as much at ease as possible. He will give instructions, tell you when to begin, check to see that you are marking your answer sheet correctly, and so on. He is not there to guard you, although he will see that your competitors do not take unfair advantage. He wants to help you do your best.

2) Listen to all instructions

Don't jump the gun! Wait until you understand all directions. In most civil service tests you get more time than you need to answer the questions. So don't be in a hurry. Read each word of instructions until you clearly understand the meaning. Study the examples, listen to all announcements and follow directions. Ask questions if you do not understand what to do.

3) Identify your papers

Civil service exams are usually identified by number only. You will be assigned a number; you must not put your name on your test papers. Be sure to copy your number correctly. Since more than one exam may be given, copy your exact examination title.

4) Plan your time

Unless you are told that a test is a "speed" or "rate of work" test, speed itself is usually not important. Time enough to answer all the questions will be provided, but this does not mean that you have all day. An overall time limit has been set. Divide the total time (in minutes) by the number of questions to determine the approximate time you have for each question.

5) Do not linger over difficult questions

If you come across a difficult question, mark it with a paper clip (useful to have along) and come back to it when you have been through the booklet. One caution if you do this – be sure to skip a number on your answer sheet as well. Check often to be sure that you have not lost your place and that you are marking in the row numbered the same as the question you are answering.

6) Read the questions

Be sure you know what the question asks! Many capable people are unsuccessful because they failed to *read* the questions correctly.

7) Answer all questions

Unless you have been instructed that a penalty will be deducted for incorrect answers, it is better to guess than to omit a question.

8) Speed tests

It is often better NOT to guess on speed tests. It has been found that on timed tests people are tempted to spend the last few seconds before time is called in marking answers at random – without even reading them – in the hope of picking up a few extra points. To discourage this practice, the instructions may warn you that your score will be "corrected" for guessing. That is, a penalty will be applied. The incorrect answers will be deducted from the correct ones, or some other penalty formula will be used.

9) Review your answers

If you finish before time is called, go back to the questions you guessed or omitted to give them further thought. Review other answers if you have time.

10) Return your test materials

If you are ready to leave before others have finished or time is called, take ALL your materials to the monitor and leave quietly. Never take any test material with you. The monitor can discover whose papers are not complete, and taking a test booklet may be grounds for disqualification.

VIII. EXAMINATION TECHNIQUES

1) Read the general instructions carefully. These are usually printed on the first page of the exam booklet. As a rule, these instructions refer to the timing of the examination; the fact that you should not start work until the signal and must stop work at a signal, etc. If there are any *special* instructions, such as a choice of questions to be answered, make sure that you note this instruction carefully.

2) When you are ready to start work on the examination, that is as soon as the signal has been given, read the instructions to each question booklet, underline any key words or phrases, such as *least, best, outline, describe* and the like. In this way you will tend to answer as requested rather than discover on reviewing your paper that you *listed without describing*, that you selected the *worst* choice rather than the *best* choice, etc.

3) If the examination is of the objective or multiple-choice type – that is, each question will also give a series of possible answers: A, B, C or D, and you are called upon to select the best answer and write the letter next to that answer on your answer paper – it is advisable to start answering each question in turn. There may be anywhere from 50 to 100 such questions in the three or four hours allotted and you can see how much time would be taken if you read through all the questions before beginning to answer any. Furthermore, if you come across a question or group of questions which you know would be difficult to answer, it would undoubtedly affect your handling of all the other questions.

4) If the examination is of the essay type and contains but a few questions, it is a moot point as to whether you should read all the questions before starting to answer any one. Of course, if you are given a choice – say five out of seven and the like – then it is essential to read all the questions so you can eliminate the two that are most difficult. If, however, you are asked to answer all the questions, there may be danger in trying to answer the easiest one first because you may find that you will spend too much time on it. The best technique is to answer the first question, then proceed to the second, etc.

5) Time your answers. Before the exam begins, write down the time it started, then add the time allowed for the examination and write down the time it must be completed, then divide the time available somewhat as follows:
   - If 3-1/2 hours are allowed, that would be 210 minutes. If you have 80 objective-type questions, that would be an average of 2-1/2 minutes per question. Allow yourself no more than 2 minutes per question, or a total of 160 minutes, which will permit about 50 minutes to review.
   - If for the time allotment of 210 minutes there are 7 essay questions to answer, that would average about 30 minutes a question. Give yourself only 25 minutes per question so that you have about 35 minutes to review.

6) The most important instruction is to *read each question* and make sure you know what is wanted. The second most important instruction is to *time yourself properly* so that you answer every question. The third most important instruction is to *answer every question*. Guess if you have to but include something for each question. Remember that you will receive no credit for a blank and will probably receive some credit if you write something in answer to an essay question. If you guess a letter – say "B" for a multiple-choice question – you may have guessed right. If you leave a blank as an answer to a multiple-choice question, the examiners may respect your feelings but it will not add a point to your score. Some exams may penalize you for wrong answers, so in such cases *only*, you may not want to guess unless you have some basis for your answer.

7) Suggestions
   a. Objective-type questions
      1. Examine the question booklet for proper sequence of pages and questions
      2. Read all instructions carefully
      3. Skip any question which seems too difficult; return to it after all other questions have been answered
      4. Apportion your time properly; do not spend too much time on any single question or group of questions

5. Note and underline key words – *all, most, fewest, least, best, worst, same, opposite,* etc.
6. Pay particular attention to negatives
7. Note unusual option, e.g., unduly long, short, complex, different or similar in content to the body of the question
8. Observe the use of "hedging" words – *probably, may, most likely,* etc.
9. Make sure that your answer is put next to the same number as the question
10. Do not second-guess unless you have good reason to believe the second answer is definitely more correct
11. Cross out original answer if you decide another answer is more accurate; do not erase until you are ready to hand your paper in
12. Answer all questions; guess unless instructed otherwise
13. Leave time for review

b. Essay questions
1. Read each question carefully
2. Determine exactly what is wanted. Underline key words or phrases.
3. Decide on outline or paragraph answer
4. Include many different points and elements unless asked to develop any one or two points or elements
5. Show impartiality by giving pros and cons unless directed to select one side only
6. Make and write down any assumptions you find necessary to answer the questions
7. Watch your English, grammar, punctuation and choice of words
8. Time your answers; don't crowd material

8) Answering the essay question

Most essay questions can be answered by framing the specific response around several key words or ideas. Here are a few such key words or ideas:

M's: manpower, materials, methods, money, management
P's: purpose, program, policy, plan, procedure, practice, problems, pitfalls, personnel, public relations

a. Six basic steps in handling problems:
1. Preliminary plan and background development
2. Collect information, data and facts
3. Analyze and interpret information, data and facts
4. Analyze and develop solutions as well as make recommendations
5. Prepare report and sell recommendations
6. Install recommendations and follow up effectiveness

b. Pitfalls to avoid
1. *Taking things for granted* – A statement of the situation does not necessarily imply that each of the elements is necessarily true; for example, a complaint may be invalid and biased so that all that can be taken for granted is that a complaint has been registered

2. *Considering only one side of a situation* – Wherever possible, indicate several alternatives and then point out the reasons you selected the best one
3. *Failing to indicate follow up* – Whenever your answer indicates action on your part, make certain that you will take proper follow-up action to see how successful your recommendations, procedures or actions turn out to be
4. *Taking too long in answering any single question* – Remember to time your answers properly

IX. AFTER THE TEST

Scoring procedures differ in detail among civil service jurisdictions although the general principles are the same. Whether the papers are hand-scored or graded by machine we have described, they are nearly always graded by number. That is, the person who marks the paper knows only the number – never the name – of the applicant. Not until all the papers have been graded will they be matched with names. If other tests, such as training and experience or oral interview ratings have been given, scores will be combined. Different parts of the examination usually have different weights. For example, the written test might count 60 percent of the final grade, and a rating of training and experience 40 percent. In many jurisdictions, veterans will have a certain number of points added to their grades.

After the final grade has been determined, the names are placed in grade order and an eligible list is established. There are various methods for resolving ties between those who get the same final grade – probably the most common is to place first the name of the person whose application was received first. Job offers are made from the eligible list in the order the names appear on it. You will be notified of your grade and your rank as soon as all these computations have been made. This will be done as rapidly as possible.

People who are found to meet the requirements in the announcement are called "eligibles." Their names are put on a list of eligible candidates. An eligible's chances of getting a job depend on how high he stands on this list and how fast agencies are filling jobs from the list.

When a job is to be filled from a list of eligibles, the agency asks for the names of people on the list of eligibles for that job. When the civil service commission receives this request, it sends to the agency the names of the three people highest on this list. Or, if the job to be filled has specialized requirements, the office sends the agency the names of the top three persons who meet these requirements from the general list.

The appointing officer makes a choice from among the three people whose names were sent to him. If the selected person accepts the appointment, the names of the others are put back on the list to be considered for future openings.

That is the rule in hiring from all kinds of eligible lists, whether they are for typist, carpenter, chemist, or something else. For every vacancy, the appointing officer has his choice of any one of the top three eligibles on the list. This explains why the person whose name is on top of the list sometimes does not get an appointment when some of the persons lower on the list do. If the appointing officer chooses the second or third eligible, the No. 1 eligible does not get a job at once, but stays on the list until he is appointed or the list is terminated.

X. HOW TO PASS THE INTERVIEW TEST

The examination for which you applied requires an oral interview test. You have already taken the written test and you are now being called for the interview test – the final part of the formal examination.

You may think that it is not possible to prepare for an interview test and that there are no procedures to follow during an interview. Our purpose is to point out some things you can do in advance that will help you and some good rules to follow and pitfalls to avoid while you are being interviewed.

What is an interview supposed to test?

The written examination is designed to test the technical knowledge and competence of the candidate; the oral is designed to evaluate intangible qualities, not readily measured otherwise, and to establish a list showing the relative fitness of each candidate – as measured against his competitors – for the position sought. Scoring is not on the basis of "right" and "wrong," but on a sliding scale of values ranging from "not passable" to "outstanding." As a matter of fact, it is possible to achieve a relatively low score without a single "incorrect" answer because of evident weakness in the qualities being measured.

Occasionally, an examination may consist entirely of an oral test – either an individual or a group oral. In such cases, information is sought concerning the technical knowledges and abilities of the candidate, since there has been no written examination for this purpose. More commonly, however, an oral test is used to supplement a written examination.

Who conducts interviews?

The composition of oral boards varies among different jurisdictions. In nearly all, a representative of the personnel department serves as chairman. One of the members of the board may be a representative of the department in which the candidate would work. In some cases, "outside experts" are used, and, frequently, a businessman or some other representative of the general public is asked to serve. Labor and management or other special groups may be represented. The aim is to secure the services of experts in the appropriate field.

However the board is composed, it is a good idea (and not at all improper or unethical) to ascertain in advance of the interview who the members are and what groups they represent. When you are introduced to them, you will have some idea of their backgrounds and interests, and at least you will not stutter and stammer over their names.

What should be done before the interview?

While knowledge about the board members is useful and takes some of the surprise element out of the interview, there is other preparation which is more substantive. It *is* possible to prepare for an oral interview – in several ways:

1) Keep a copy of your application and review it carefully before the interview

This may be the only document before the oral board, and the starting point of the interview. Know what education and experience you have listed there, and the sequence and dates of all of it. Sometimes the board will ask you to review the highlights of your experience for them; you should not have to hem and haw doing it.

2) Study the class specification and the examination announcement

Usually, the oral board has one or both of these to guide them. The qualities, characteristics or knowledges required by the position sought are stated in these documents. They offer valuable clues as to the nature of the oral interview. For example, if the job involves supervisory responsibilities, the announcement will usually indicate that knowledge of modern supervisory methods and the qualifications of the candidate as a supervisor will be tested. If so, you can expect such questions, frequently in the form of a hypothetical situation which you are expected to solve. NEVER go into an oral without knowledge of the duties and responsibilities of the job you seek.

3) Think through each qualification required

Try to visualize the kind of questions you would ask if you were a board member. How well could you answer them? Try especially to appraise your own knowledge and background in each area, *measured against the job sought*, and identify any areas in which you are weak. Be critical and realistic – do not flatter yourself.

4) Do some general reading in areas in which you feel you may be weak

For example, if the job involves supervision and your past experience has NOT, some general reading in supervisory methods and practices, particularly in the field of human relations, might be useful. Do NOT study agency procedures or detailed manuals. The oral board will be testing your understanding and capacity, not your memory.

5) Get a good night's sleep and watch your general health and mental attitude

You will want a clear head at the interview. Take care of a cold or any other minor ailment, and of course, no hangovers.

What should be done on the day of the interview?

Now comes the day of the interview itself. Give yourself plenty of time to get there. Plan to arrive somewhat ahead of the scheduled time, particularly if your appointment is in the fore part of the day. If a previous candidate fails to appear, the board might be ready for you a bit early. By early afternoon an oral board is almost invariably behind schedule if there are many candidates, and you may have to wait. Take along a book or magazine to read, or your application to review, but leave any extraneous material in the waiting room when you go in for your interview. In any event, relax and compose yourself.

The matter of dress is important. The board is forming impressions about you – from your experience, your manners, your attitude, and your appearance. Give your personal appearance careful attention. Dress your best, but not your flashiest. Choose conservative, appropriate clothing, and be sure it is immaculate. This is a business interview, and your appearance should indicate that you regard it as such. Besides, being well groomed and properly dressed will help boost your confidence.

Sooner or later, someone will call your name and escort you into the interview room. *This is it.* From here on you are on your own. It is too late for any more preparation. But remember, you asked for this opportunity to prove your fitness, and you are here because your request was granted.

What happens when you go in?

The usual sequence of events will be as follows: The clerk (who is often the board stenographer) will introduce you to the chairman of the oral board, who will introduce you to the other members of the board. Acknowledge the introductions before you sit down. Do not be surprised if you find a microphone facing you or a stenotypist sitting by. Oral interviews are usually recorded in the event of an appeal or other review.

Usually the chairman of the board will open the interview by reviewing the highlights of your education and work experience from your application – primarily for the benefit of the other members of the board, as well as to get the material into the record. Do not interrupt or comment unless there is an error or significant misinterpretation; if that is the case, do not hesitate. But do not quibble about insignificant matters. Also, he will usually ask you some question about your education, experience or your present job – partly to get you to start talking and to establish the interviewing "rapport." He may start the actual questioning, or turn it over to one of the other members. Frequently, each member undertakes the questioning on a particular area, one in which he is perhaps most competent, so you can expect each member to participate in the examination. Because time is limited, you may also expect some rather abrupt switches in the direction the questioning takes, so do not be upset by it. Normally, a board member will not pursue a single line of questioning unless he discovers a particular strength or weakness.

After each member has participated, the chairman will usually ask whether any member has any further questions, then will ask you if you have anything you wish to add. Unless you are expecting this question, it may floor you. Worse, it may start you off on an extended, extemporaneous speech. The board is not usually seeking more information. The question is principally to offer you a last opportunity to present further qualifications or to indicate that you have nothing to add. So, if you feel that a significant qualification or characteristic has been overlooked, it is proper to point it out in a sentence or so. Do not compliment the board on the thoroughness of their examination – they have been sketchy, and you know it. If you wish, merely say, "No thank you, I have nothing further to add." This is a point where you can "talk yourself out" of a good impression or fail to present an important bit of information. Remember, *you close the interview yourself*.

The chairman will then say, "That is all, Mr. _____, thank you." Do not be startled; the interview is over, and quicker than you think. Thank him, gather your belongings and take your leave. Save your sigh of relief for the other side of the door.

How to put your best foot forward

Throughout this entire process, you may feel that the board individually and collectively is trying to pierce your defenses, seek out your hidden weaknesses and embarrass and confuse you. Actually, this is not true. They are obliged to make an appraisal of your qualifications for the job you are seeking, and they want to see you in your best light. Remember, they must interview all candidates and a non-cooperative candidate may become a failure in spite of their best efforts to bring out his qualifications. Here are 15 suggestions that will help you:

1) Be natural – Keep your attitude confident, not cocky

If you are not confident that you can do the job, do not expect the board to be. Do not apologize for your weaknesses, try to bring out your strong points. The board is interested in a positive, not negative, presentation. Cockiness will antagonize any board member and make him wonder if you are covering up a weakness by a false show of strength.

2) Get comfortable, but don't lounge or sprawl

Sit erectly but not stiffly. A careless posture may lead the board to conclude that you are careless in other things, or at least that you are not impressed by the importance of the occasion. Either conclusion is natural, even if incorrect. Do not fuss with your clothing, a pencil or an ashtray. Your hands may occasionally be useful to emphasize a point; do not let them become a point of distraction.

3) Do not wisecrack or make small talk

This is a serious situation, and your attitude should show that you consider it as such. Further, the time of the board is limited – they do not want to waste it, and neither should you.

4) Do not exaggerate your experience or abilities
    In the first place, from information in the application or other interviews and sources, the board may know more about you than you think. Secondly, you probably will not get away with it. An experienced board is rather adept at spotting such a situation, so do not take the chance.

5) If you know a board member, do not make a point of it, yet do not hide it
    Certainly you are not fooling him, and probably not the other members of the board. Do not try to take advantage of your acquaintanceship – it will probably do you little good.

6) Do not dominate the interview
    Let the board do that. They will give you the clues – do not assume that you have to do all the talking. Realize that the board has a number of questions to ask you, and do not try to take up all the interview time by showing off your extensive knowledge of the answer to the first one.

7) Be attentive
    You only have 20 minutes or so, and you should keep your attention at its sharpest throughout. When a member is addressing a problem or question to you, give him your undivided attention. Address your reply principally to him, but do not exclude the other board members.

8) Do not interrupt
    A board member may be stating a problem for you to analyze. He will ask you a question when the time comes. Let him state the problem, and wait for the question.

9) Make sure you understand the question
    Do not try to answer until you are sure what the question is. If it is not clear, restate it in your own words or ask the board member to clarify it for you. However, do not haggle about minor elements.

10) Reply promptly but not hastily
    A common entry on oral board rating sheets is "candidate responded readily," or "candidate hesitated in replies." Respond as promptly and quickly as you can, but do not jump to a hasty, ill-considered answer.

11) Do not be peremptory in your answers
    A brief answer is proper – but do not fire your answer back. That is a losing game from your point of view. The board member can probably ask questions much faster than you can answer them.

12) Do not try to create the answer you think the board member wants
    He is interested in what kind of mind you have and how it works – not in playing games. Furthermore, he can usually spot this practice and will actually grade you down on it.

13) Do not switch sides in your reply merely to agree with a board member
    Frequently, a member will take a contrary position merely to draw you out and to see if you are willing and able to defend your point of view. Do not start a debate, yet do not surrender a good position. If a position is worth taking, it is worth defending.

14) Do not be afraid to admit an error in judgment if you are shown to be wrong

The board knows that you are forced to reply without any opportunity for careful consideration. Your answer may be demonstrably wrong. If so, admit it and get on with the interview.

15) Do not dwell at length on your present job

The opening question may relate to your present assignment. Answer the question but do not go into an extended discussion. You are being examined for a *new* job, not your present one. As a matter of fact, try to phrase ALL your answers in terms of the job for which you are being examined.

Basis of Rating

Probably you will forget most of these "do's" and "don'ts" when you walk into the oral interview room. Even remembering them all will not ensure you a passing grade. Perhaps you did not have the qualifications in the first place. But remembering them will help you to put your best foot forward, without treading on the toes of the board members.

Rumor and popular opinion to the contrary notwithstanding, an oral board wants you to make the best appearance possible. They know you are under pressure – but they also want to see how you respond to it as a guide to what your reaction would be under the pressures of the job you seek. They will be influenced by the degree of poise you display, the personal traits you show and the manner in which you respond.

ABOUT THIS BOOK

This book contains tests divided into Examination Sections. Go through each test, answering every question in the margin. We have also attached a sample answer sheet at the back of the book that can be removed and used. At the end of each test look at the answer key and check your answers. On the ones you got wrong, look at the right answer choice and learn. Do not fill in the answers first. Do not memorize the questions and answers, but understand the answer and principles involved. On your test, the questions will likely be different from the samples. Questions are changed and new ones added. If you understand these past questions you should have success with any changes that arise. Tests may consist of several types of questions. We have additional books on each subject should more study be advisable or necessary for you. Finally, the more you study, the better prepared you will be. This book is intended to be the last thing you study before you walk into the examination room. Prior study of relevant texts is also recommended. NLC publishes some of these in our Fundamental Series. Knowledge and good sense are important factors in passing your exam. Good luck also helps. So now study this Passbook, absorb the material contained within and take that knowledge into the examination. Then do your best to pass that exam.

EXAMINATION SECTION

EXAMINATION SECTION

TEST 1

DIRECTIONS: Each question or incomplete statement is followed by several suggested answers or completions. Select the one that BEST answers the question or completes the statement. *PRINT THE LETTER OF THE CORRECT ANSWER IN THE SPACE AT THE RIGHT.*

Questions 1-5.

DIRECTIONS: Questions 1 through 5 are to be answered on the basis of the extracts from Federal income tax withholding and Social Security tax tables shown below. These tables indicate the amounts which must be withheld from the employee's salary by his employer for Federal income tax and for Social Security. They are based on weekly earnings.

INCOME TAX WITHHOLDING TABLE							
The wages are		And the number of withholding allowances is					
At Least	But Less Than	5	6	7	8	9	10 or More
		The amount of income tax to be withheld shall be					
$300	$320	$24.60	$19.00	$13.80	$ 8.60	$4.00	$ 0
320	340	28.80	22.80	17.40	12.20	7.00	2.80
340	360	33.00	27.00	21.00	15.80	10.60	5.60
360	380	37.20	31.20	25.20	19.40	14.20	9.00
380	400	41.40	34.40	29.40	23.40	17.80	12.60
400	420	45.60	39.60	33.60	27.60	21.40	16.20
420	440	49.80	43.80	37.80	31.80	25.60	19.80
440	460	54.00	48.00	42.00	36.00	29.80	23.80
460	480	58.20	52.20	46.20	40.20	34.00	38.00
480	500	62.40	46.40	40.40	44.40	38.20	32.20

SOCIAL SECURITY TABLE					
WAGES			WAGES		
At Least	But Less Than	Tax to be Withheld	At Least	But Less Than	Tax to be Withheld
$333.18	$333.52	$19.50	$336.60	$336.94	$19.70
333.52	333.86	19.52	336.94	337.28	19.72
333.86	334.20	19.54	337.28	337.62	19.74
334.20	334.54	19.56	337.62	337.96	19.76
334.54	334.88	19.58	337.96	338.30	19.78
334.88	335.22	19.60	338.30	338.64	19.80
335.22	335.56	19.62	338.64	338.98	19.82
335.56	335.90	19.64	338.98	339.32	19.84
335.90	336.24	19.66	339.32	339.66	19.86
336.24	336.60	19.68	339.66	340.00	19.88

1. If an employee has a weekly wage of $379.50 and claims 6 withholding allowances, the amount of income tax to be withheld is
   A. $27.00   B. $31.20   C. $35.40   D. $37.20

2. An employee had wages of $335.60 for one week.
   With eight withholding allowances claimed, how much income tax will be withheld from his salary?
   A. $8.60   B. $12.00   C. $13.80   D. $17.40

3. How much social security tax will an employee with weekly wages of $335.60 pay?
   A. $19.60   B. $19.62   C. $19.64   D. $19.66

4. Mr. Wise earns $339.80 a week and claims seven withholding allowances.
   What is his take-home pay after income tax and social security tax are deducted?
   A. $300.32   B. $302.52   C. $319.92   D. $322.40

5. If an employee pays $19.74 in social security tax and claims eight withholding allowances, the amount of income tax that should be withheld from his wages is
   A. $8.60   B. $12.20   C. $13.80   D. $15.80

6. A fundamental rule of bookkeeping states that an individual's assets equal his liabilities plus his proprietorship (ASSETS = LIABILITIES − PROPRIETORSHIP).
   Which of the following statements logically follows from this rule?
   A. ASSETS = PROPRIETORSHIP − LIABILITIES
   B. LIABILITIES = ASSETS + PROPRIETORSHIP
   C. PROPRIETORSHIP = ASSETS − LIABILITIES
   D. PROPRIETORSHIP = LIABILITIES + ASSETS

7. Mr. Martin's assets consist of the following:
   Cash on Hand: $5,233.74
   Furniture: $4,925.00
   Government Bonds: $5,500.00
   What are his TOTAL assets?
   A. $10,158.74 $10,425.00   C. $10,733.74   D. $15,658.74

8. If Mr. Mitchell has $627.04 in his checking account and then writes three checks for $241.74, $13.24, and $101.97, what will be his new balance?
   A. $257.88   B. $269.08   C. $357.96   D. $368.96

9. An employee's net pay is equal to his total earnings less all deductions.
   If an employee's total earnings in a pay period are $497.05, what is his NET pay if he has the following deductions: Federal income tax, $90.32; FICA: $28.74; State tax: $18.79; City tax: $7.25; Pension: $1.88?
   A. $351.17   B. $351.07   C. $350.17   D. $350.07

10. A petty cash fund had an opening balance of $85.75 on December 1. Expenditures of $23.00, $15.65, $5.23, $14.75, and $26.38 were made out of his fund during the first 14 days of the month. Then, on December 17, another $38.50 was added to the fund.
If additional expenditures of $17.18, $3.29, and $11.64 were made during the remainder of the month, what was the FINAL balance of the petty cash fund at the end of December?

10.____

    A. $6.93   B. $7.13   C. $46.51   D. $91.40

Questions 11-15.

DIRECTIONS: Questions 11 through 15 are to be answered on the basis of the following instructions.

The chart below is used by the loan division of a city retirement system for the following purposes: (1) to calculate the monthly payment a member must pay on an outstanding loan; (2) to calculate how much a member owes on an outstanding loan after he has made a number of payments.

To calculate the amount a member must pay each month in repaying his loan, look at Column II on the chart. You will notice that each entry in Column II corresponds to a number appearing under the *Months* column; for example, 1.004868 corresponds to 1 month, 0.503654 corresponds to 2 months, etc. To calculate the amount a member must pay each month, use the following procedure: multiply the amount of the load by the entry in Column II which corresponds to the number of months over which the load will be paid back. For example, if a loan of $200 is taken out for six months, multiply $200 by 0.169518, the entry in Column II which corresponds to six months.

In order to calculate the balance still owed on an outstanding loan, multiply the monthly payment by the number in Column I which corresponds to the number of monthly payments which remain to be paid on the loan. For example, if a member is supposed to pay $106.00 a month for twelve months, after seven payments, five monthly payments remain. To calculate the balance owed on the loan at this point, multiply the $106.00 monthly payment by 4.927807, the number in Column I that corresponds to five months.

Months	Column I	Column II
1	0.995156	1.004868
2	1.985491	0.503654
3	2.971029	0.336584
4	3.951793	0.253050
5	4.927807	0.202930
6	5.899092	0.169518
7	6.865673	0.145652
8	7.827572	0.127754
9	8.784811	0.113833
10	9.737414	0.102697
11	10.685402	0.093586
12	11.628798	0.085994
13	12.567624	0.079570
14	13.501902	0.074064
15	14.431655	0.069292

11. If Mr. Carson borrows $1,500 for eight months, how much will he have to pay back each month?
    A. $187.16   B. $191.63   C. $208.72   D. $218.65

12. If a member borrows $2,400 for one year, the amount he will have to pay back each month is
    A. $118.78   B. $196.18   C. $202.28   D. $206.38

13. Mr. Elliott borrowed $1,700 for a period of fifteen months. Each month he will have to pay back
    A. $117.80   B. $116.96   C. $107.79   D. $101.79

14. Mr. Aylward is paying back a thirteen-month loan at the rate of $173.13 a month.
If he has already made six monthly payments, how much does he owe on the outstanding loan?
    A. $1,027.38   B. $1,178.75   C. $1,188.65   D. $1,898.85

15. A loan was taken out for 15 months, and the monthly payment was $104.75. After two monthly payments, how much was still owed on this load?
    A. $515.79   B. $863.89   C. $1,116.76   D. $1,316.46

16. The ABC Corporation had a gross income of $125,500.00 in 2015. Of this, it paid 60% for overhead.
If the gross income for 2016 increased by $6,500 and the cost of overhead increased to 61% of gross income, how much more did it pay for overhead in 2016 than in 2015?
    A. $1,320   B. $5,220   C. $7,530   D. $8,052

17. After one year, Mr. Richards paid back a total of $1,695.00 as payment for 17.____
a $1,500.00 loan. All the money paid over $1,500.00 was simple interest.
The interest charge was MOST NEARLY
   A. 13%   B. 11%   C. 9%   D. 7%

18. A checking account has a balance of $253.36. 18.____
If deposits of $36.95, $210.23, and $7.34 and withdrawals of $117.35, $23.37,
and $15.98 are made, what is the NEW balance of the account?
   A. $155.54   B. $351.18   C. $364.58   D. $664.58

19. In 2015, the W Realty Company spent 27% of its income on rent. 19.____
If it earned $97,254.00 in 2015, the amount it paid for rent was
   A. $26.258.58   B. $26,348.58   C. $27,248.58   D. $27,358.58

20. Six percent simple annual interest on $2,436.18 is MOST NEARLY 20.____
   A. $145.08   B. $145.17   c. $146.08   D. $146.17

21. Assume that the XYZ Company has $10,402.72 cash on hand. 21.____
If it pays $699.83 of this for rent, the amount of cash on hand would be
   A. $9,792.89   B. $9,702.89   C. $9,692.89   D. $9,602.89

22. On January 31, Mr. Warren's checking account had a balance of $933.68. 22.____
If he deposited $36.40 on February 2, $126.00 on February 9, and $90.02 on
February 16 and wrote no checks during this period, what was the balance of his
account on February 17?
   A. $680.26   B. $681.26   C. $1,186.10   D. $1,187.00

23. Multiplying a number by .75 is the same as 23.____
   A. multiplying it by 2/3   B. dividing it by 2/3
   C. multiplying it by 3/4   D. dividing it by 3/4

24. In City Agency A, 2/3 of the employees are enrolled in a retirement system. 24.____
City Agency B has the same number of employees as Agency A, and 60% of
these are enrolled in a retirement system.
If Agency A has a total of 660 employees, how many MORE employees does it
have enrolled in a retirement system than does Agency B?
   B. 36   B. 44   C. 56   D. 66

25. Net Worth is equal to Assets minus Liabilities. 25.____
If, at the end of year, a textile company had assets of $98,695.83 and liabilities of
$59,238.29, what was its net worth?
   A. $38,478.54   B. $38,488.64   C. $39,457.54   D. $48,557.54

KEY (CORRECT ANSWERS)

1. B
2. B
3. C
4. B
5. B

6. C
7. D
8. B
9. D
10. B

11. B
12. D
13. A
14. C
15. D

16. B
17. A
18. B
19. A
20. D

21. B
22. C
23. C
24. B
25. C

TEST 2

DIRECTIONS: Each question or incomplete statement is followed by several suggested answers or completions. Select the one that BEST answers the question or completes the statement. *PRINT THE LETTER OF THE CORRECT ANSWER IN THE SPACE AT THE RIGHT.*

Questions 1-10.

DIRECTIONS: Questions 1 through 10 below present the identification numbers, initials, and last names of employees enrolled in a city retirement system. You are to choose the option (A, B, C, or D) that has the IDENTICAL identification number, initials, and last name as those given in each question.

Sample Question
B145698 JL Jones
    A.   B146798 JL Jones   B. B145698 JL Jonas
    C.   P145698 JL Jones   D. B145698 JL Jones

The correct answer is D. Only Option D shows the identification number, initials, and last name exactly as they are in the sample question. Options A, B, and C have errors in the identification number or last name.

1. J297483 PL Robinson
   - A. J294783 PL Robinson
   - B. J297483 PL Robinson
   - C. J297483 Pl Robinson
   - D. J297843 PL Robinson

2. S497662 JG Schwartz
   - B. S497662 JG Schwarz
   - B. S497762 JG Schwartz
   - C. S497662 JG Schwartz
   - D. S497663 JG Schwartz

3. G696436 LN Alberton
   - A. G696436 LM Alberton
   - B. G696436 LN Albertson
   - C. G696346 LN Albertson
   - D. G696436 LN Alberton

4. R774923 AD Aldrich
   - A. R774923 AD Aldrich
   - B. R744923 AD Aldrich
   - C. R774932 AP Aldrich
   - D. R774932 AD Allrich

5. N239638 RP Hrynyk
   - A. N236938 PR Hrynyk
   - B. N236938 RP Hrynyk
   - C. N239638 PR Hrynyk
   - D. N239638 Hrynyk

6. R156949 LT Carlson
   - A. R156949 LT Carlton
   - B. R156494 LT Carlson
   - C. R159649 LT Carlton
   - D. R156949 LT Carlson

7. T524697 MN Orenstein
   - A. T524697 MN Orenstein
   - B. T524967 MN Orinstein
   - C. T524697 NM Ornstein
   - D. T524967 NM Orenstein

8. L346239 JD Remsen
   A. L346239 JD Remson
   B. L364239 JD Remsen
   C. L346329 JD Remsen
   D. L346239 JD Remsen

9. P966438 SB Rieperson
   A. P996438 SB Rieperson
   B. P466438 SB Reiperson
   C. R996438 SB Rieperson
   D. P966438 SB Rieperson

10. D749382 CD Thompson
    A. P749382 CD Thompson
    B. D749832 CD Thomsonn
    C. D749382 CD Thompson
    D. D749823 CD Thomspon

Questions 11-20.

DIRECTIONS: Assume that each of the capital letters in the table below represents the name of an employee enrolled in the city's employees' personnel system. The number directly beneath the letter represents the agency for which the employee works, and the small letter directly beneath represents the code for the employee's account.

Name of Employee	L	O	T	Q	A	M	R	N	C
Agency	3	4	5	9	8	7	2	1	6
Account Code	r	f	b	i	d	t	g	e	n

In each of the following Questions 11 through 20, the agency code numbers and the account code letters in Columns 2 and 3 should correspond to the capital letters in Column 1 and should be in the same consecutive order. For each question, look at each column carefully and mark your answer as follows:

If there are one or more errors in Column 2 only, mark your answer A.
If there are one or more errors in Column 3 only, mark your answer B.
I there are one or more errors in Column 2 and one or more errors in Column 3, mark your answer C.
If there are NO errors in either column, mark your answer D.

Sample Question

Column 1   Column 2   Column 3
TQLMOC   583746   birtfn

In Column 2, the second agency code number (corresponding to letter Q) should be 9, not 8. Column 3 is coded correctly to Column 1. Since there is an error only in Column 2, the correct answer is A.

	COLUMN 1	COLUMN 2	COLUMN 3	
11.	QLNRCA	931268	iregnd	11._____
12.	NRMOTC	127546	egftbn	12._____
13.	RCTALM	265837	gndbrt	13._____
14.	TAMLON	578341	bdtrfe	14._____
15.	ANTORM	815427	debigt	15._____
16.	MRALON	728341	tgdrfe	16._____
17.	CTNQRO	657924	ndeigf	17._____
18.	QMROTA	972458	itgfbd	18._____
19.	RQMCOL	297463	gitnfr	19._____
20.	NOMRTQ	147259	eftgbi	20._____

Questions 21-25.

DIRECTIONS: Questions 21 through 25 are to be answered SOLELY on the basis of the following passage.

    The city may issue its own bonds or it may purchase bonds as an investment. Bonds may be issued in various denominations, and the face value of the bond is its par value. Before purchasing a bond, the investor desires to know the rate of income that the investment may yield in computing the yield on a bond, it is assumed that the investor will keep the bond until the date of maturity, except for callable bonds which are not considered in this passage. To compute exact yield is a complicated mathematical problem, and scientifically prepared tables are generally used to avoid such computation. However, the approximate yield can be computed much more easily. In computing approximate yield, the accrued interest on the date of purchase should be ignored because the buyer who pays accrued interest to the seller receives it again at the next interest date. Bonds bought at a premium (which cost more) yield a lower rate of income than the same bonds bought at par (face value), and bounds bought at a discount (which cost less) yield a higher rate of income than the same bonds bought at par.

21. An investor bought a $10,000 city bond paying 6% interest.   21._____
 Which of the following purchase prices would indicate that the bond was bought at a premium?
   A. $9,000   B. $9,400   C. $10,000   D. $10,600

22. During 2016, a particular $10,000 bond paying 7 ½% sold at fluctuating prices.   22._____
 Which of the following prices would indicate that the bond was bought at a discount?
   A. $9,800   B. $10,000   C. $10,200   D. $10,750

23. A certain group of bonds was sold in denominations of $5,000, $10,000, $20,000, and $50,000.
In the following list of four purchase prices, which one is MOST likely to represent a bond sold at par value?
   A. $10,500   B. $20,000   C. $22,000   D. $49,000

24. When computing the approximate yield on a bond, it is DESIRABLE to
   A. assume the bond was purchased at par
   B. consult scientifically prepared tables
   C. ignore accrued interest on the date of purchase
   D. wait until the bond reaches maturity

25. Which of the following is MOST likely to be an exception to the information provided in the above passage?
Bonds
   A. purchased at a premium
   B. sold at par
   C. sold before maturity
   D. which are callable

KEY (CORRECT ANSWERS)

1.	B		11.	D
2.	C		12.	C
3.	D		13.	B
4.	A		14.	A
5.	D		15.	B
6.	D		16.	D
7.	A		17.	C
8.	D		18.	D
9.	D		19.	A
10.	C		20.	D

21.	D
22.	A
23.	B
24.	C
25.	D

TEST 3

DIRECTIONS: Each question or incomplete statement is followed by several suggested answers or completions. Select the one that BEST answers the question or completes the statement. *PRINT THE LETTER OF THE CORRECT ANSWER IN THE SPACE AT THE RIGHT.*

Questions 1-6.

DIRECTIONS: Questions 1 through 6 consist of computations of addition, subtraction, multiplication, and division. For each question, do the computation indicated, and choose the correct answer from the four choices given.

1. ADD: 8936
   7821
   8953
   4297
   9785
   6579

   A. 45371   B. 45381   C. 46371   D. 46381

2. SUBTRACT: 95,432
   67,596

   A. 27,836   B. 27,846   C. 27,936   D. 27,946

3. MULTIPLY: 987
   867

   A. 854609   B. 854729   C. 855709   D. 855729

4. DIVIDE: 59)321439.0

   A. 5438.1   B. 5447.1   C. 5448.1   D. 5457.1

5. DIVIDE: .057)721

   A. 12,648.0   B. 12,648.1   C. 12,649.0   D. 12,649.1

6. ADD: 1/2 + 5/7
   A. 1 3/14   B. 1 2/7   C. 1 5/14   D. 1 3/7

7. If the total number of employees in one city agency increased from 1,927 to 2,006 during a certain year, the percentage increase in the number of employees for that year is MOST NEARLY
   A. 4%   B. 5%   C. 6%   D. 7%

2 (#3)

8. During a single fiscal year, which totaled 248 workdays, one account clerk verified 1,488 purchase vouchers.
Assuming a normal work week of five days, what is the average number of vouchers verified by the account clerk in a one-week period during this fiscal year?
   A. 25   B. 30   C. 35   D. 40

9. If the city department of purchase bought 190 computers for $793.50 each and 208 computers for $839.90 each, the TOTAL price paid for these computers is
   A. $315,813.00
   B. $325,464.20
   C. $334,279.20
   D. $335,863.00

Questions 10-14.

DIRECTIONS: Questions 10 through 14 are to be answered SOLELY on the basis of the information given in the following paragraph.

Since discounts are in common use in the commercial world and apply to purchases made by government agencies as well as business firms, it is essential that individuals in both public and private employment who prepare bills, check invoices, prepare payment vouchers, or write checks to pay bills have an understanding of the terms used. These include cash or time discount, trade discount, and disconnect series. A cash or time discount offers a reduction in price to the buyer for the prompt payment of the bill and is usually expressed as a percentage with a time requirement, stated in days, within which the bill must be paid in order to earn the discount. An example would be 3/10, meaning a 3% discount may be applied to the bill if the payment is forwarded to the vendor within ten days. On an invoice, the cash discount terms are usually followed by the net terms, which is the time in days allowed for ordinary payment of the bill. Thus, 3/10, Net 30 means that full payment is expected in thirty days if the cash discount of 3% is not taken for having paid the bill within ten days. When the expression Terms Net Cash is listed on a bill, it means that no deduction for early payment is allowed. A trade discount is normally applied to list prices by a manufacturer to show the actual price to retailers so that they may know their cost and determine markups that will allow them to operate competitively and at a profit. A trade discount is applied by the seller to the list price and is independent of a cash or time discount. Discounts may also be used by manufacturers to adjust prices charged to retailers without changing list prices. This is usually done by series discounting and is expressed as a series of percentages. To compute a series discount, such as 40%, 20%, 10%, first apply the 40% discount to the list price, then apply the 20% discount to the remainder, and finally apply the 10% discount to the second remainder.

10. According to the above passage, trade discounts are
    A. applied by the buyer
    B. independent of cash discounts
    C. restricted to cash sales
    D. used to secure rapid payment of bills

11. According to the above passage, if the sales terms 5/10, Net 60 appear on a bill in the amount of $100 dated December 5, 2016 and the buyer submits his payment on December 15, 2016, his PROPER payment should be
    A. $60   B. $90   C. $95   D. $100

12. According to the above passage, if a manufacturer gives a trade discount of 40% for an item with a list price of $250 and the terms are Net Cash, the price a retail merchant is required to pay for this item is
    A. $250 B. $210 C. $150 D. $100

    12.____

13. According to the above passage, a series discount of 25%, 20%, 10% applied to a list price of $200 results in an ACTUAL price to the buyer of
    A. $88 B. $90 C. $108 D. $110

    13.____

14. According to the above passage, if a manufacturer gives a trade discount of 50% and the terms are 6/10, Net 30, the cost to a retail merchant of an item with a list price of $500 and for which he takes the time discount is
    A. $220 B. $235 C. $240 D. $250

    14.____

Questions 15-22.

DIRECTIONS: Questions 15 through 22 each show in Column I the information written on five cards (lettered j, k, l, m, n) which have to be filed. You are to choose the option (lettered A, B, C, or D) in Column II which BEST represents the proper order of filing according to the information, rules, and sample question given below.

A file card record is kept of the work assignments for all the employees in a certain bureau. On each card is the employee's name, the date of work assignment, and the work assignment code number. The cards are to be filed according to the following rules:

FIRST: File in alphabetical order according to employee's name.

SECOND: When two or more cards have the same employee's name, file according to the assignment date, beginning with the earliest date.

THIRD: When two or more cards have the same employee's name and the same date, file according to the work assignment number beginning with the lowest number.

Column II shows the cards arranged in four different orders. Pick the option (A, B, C, or D) in Column II which shows the correct arrangement of the cards according to th above filing rules.

SAMPLE QUESTION

Column I
j. Cluney 4/8/02 (486503)
k. Roster 5/10/01 (246611)
l. Altool 10/15/02 (711433)
m. Cluney 12/18/02 (527610)
n. Cluney 4/8/02 (486500)

Column II
A. k, l, m, j, n
B. k, n, j, l, m
C. l, k, j, m, n
D. l, n, j, m, k

4 (#3)

The correct way to file the cards is:
- l. Altool 10/15/02 (71143)
- n. Cluney 4/8/02 (486500)
- j. Cluney 4/8/02 (486503)
- m. Cluney 12/18/02 (527610)
- k. Roster 5/10/01 (246611)

The correct filing order is shown by the letters l, n, j, m, k. The answer to the sample question is the letter D, which appears in front of the letters l, n, j, m, k in Column II.

COLUMN I   COLUMN II

15. j. Smith 3/19/03 (662118)   A. j, m, l, n, k   15.____
    k. Turner 4/16/99 (481349)   B. j, l, n, m, k
    l. Terman 3/20/02 (210229)   C. k, n, m, l, j
    m. Smyth 3/20/02 (481359)   D. j, n, k, l, m
    n. Terry 5/11/01 (672128)

16. j. Ross 5/29/02 (396118)   A. l, m, k, n, j   16.____
    k. Rosner 5/29/02 (439281)   B. m, l, k, n, j
    l. Rose 7/19/02 (723456)   C. l, m, k, j, n
    m. Rosen 5/29/03 (829692)   D. m, l, j, n, k
    n. Ross 5/29/02 (399118)

17. j. Sherd 10/12/99 (552368)   A. n, m, k, j, l   17.____
    k. Snyder 11/12/99 (539286)   B. j, m, l, k, n
    l. Shindler 10/13/98 (426798)   C. m, k, n, j. l
    m. Scherld 10/12/99 (552386)   D. m, n, j, l, k
    n. Schneider 11/12/99 (798213)

18. j. Carter 1/16/02 (489636)   A. k, n, j, l, m   18.____
    k. Carson 2/16/01 (392671)   B. n, k, m, l, j
    l. Carter 1/16/01 (486936)   C. n, k, l, j, m
    m. Carton 3/15/00 (489639)   D. k, n, l, j, m
    n. Carson 2/16/01 (392617)

19. j. Thomas 3/18/99 (763182)   A. m, l, j, k, n   19.____
    k. Tompkins 3/19/00 (928439)   B. j, m, l, k, n
    l. Thomson 3/21/00 (763812)   C. j, l, n, m, k
    m. Thompson 3/18/99 (924893)   D. l, m, j, n, k
    n. Tompson 3/19/99 (928793)

20. j. Breit 8/10/03 (345612)   A. m, j, n, k, l   20.____
    k. Briet 5/21/00 (837543)   B. n, m, j, k, l
    l. Bright 9/18/99 (931827)   C. m, j, k, l, n
    m. Breit 3/7/98 (553984)   D. j, m, k, l, n
    n. Brent 6/14/04 (682731)

COLUMN I   COLUMN II

21. j. Roberts 10/19/02 (581932)   A. n, k, l, m, j   21. **D**
    k. Rogers 8/9/00 (638763)   B. n, k, l, j, m
    l. Rogerts 7/15/97 (105689)   C. k, n, l, m, j
    m. Robin 3/8/92 (287915)   D. j, m, k, n, l
    n. Rogers 4/2/04 (736921)

22. j. Hebert 4/28/02 (719468)   A. n, k, j, m, l   22. **D**
    k. Herbert 5/8/01 (938432)   B. j, l, n, k, m
    l. Helbert 9/23/04 (832912)   C. l, j, k, n, m
    m. Herbst 7/10/03 (648599)   D. l, j, n, k, m
    n. Herbert 5/8/01 (487627)

23. In order to pay its employees, the Convex Company obtained bills and coins   23. **A**
    in the following denominations:

Denomination	$20	$10	$5	$1	$.50	$.25	$.10	$.05	$.01
Number	317	122	38	73	69	47	39	25	36

What was the TOTAL amount of cash obtained?
A. $7,874.76   B. $7,878.00   C. $7,889.25   D. $7,924.35

24. H. Partridge receives a weekly gross salary (before deductions) of $596.25.   24. **C**
    Through weekly payroll deductions of $19.77, he is paying back a load he took
    from his pension fund.
    If other fixed weekly deductions amount to $184.14, how much pay would Mr.
    Partridge take home over a period of 33 weeks?
    A. $11,446.92   B. $12,375.69   C. $12,947.22   D. $19,676.25

25. Mr. Robertson is a city employee enrolled in a city retirement system. He has   25. **A**
    taken out a loan from the retirement fund and is paying it back at the rate of
    $14.90 every two weeks.
    In eighteen weeks, how much money will he have paid back on the loan?
    A. $268.20   B. $152.80   C. $124.10   D. $67.05

26. In 2015, the Iridor Book Company had the following expenses: rent, $6,500;   26. **D**
    overhead, $52,585; inventory, $35,700; and miscellaneous, $1,275.
    If all of these expenses went up 18% in 2016, what would they TOTAL in 2016?
    A. $17,290.80   B. $78,768.20   C. $96,060.00   D. $113,350.80

27. Ms. Ranier had a gross salary of $355.36, paid once every week.   27. **A**
    If the deductions from each paycheck are $62.72, $25.13, $6.29, and $1.27, how
    much money would Ms. Ranier take home in four weeks?
    A. $1,039.80   B. $1,421.44   C. $2,079.60   D. $2,842.88

6 (#3)

28. Mr. Martin had a net income of $19,100 for the year.
If he spent 34% on rent and household expenses, 3% on house furnishings, 25% on clothes, and 36% on food, how much was left for savings and other expenses?
   A. $196.00   B. $382.00   C. $649.40   D. $1,960.00

28.____

29. Mr. Elsberg can pay back a loan of $1,800 from the city employees' retirement system if he pays back $36.69 every two weeks for two full years.
At the end of the two years, how much more than the original $1,800 he borrowed will Mr. Elsberg have paid back?
   A. $53.94   B. $107.88   C. $190.79   D. $214.76

29.____

30. Mrs. Nusbaum is a city employee, receiving a gross salary (salary before deductions) of $31,200. Every two weeks, the following deductions are taken out of her salary: Federal Income Tax, $243.96; FICA, $66.39; State Tax, $44.58; City Tax, $20.91; Health Insurance, $4.71.
If Mrs. Nusbaum's salary and deductions remained the same for a full calendar year, what would her NET salary (gross salary less deductions) be in that year?
   A. $9,894.30   B. $21,305.70   C. $28,118.25   D. $30,819.45

30.____

KEY (CORRECT ANSWERS)

1.	C	11.	C	21.	D
2.	A	12.	C	22.	B
3.	D	13.	C	33.	A
4.	C	14.	B	24.	C
5.	D	15.	A	25.	C
6.	A	16.	C	26.	D
7.	A	17.	D	27.	A
8.	B	18.	C	28.	B
9.	B	19.	B	29.	B
10.	B	20.	A	30.	B

EXAMINATION SECTION
TEST 1

DIRECTIONS: Each question or incomplete statement is followed by several suggested answers or completions. Select the one that BEST answers the question or completes the statement. *PRINT THE LETTER OF THE CORRECT ANSWER IN THE SPACE AT THE RIGHT.*

Questions 1-7.

DIRECTIONS: Questions 1 through 7 are to be answered on the basis of the following income statement.

Laura Lee's Bridal Shop
Income Statement
For the Year Ended December 31, 2018

Revenue:		
New & Used Bridal Gowns & Accessories		$55,000
Expenses:		
Advertisement Expense	$ 2,000	
Salaries Expense	12,000	
Dry cleaning & Alterations	10,000	
Utilities	1,500	
Total Expenses		25,500
Net Income		$29,500

1. What is the period of time covered by this income statement?   1.____

   A. January-December 2017
   B. December 2018
   C. January 2017-December 2018
   D. January-December 2018

2. What is the source of the revenue?   2.____

   A. New and used bridal gowns, advertisements, salaries, dry cleaning, and utilities
   B. Advertisements, salaries, dry cleaning, alterations, and utilities
   C. New and used bridal gowns and accessories
   D. Net income

3. What is the total revenue?   3.____

   A. $25,500   B. $55,000   C. $29,500   D. $79,500

4. Which of the following are expenses?   4.____

   A. Salaries
   B. New and used bridal gowns and accessories
   C. Revenue
   D. New and used bridal gowns, advertisements, and dry cleaning

5. What are the total expenses?   5.____

   A. $55,000   B. $29,500   C. $79,500   D. $25,500

17

6. There is a resulting net income because

   A. total revenue and total expenses are combined
   B. net income is greater than total revenue
   C. the total revenue is greater than total expenses
   D. the total revenue is less than total expenses

7. Is this statement an interim statement?

   A. *Yes*, because it covers an entire accounting period
   B. *No*, because it covers an entire accounting period
   C. *Yes*, because it covers a period of less than a year
   D. *No*, because it covers a period of more than a year

8. What is the name of the accounting report that may show either a net profit or a net loss for an accounting period?

   A. Income statement
   B. Balance sheet
   C. Statement of capital
   D. Classified balance sheet

9. What are the two main parts of the body of the income statement?

   A. Cash and Capital
   B. Revenue and Expenses
   C. Liabilities and Capital
   D. Assets and Notes Payable

10. If total revenue exceeds total expenses for an accounting period, what is the difference called?

    A. Gross income
    B. Total liabilities
    C. Total assets
    D. Net income

11. In the body of a balance sheet, what are the three sections called?

    A. Assets and liabilities
    B. Cash, liabilities, and revenue
    C. Assets, liabilities, and capital
    D. Revenue, assets, and capital

12. What business record shows the results of the proprietor's borrowing assets from the business, usually in anticipation of profits?

    A. Proprietor's withdrawals
    B. Accounts payable
    C. Liabilities and Capital
    D. Total liabilities

Questions 13-24.

DIRECTIONS: For each transaction given for Mona's Magic Moments Hair Salon in Questions 13 through 24, identify which journal the transaction should be recorded in.

13. April 1: Mona, the owner, paid the month's rent - $600.00; check no. 356.

    A. General
    B. Cash disbursements
    C. Purchases
    D. Sales

14. April 6: the salon purchased $300.00 worth of styling products on account from Pomme de Terre Company.   14.____

     A. Cash disbursements   B. General
     C. Sales   D. Purchases

15. April 8: sold $100.00 worth of hair products on account to Mrs. Angela Bray.   15.____

     A. Sales   B. Purchases
     C. Cash disbursements   D. General

16. April 11: the owner, Mona Ramen, withdrew $80.00 of styling products for personal use.   16.____

     A. Sales   B. Cash receipts
     C. General   D. Cash disbursements

17. April 13: paid Pomme de Terre Company $300.00 on account; check 357.   17.____

     A. Purchases   B. Cash disbursements
     C. Cash receipts   D. General

18. April 15: cash sales to date were $4,607.00.   18.____

     A. Cash disbursements   B. Purchases
     C. Sales   D. General

19. April 17: issued credit slip #17 to Mrs. Angela Bray for $25.00 for merchandise returned.   19.____

     A. Cash disbursements   B. Cash receipts
     C. Sales   D. General

20. April 19: paid electric bill for $250.00; check no. 358.   20.____

     A. Cash disbursements   B. Purchases
     C. General   D. Cash receipts

21. April 21: received $75.00 from Mrs. Angela Bray for balance due on account.   21.____

     A. Sales   B. Cash disbursements
     C. Cash receipts   D. Purchases

22. April 23: sold $88.00 of hair products on account to Ms. Tania Alioto.   22.____

     A. Purchases   B. Sales
     C. Cash disbursements   D. Cash receipts

23. April 27: purchased $500.00 of equipment from Salon Stylings Merchandisers on account.   23.____

     A. Cash disbursements   B. Sales
     C. General   D. Purchases

24. April 30: cash sales to date were $5023.00.   24.____

     A. Purchases   B. Sales
     C. Cash receipts   D. General

Questions 25-30.

DIRECTIONS: Questions 25 through 30 are to be answered on the basis of the following ledger for a barbecue take-out restaurant owned and operated by Ruby Joiner.

Cash		Accounts Receivable		Delivery Equipment	
450	150	360	170	5,000	
212	125	250	100	4,000	
328	440	165	120	3,000	
172	125	100	60		
250	70				
275	150				
325	50				

Supplies		Ruby Joiner, Capital		Accounts Payable	
40			8,200	10	600
65			2,000	15	300
30			2,097		200
25					

Ruby Joiner, Drawing		Advertising Expense		Delivery Income	
225		40			400
175		45			350
200					250
					100

Trucking Expense		Telephone Expense	
100		80	
50		40	
		20	

25. What is the balance on the Cash account shown above?   25.____

    A. 2,012.00   B. 1,110.00   C. 3,122.00   D. 902.00

26. What is the balance on the Accounts receivable account shown above?   26.____

    A. 425.00   B. 875.00   C. 450.00   D. 1315.00

27. What is the balance on the Accounts payable account shown above?   27.____

    A. 1100.00   B. 1075.00   C. 25.00   D. 1125.00

28. Which of the above accounts has a balance of 1100.00?   28.____

    A. Accounts payable   B. Delivery Income
    C. Cash   D. Delivery equipment

29. Which of the above accounts has a balance of 12,000.00?   29.____

    A. Ruby Joiner, Capital
    B. Cash and Accounts receivable combined
    C. Delivery equipment
    D. None of the accounts

30. If you made a balance sheet out of the information listed above, Ruby Joiner's total assets would be   30.____

    A. 14,472.00   B. 12,297.00   C. 13,392.00   D. 13,487.00

Questions 31-34.

DIRECTIONS: Questions 31 through 34 are to be answered on the basis of the following information, to be included on a checking deposit ticket.

Five $20 bills; 11 $10 bills; 6 $5 bills; 47 $1 bills; 200 half dollars; 120 quarters; 112 dimes; 320 nickels; 67 pennies. Second National Bank (73-124) check of 152.34; Bank of the Midwest (13-298) check of 68.37; Great National Bank (32-165) check of 185.06.

31. What is the TOTAL currency for this deposit? 31.____
    A. $387   B. $287   C. $444.87   D. $157.87

32. What is the TOTAL coin for this deposit? 32.____
    A. $387   B. $287   C. $444.87   D. $157.87

33. What is the check total for this deposit? 33.____
    A. $692.77   B. $406   C. $405.77   D. $850.64

34. What is the TOTAL deposit? 34.____
    A. $444.87   B. $692.77   C. $851   D. $850.64

Questions 35-37.

DIRECTIONS: Questions 35 through 37 are to be answered on the basis of the following petty cash journal.

Date	Receipt No.	To Whom Paid	For What	Acct.#	Amount
10/2	1	Anna Jones - Mail	Postage	548	13.50
10/2	2	Jim Collins	Messenger	525	5.75
10/4	3	Anna Jones - Mail	Postage	548	13.50
10/5	4	Lucky Stores	Coffee	515	7.34
10/6	5	Tom Allen	Lunch w/customer	525	11.38

35. What is the TOTAL disbursement from this fund for the time period 10/1 through 10/6? 35.____
    A. $51.47   B. $40.09   C. $61.47   D. $26.59

36. How much money was disbursed to Account #548 during the time period 10/1-10/16? 36.____
    A. $51.47   B. $26   C. $27   D. $34.34

37. If the fund began the month with a total of $100.00, what amount was left in the fund at the end of business on 10/5? 37.____
    A. $48.53   B. $59.91   C. $51.47   D. $40.09

Questions 38-40.

DIRECTIONS: Questions 38 through 40 are to be answered on the basis of the following information.

A promissory note dated December 1, 2018, bearing interest at a rate of 12% and due in 90 days, is sent to a creditor. The face value of the note is $900.

38. What is the due date of the promissory note? 38.____

   A. January 15, 2019
   B. March 1, 2019
   C. February 1, 2019
   D. December 31, 2018

39. What is the TOTAL interest that will be earned on the note? 39.____

   A. $27   B. $270   C. $108   D. $10.80

40. What interest will be earned on the note for the old accounting period (December 1-31)? 40.____

   A. $90   B. $36   C. $9   D. $3.60

KEY (CORRECT ANSWERS)

1.	D	11.	C	21.	C	31.	B
2.	C	12.	A	22.	B	32.	D
3.	B	13.	B	23.	D	33.	C
4.	A	14.	D	24.	B	34.	D
5.	D	15.	A	25.	D	35.	A
6.	C	16.	C	26.	A	36.	C
7.	B	17.	B	27.	B	37.	B
8.	A	18.	C	28.	B	38.	B
9.	B	19.	D	29.	C	39.	A
10.	D	20.	A	30.	D	40.	C

TEST 2

DIRECTIONS: Each question or incomplete statement is followed by several suggested answers or completions. Select the one that BEST answers the question or completes the statement. *PRINT THE LETTER OF THE CORRECT ANSWER IN THE SPACE AT THE RIGHT.*

Questions 1-4.

DIRECTIONS: Questions 1 through 4 are to be answered on the basis of the following information, to be included in a deposit slip.

    14 twenty dollar bills   63 quarters
    52 ten dollar bills   22 dimes
    12 five dollar bills   44 nickels
    43 one dollar bills   70 pennies

Checks: $236.34 and $129.72

1. What is the TOTAL amount of currency for this deposit?   1.____
   A. $923.85   B. $1269.06   C. $903.00   D. $1299.91

2. What is the TOTAL amount of coin for this deposit?   2.____
   A. $20.85   B. $923.85   C. $903.00   D. $1299.91

3. What is the TOTAL amount of check for this deposit?   3.____
   A. $20.85   B. $366.06   C. $1299.91   D. $903.00

4. What is the TOTAL deposit for this slip?   4.____
   A. $1269.06   B. $903.00   C. $923.85   D. $1289.91

Questions 5-7.

DIRECTIONS: Questions 5 through 7 are to be answered on the basis of the following information.

Angela Martinez's last check stub balance was $675.50. Her bank statement balance dated April 30 was $652.00. A $250 deposit was in transit on that date. Outstanding checks were as follows: No. 127, $65.00; No. 129, $203.50; No. 130, $50.00. The bank service charge for the month was $5.00.

5. What was Angela Martinez's available checkbook balance on April 30?   5.____
   A. $652.00   B. $338.50   C. $583.50   D. $675.50

6. In order to reconcile her checkbook balance with her bank statement balance, what must Angela Martinez do?   6.____

   A. Add her checkbook balance to the balance on her bank statement
   B. Subtract her checkbook balance from the balance on her bank statement

C. Ignore her checkbook balance and adopt the balance on her bank statement
D. Adjust the checkbook balance by adding deposits and debiting outstanding checks and charges

7. The check stub balance referred to in the problem refers to the 7.____

   A. last check Angela Martinez recorded in her checkbook
   B. amount of money left in Angela Martinez's account according to her own calculations based on the checks, charges, and deposits she has written and recorded
   C. amount of money left in Angela Martinez's account according to the bank's calculations based on the checks, charges, and deposits posted to her account
   D. number of checks left in her checkbook

Questions 8-9.

DIRECTIONS: Questions 8 and 9 are to be answered on the basis of the following information.

Tu Nguyen, an interior designer, received his June bank statement on July 2. The balance was $622.66. His last check stub balance was $700. On comparing the two, he noticed that a deposit of $275 made on June 30 was not included on the statement; also, a bank service charge of $4 was deducted. Outstanding checks were as follows: No. 331, $97.50; No. 332, $207; No. 335, $25.40; and No. 336, $68.97.

8. What is Nguyen's CORRECT available bank balance? 8.____

   A. $494.79   B. $897.66   C. $700.00   D. $219.79

9. The bank statement balance referred to in the problem refers to the 9.____

   A. last check Tu Nguyen recorded in his checkbook
   B. last check presented for payment to Tu Nguyen's account
   C. amount of money left in Tu Nguyen's account according to the bank's calculations based on the checks, charges, and deposits posted to his account
   D. amount of money left in Tu Nguyen's account based on his own calculations of the checks, charges, and deposits he has written and recorded

10. What of the following endorsements would be an example of a simple Endorsement in Blank? 10.____

    A. Pay to the Order of Joanie Anderson
    B. Joanie Anderson
    C. For deposit only; Acct. No. 12345; Joanie Anderson
    D. Without Recourse; Joanie Anderson

11. Which of the following endorsements would limit the further purpose or use of the endorsed check? 11.____

    A. Pay to the Order of Joanie Anderson
    B. Joanie Anderson
    C. For deposit only; Acct. No. 12345; Joanie Anderson,
    D. Without Recourse; Joanie Anderson

12. Which of the following endorsements would protect the endorser from legal responsibility for payment, should the drawer have insufficient funds to honor his/her own check? 12.____

    A. Pay to the Order of Joanie Anderson
    B. Joanie Anderson
    C. For deposit only; Acct. No. 12345; Joanie Anderson
    D. Without Recourse; Joanie Anderson

Questions 13-24.

DIRECTIONS: Questions 13 - 24 are to be answered on the basis of the following ledger accounts for Wheelsmith Organic Farms.

Wheelsmith Organic Farms
Ledger Accounts

Cash	Accounts Payable	Service Supplies
Jan. 1 4,000	Jan. 1 2,000	Jan. 1 2,000

Shelley Wheelsmith, Capital	Machinery
Jan. 1 11,000	Jan. 1 7,000

13. Transaction #1: On January 5, Shelley Wheelsmith, the proprietor, received cash amounting to $5,000 as a result of returning machinery that had recently been purchased. What account(s) should this transaction be posted to? 13.____

    A. Cash
    B. Cash and Machinery
    C. Machinery
    D. Cash, Machinery, and Service Supplies

14. Transaction #2: On January 8, Shelley Wheelsmith, the proprietor, sent out a check for $600 in partial payment of the accounts payable. What account(s) should this transaction be posted to? 14.____

    A. Accounts Payable
    B. Accounts Payable and Cash
    C. Accounts Payable and Capital
    D. Cash

15. Transaction #3: On January 14, Shelley Wheelsmith, proprietor, made an additional investment in the business by contributing machinery valued at $1,500. What account(s) should this transaction be posted to? 15.____

    A. Machinery
    B. Machinery and Capital
    C. Capital
    D. Machinery and Cash

16. Transaction #4: On January 26, Shelley Wheelsmith, proprietor, purchased additional service supplies for $200. She agreed to pay the obligation in 30 days. What account(s) should this transaction be posted to? 16.____

A. Accounts Payable and Liabilities
B. Service supplies
C. Accounts Payable
D. Accounts Payable and Service supplies

17. Transaction #5: On January 31, Shelley Wheelsmith, proprietor, purchased service supplies paying cash of $50. What account(s) should this transaction be posted to? 17._____

   A. Service supplies
   B. Service supplies and Accounts Payable
   C. Cash and Service supplies
   D. Cash

18. What is the balance in the Cash account after all of these transactions are posted? 18._____

   A. $9,000   B. $1,000   C. $5,000   D. $8,350

19. What is the balance in the Machinery account after all of these transactions are posted? 19._____

   A. $7,000   B. $5,000   C. $3,500   D. $13,500

20. What is the balance in the Accounts Payable account after all of these transactions are posted? 20._____

   A. $800   B. $600   C. $2,600   D. $1,600

21. What is the balance in the Capital account after all of these transactions are posted? 21._____

   A. $12,500   B. $800   C. $11,600   D. $10,400

22. What is the balance in the Service supplies account after all of these transactions are posted? 22._____

   A. $2,000   B. $2,250   C. $750   D. $2,200

23. What are the total assets of Wheelsmith Organic Farms after these transactions have been posted? 23._____

   A. $10,600   B. $11,850   C. $14,100   D. $10,750

24. What are the total liabilities and capital for Wheelsmith Organic Farms after these transactions have been posted? 24._____

   A. $14,100   B. $12,500   C. $11,850   D. $10,600

Questions 25-28.

DIRECTIONS: Questions 25 through 28 are to be answered on the basis of the following information.

At the end of an accounting period, Andy's Framing Gallery recorded the following information: Sales, $125,225; Merchandise Inventory, December 31, $95,325; Purchases Returns and Allowances, $3,500; Merchandise Inventory, January 1, $98,725; Freight on Purchases, $2,500; Purchases, $120,000.

25. What are the net purchases for Andy's Framing Gallery during the accounting period?   25._____
    A. $120,000   B. $119,000   C. $3,500   D. $122,500

26. What is the cost of goods available for sale?   26._____
    A. $119,000   B. $98,725   C. $95,325   D. $217,725

27. What is the total cost of goods sold for this accounting period?   27._____
    A. $217,725   B. $95,325   C. $122,400   D. $125,225

28. What is the gross profit on sales for this accounting period?   28._____
    A. $2825   B. $2500   C. $125,225   D. $122,400

Questions 29-40.

DIRECTIONS: Questions 29 through 40 are to be answered on the basis of the following information.

The Joie de Vivre Co. received the promissory notes listed below during the last quarter of its calendar year:

	Date	Face Amount	Terms	Interest Rate	Date Discounted	Discount Rate
(1)	10/8	$3,600	30 days	-	10/18	9%
(2)	9/22	$8,000	60 days	6%	10/1	7%
(3)	11/15	$3,000	90 days	7%	11/20	8%

29. What is the due date for the first note?   29._____
    A. 12/31   B. 11/7   C. 12/7   D. 10/31

30. What interest will be due when the first note matures?   30._____
    A. $3   B. $3,600   C. $30   D. $0

31. What is the maturity value of the first note?   31._____
    A. $3,600   B. $3,630   C. $0   D. $3,603

32. What is the discount period for the first note?   32._____
    A. One fiscal year   B. 10 days
    C. 20 days   D. One month

33. What is the due date for the second note?   33._____
    A. 12/21   B. 11/21   C. 10/21   D. 1/21

34. What interest will be due when the second note matures?   34._____
    A. $60   B. $800.00   C. $8.00   D. $80.00

35. What is the maturity value of the second note?   35._____
    A. $8,000   B. $8,080   C. $8,800   D. $8,008

36. What is the discount period for the second note?
    A. 51 days   B. 10 days   C. 360 days   D. 60 days

37. What is the due date for the third note?
    A. 1/14   B. 12/15   C. 12/31   D. 2/13

38. What interest will be due when the third note matures?
    A. $5.25   B. $52.50   C. $525   D. $90

39. What is the maturity value of the third note?
    A. $3525   B. $3005.25   C. $3052.50   D. $3090

40. What is the discount period for the third note?
    A. 60 days   B. 85 days   C. 5 days   D. 90 days

KEY (CORRECT ANSWERS)

1. C	11. C	21. A	31. A
2. A	12. D	22. B	32. C
3. B	13. B	23. C	33. B
4. D	14. B	24. A	34. D
5. C	15. B	25. B	35. B
6. D	16. D	26. D	36. A
7. B	17. C	27. C	37. D
8. A	18. D	28. A	38. B
9. C	19. C	29. B	39. C
10. B	20. D	30. D	40. B

TEST 3

DIRECTIONS: Each question or incomplete statement is followed by several suggested answers or completions. Select the one that BEST answers the question or completes the statement. *PRINT THE LETTER OF THE CORRECT ANSWER IN THE SPACE AT THE RIGHT.*

Questions 1-8.

DIRECTIONS: Questions 1 through 8 are to be answered on the basis of the following Balance Sheet.

Laura Lee's Bridal Shop
Balance Sheet
December 31, 2018

Assets

Cash	$14,000	
Accounts Receivable	3,000	
Bridal Accessories	10,000	
Gowns and Other Inventory	30,000	
Total Assets		$57,000

Liabilities and Capital

Accounts Payable	$ 4,000	
Notes Payable	28,000	
Total Liabilities		$32,000
Laura Lee, Capital		25,000
Total Liabilities and Capital		$57,000

1. When was the balance sheet prepared?

   A. January 2019
   B. December 31, 2018
   C. After the close of the 2018 fiscal year
   D. December 1, 2018

2. How does the date on this balance sheet differ from the date on the statement of capital or income statement?

   A. It doesn't differ. The dates for each statement signify the same time period.
   B. The date on a balance sheet represents the period during which any changes indicated on the statement took place, whereas the other financial statements represent the moment in time when the statement was prepared.
   C. The date on a balance sheet represents the moment in time when the statement was prepared, whereas the other financial statements represent the period during which any changes indicated on the statement took place.
   D. The date on a balance sheet indicates an entire year, whereas the dates on the other statements indicate a single month.

3. Can Laura Lee purchase more bridal gowns for the business paying cash of $16,000?

   A. No, because the business has only $14,000 cash available
   B. Yes, because the business has $57,000 cash available
   C. Yes, because the business has $57,000 available in assets
   D. No, because the business has $57,000 in liabilities

1.____

2.____

3.____

29

4. What is the owner's equity of Laura Lee's Bridal Shop?
   Since total equity consists of total _____, total equity is _____.

   A. assets minus total liabilities and proprietor's capital; $0
   B. assets minus total liabilities; $25,000
   C. assets; $57,000
   D. liabilities and proprietor's capital; $57,000

5. What is the TOTAL amount of Laura Lee's claim against the total assets of the business?

   A. $57,000   B. $25,000   C. $0   D. $39,000

6. What is the amount of the creditors' claims against the assets of the business?

   A. $4,000   B. $57,000   C. $32,000   D. $28,000

7. What is the net income for the period?

   A. $57,000
   B. $0
   C. $25,000
   D. This information cannot be obtained from the balance sheet

8. What was the value of Laura Lee's ownership in this business on January 1, 2004?

   A. $25,000
   B. $57,000
   C. $14,000
   D. This information cannot be obtained from the balance sheet

Questions 9-21.

DIRECTIONS: Each of the transactions described in Questions 9 through 21 occurred within an accounting period. For each question, indicate which of the four journals the transaction would be recorded in.

9. Sale of goods on account

   A. Cash receipts   B. Cash payments
   C. General   D. Sales

10. Cash payment of a promissory note

    A. Cash payments   B. Cash receipts
    C. Sales   D. General

11. Received a credit memo from a creditor

    A. Purchases   B. General
    C. Sales   D. Cash payments

12. Sale of merchandise for cash

    A. Purchases   B. General
    C. Cash receipts   D. Cash payments

13. Received a check from a customer in partial payment of an oral agreement 13.____

    A. Purchases B. Sales
    C. General   D. Cash receipts

14. Issued a credit memo to a customer 14.____

    A. Purchases   B. General
    C. Cash payments D. Sales

15. Received a promissory note in place of an oral agreement from a customer 15.____

    A. General   B. Cash payments
    C. Cash receipts D. Sales

16. Paid monthly rent 16.____

    A. General   B. Purchases
    C. Cash payments D. Cash receipts

17. Sale of a service on credit 17.____

    A. Cash receipts B. General
    C. Purchases   D. Sales

18. Purchase of office furniture on credit 18.____

    A. General   B. Purchases
    C. Cash payments D. Cash receipts

19. Purchased merchandise for cash 19.____

    A. Cash payments B. Cash receipts
    C. Sales   D. General

20. Cash refund to a customer 20.____

    A. Cash receipts B. Sales
    C. General   D. Cash payments

21. Purchases made on credit 21.____

    A. Purchases   B. Sales
    C. Cash receipts D. General

Questions 22-26.

DIRECTIONS: Questions 22 through 26 are to be answered on the basis of the following inventory, purchased by International Soap and Candle Traders, Inc.

700 units at $4.50, 320 units at $3.75, 550 units at $2.75, and 475 units at $1.90

22. Calculate the total price of the units that cost $4.50. 22.____

    A. $315   B. $31,500   C. $3,150   D. $2,800

23. Calculate the total price of the units that cost $3.75. 23.____

    A. $2062.50   B. $12,000   C. $120   D. $1,200

24. Calculate the total price of the units that cost $2.75.

    A. $1,512.50   B. $15,125   C. $151.25   D. $550

25. Calculate the total price of the units that cost $1.90.

    A. $90.25   B. $9025   C. $902.50   D. $475

26. Calculate the average cost per unit.

    A. $27   B. $33.10   C. $0.30   D. $3.31

27. The interest on a promissory note is recorded at which of the following times?

    A. When the debt is incurred
    B. At the end of the accounting period
    C. When the note is paid
    D. At the beginning of each month

28. The interest on a promissory note begins accruing at which of the following times?

    A. When the debt is incurred
    B. At the end of the accounting period
    C. When the note is paid
    D. At the beginning of each month

29. The maturity value of an interest-bearing note is the

    A. interest accrued on the note plus a service charge imposed by the lender
    B. interest accrued on the note
    C. face value of the note
    D. principal of the note plus interest

30. A cash receipts journal is used to record the

    A. number of cash sales a business makes
    B. number of credit sales a business makes
    C. collection of cash made by the business
    D. expenditure of cash made by the business

31. Calculate the interest on a promissory note issued for $3,000 at an interest rate of 8%, due in 360 days. (Assume a banking year of 360 days.)

    A. $300   B. $240   C. $60   D. $360

32. Calculate the total payment due for a promissory note issued for $1,000 at an interest rate of 10%, due in 90 days. (Assume a banking year of 360 days.)

    A. $25   B. $1050   C. $1000   D. $1025

33. Calculate the total payment due for a promissory note issued for $5,000 at an interest rate of 6%, due in 60 days. (Assume a banking year of 360 days.)

    A. $5,050   B. $50   C. $5,000   D. $5,300

34. Calculate the interest on a promissory note issued for $1,700 at an interest rate of 12%, due in 45 days. (Assume a banking year of 360 days.) 34.____

   A. $204   B. $1725.50   C. $25.50   D. $1904

35. Calculate the interest on a promissory note issued for $600 at an interest rate of 9%, due in 90 days. (Assume a banking year of 360 days.) 35.____

   A. $13.50   B. $135   C. $54   D. $540

KEY (CORRECT ANSWERS)

1.	B	16.	C
2.	C	17.	D
3.	A	18.	B
4.	B	19.	A
5.	B	20.	D
6.	C	21.	A
7.	D	22.	C
8.	D	23.	D
9.	D	24.	A
10.	A	25.	C
11.	B	26.	D
12.	C	27.	C
13.	D	28.	A
14.	B	29.	D
15.	A	30.	C

31. B
32. D
33. A
34. C
35. A

EXAMINATION SECTION
TEST 1

DIRECTIONS: Each question or incomplete statement is followed by several suggested answers or completions. Select the one that BEST answers the question or completes the statement. *PRINT THE LETTER OF THE CORRECT ANSWER IN THE SPACE AT THE RIGHT.*

Questions 1-20.

DIRECTIONS: Listed below in T accounts are the five MAJOR classifications of accounts. Consider carefully each of the following statements and indicate the change by writing the appropriate letter from the T accounts in the space at the right.

ASSETS	LIABILITIES	PROPRIETORSHIP	INCOME	EXPENSES
A | B	C | D	E | F	G | H	I | J

Sample Question:
A decrease in cash
The CORRECT answer is B.

1. An increase in equipment   1.____
2. An increase in the proprietorship   2.____
3. An increase in office salaries   3.____
4. A decrease in accounts payable   4.____
5. An increase in merchandise inventory   5.____
6. A decrease in office equipment   6.____
7. A decrease in office supplies   7.____
8. An increase in the proprietor's drawing account   8.____
9. A withdrawal of capital by the proprietor   9.____
10. An increase in sales   10.____
11. An increase in salaries payable   11.____
12. An increase in the net profit for the period   12.____
13. An increase in the sales returns and allowances   13.____

14. A decrease in purchases   14._____

15. A decrease in the accounts receivable   15._____

16. An increase in the mortgage payable   16._____

17. An increase in delivery expense   17._____

18. An increase in notes payable   18._____

19. An increase in purchases returns and allowances   19._____

20. A decrease in delivery equipment   20._____

Questions 21-40.

DIRECTIONS: Indicate the title of the accounts to be debited and credited in journalizing, adjusting, and closing the transactions given below by writing in the space at the right the letters that correspond to the accounts listed at the right.

Sample Question:
Paid the rent for the month, $100   Debit   Credit
                                           K   C

			Debit	Credit
21.	C.M. Smith invested $10,000 in the business	A. Accounts Payable B. Accounts Receivable C. Cash	21._____	_____
22.	Purchased merchandise on account from A.D. Hall, $875	D. Income & Expense Summary E. Insurance	22._____	_____
23.	Sold merchandise on account to L.S. Brook, $500	F. Insurance Expense G. Merchandise Inventory	23._____	_____
24.	Received $250 from cash sales	H. Office Supplies I. Office Supplies Used	24._____	_____
25.	Purchased office supplies for cash, $90	J. Purchases K. Rent Expense	25._____	_____
26.	Paid A.D. Hall $500 to apply on account	L. Salaries M. Salaries Payable N. Sales	26._____	_____
27.	Paid insurance premium for the year, $360	O. C.M. Smith, Capital P. C.M. Smith, Drawing	27._____	_____
28.	Paid C.M. Smith $100 for personal use		28._____	_____
29.	Received $300 from L.S. Brooks, to apply on account		29._____	_____

3 (#1)

30. Paid salaries for the month $500   30.____ ____

Adjusting Entries

31. The supplies used during the month   31.____ ____
    were $60

32. The salaries owed at the close of   32.____ ____
    the month were $40

33. The prepaid insurance expired was $30   33.____ ____

34. The beginning merchandise inventory   34.____ ____
    was $1200

35. The closing merchandise inventory   35.____ ____
    was $750

Closing Entries

36. The sales account has a balance   36.____ ____
    of $4500

37. The salaries for the month were $540   37.____ ____

38. The purchase account balance is $3600   38.____ ____

39. The office supplies used were $75   39.____ ____

40. The income and expense summary has   40.____ ____
    a net profit of $350

4 (#1)

KEY (CORRECT ANSWERS)

					DEBIT	CREDIT		DEBIT	CREDIT
1.	A	11.	D	21.	C	O	31.	I	H
2.	F	12.	F	22.	J	A	32.	L	M
3.	I	13.	G	23.	B	N	33.	F	E
4.	C	14.	J	24.	C	N	34.	D	G
5.	A	15.	B	25.	H	C	35.	G	D
6.	B	16.	D	26.	A	C	36.	N	D
7.	B	17.	I	27.	E	C	37.	D	L
8.	E	18.	D	28.	P	C	38.	D	J
9.	E	19.	J	29.	C	B	39.	D	I
10.	H	20.	B	30.	L	C	40.	D	O

TEST 2

DIRECTIONS: Each question or incomplete statement is followed by several suggested answers or completions. Select the one that BEST answers the question or completes the statement. *PRINT THE LETTER OF THE CORRECT ANSWER IN THE SPACE AT THE RIGHT.*

Questions 1-16.

DIRECTIONS: Read each statement carefully. If you believe that the account should be debited, place a D for DEBIT in the space at the right. If you think it should be credited, place a C for CREDIT in the space at the right.

1. When sales are made for cash, the sales account is (debited or credited).   1.____

2. When sales are made on account, the customer's account is (debited or credited).   2.____

3. When merchandise is purchased for cash, the purchases account is (debited or credited).   3.____

4. The creditor's account is (debited or credited) when payment is made on account.   4.____

5. The sales account is (debited or credited) for the total of the amount column in the Sales Journal.   5.____

6. The cash account is (debited or credited) for the total of the cash column in the Cash Receipts Journal.   6.____

7. The purchases account is (debited or credited) for the total amount of the purchases column in the Purchases Journal.   7.____

8. The accounts receivable account is (debited or credited) for the total amount of the Sales Journal.   8.____

9. Each account in the Sales Journal is posted to the (debit or credit) of the customer's account.   9.____

10. The total of the accounts payable column in the Cash Payments Journal is posted to the (debit or credit) of the accounts payable account.   10.____

11. The total of the cash column in the Cash Payments Journal is posted to the (debit or credit) of the cash account.   11.____

12. Each account with an amount entered in the General column of the Cash Receipts Journal is (debited or credited).   12.____

13. When the proprietor invests additional cash in the business, the capital account is (debited or credited). 13.____

14. When merchandise is purchased on account, the purchases account is (debited or credited). 14.____

15. When sales salaries are unpaid at the close of the fiscal period, the salaries payable account is (debited or credited). 15.____

16. When equipment is purchased on account, the creditor's account is (debited or credited). 16.____

Questions 17-30.

DIRECTIONS: The following figures have been taken from Income Statements. Certain figures have been omitted and letters have been substituted. Determine the CORRECT amounts that should be recorded for each of the letters and write this amount in the space at the right. Each line across the page is a separate income statement.

Sales	Beginning Inventory	Purchases	Closing Inventory	Cost of Goods Sold	Gross Profit	Expenses	Net Profit	Net Loss
22,000	8,000	12,000	A	15,000	B	4,000	C	
D	E	60,000	30,000	40,000	10,000	F		2,000
3,500	1,000	2,500	500	G	500	H	100	
7,500	500	I	2,000	J	1,000	800	K	
30,000	L	25,000	5,000	28,000	M	2,500		N

17. A 17.____

18. B 18.____

19. C 19.____

20. D 20.____

21. E 21.____

22. F 22.____

23. G 23.____

24. H 24.____

25. I 25.____

26. J 26.____

27. K 27.____
28. L 28.____
29. M 29.____
30. N 30.____

KEY (CORRECT ANSWERS)

1.	C	11.	C	21.	10,000
2.	D	12.	C	22.	12,000
3.	D	13.	C	23.	3,000
4.	D	14.	D	24.	400
5.	C	15.	C	25.	8,000
6.	D	16.	C	26.	6,500
7.	D	17.	5,000	27.	200
8.	D	18.	7,000	28.	8,000
9.	D	19.	3,000	29.	2,000
10.	D	20.	50,000	30.	500

TEST 3

Questions 1-25

DIRECTIONS: Each of Questions 1 through 25 consists of a statement. You are to indicate whether the statement is TRUE (T) or FALSE (F). *PRINT THE LETTER OF THE CORRECT ANSWER IN THE SPACE AT THE RIGHT.*

1. One of the primary objectives of the proprietor of a business is to increase his proprietorship by earning a profit.   1.____

2. The length of time covered by the Income and Expense Statement is of no importance or significance.   2.____

3. The length of time covered by the Balance Sheet is of no importance or significance.   3.____

4. When a customer takes advantage of a cash discount, the amount of cash received is more than the amount of the invoice for which payment is received.   4.____

5. Posting of column totals from the Cash Receipts Journal to the General Ledger is done each day.   5.____

6. After the adjustments have been entered in their appropriate column in the worksheet, their equality is proved by adding the columns.   6.____

7. The amount of unsold merchandise is found by subtracting the merchandise sales from the merchandise purchased.   7.____

8. In the Income and Expense Statement, the sales minus the cost of goods sold equals the gross profit.   8.____

9. If the operating expenses exceed the gross profit, a net loss results.   9.____

10. Only asset, liability, and capital accounts appear in the post-closing trial balance.   10.____

11. The earning of a net profit by a business results in an increase in the net worth of the business.   11.____

12. If the assets of a business are less than the liabilities, the business is solvent.   12.____

13. Small business can use accounting and data processing machines to a better advantage than large businesses.   13.____

14. The adjusting entries can be prepared from the adjustment columns of the worksheet. 14.____

15. The amount of the supplies used during the fiscal period is credited to the supplies account at the close of the fiscal period. 15.____

16. If the credit side of the income and expense summary account is larger than the debit side, the difference is a net loss to the business. 16.____

17. The discount on sales is considered to be a part of the regular operating expenses of the business. 17.____

18. In writing off a customer's uncollectible amount, the allowance for bad debts in the General Ledger is credited. 18.____

19. The amount credited to the allowance for bad debts account is an estimated amount. 19.____

20. The allowance for depreciation account usually has a credit balance. 20.____

21. The time received for a fixed asset at the time it is replaced is always equal to its book value. 21.____

22. Prepaid expenses are sometimes called deferred credits to income. 22.____

23. Expenses that are incurred but not paid are termed accrued expenses. 23.____

24. Prepaid expenses may be shown on the balance sheet as a current asset. 24.____

25. Equipment is listed on the balance sheet as a fixed asset. 25.____

Questions 26-30.

DIRECTIONS: Questions 26 through 30 are to be answered by writing the CORRECT amount in the space at the right.

26. The office supplies account has a balance of $150 at the close of the fiscal period. The actual inventory of supplies is $60. What is the amount of supplies used during the period? 26.____

27. A company receives $490 in cash from a customer for the prompt payment of an invoice. Two percent was the discount. What was the original amount of the invoice? 27.____

28. The balance of the store supplies before adjustment is $400. The total cost of the store supplies on hand at the end of the period is $150. What is the amount of the adjusting entry? 28.____

29. What is the amount necessary to pay a $300 invoice, terms 3/10, 2/20, n/30, twelve days after date? 29._____

30. If equipment costing $1,500, with an estimated life of ten years, was purchased, what is the annual rate of depreciation? 30._____

KEY (CORRECT ANSWERS)

1.	T	11.	T	21.	F
2.	F	12.	F	22.	F
3.	T	13.	F	23.	T
4.	F	14.	T	24.	T
5.	F	15.	T	25.	T
6.	T	16.	F	26.	$90
7.	F	17.	F	27.	$500
8.	T	18.	F	28.	$250
9.	T	19.	T	29.	$294
10.	T	20.	T	30.	10%

TEST 4

DIRECTIONS: Each question or incomplete statement is followed by several suggested answers or completions. Select the one that BEST answers the question or completes the statement. *PRINT THE LETTER OF THE CORRECT ANSWER IN THE SPACE AT THE RIGHT.*

Questions 1-12.

DIRECTIONS: Each of Questions 1 through 12 consists of a statement. You are to indicate whether the statement is TRUE (T) or FALSE (F). *PRINT THE LETTER OF THE CORRECT ANSWER IN THE SPACE AT THE RIGHT.*

1. The supplies used during a fiscal period are shown on the balance sheet as a current asset.   1.____

2. If the assets and liabilities increase equally, the proprietorship also increases.   2.____

3. The Income and Expense Statement shows the results of business operations over a period of time.   3.____

4. An exchange of one asset for another asset of different value causes a change in the proprietorship.   4.____

5. The recording of allowance for depreciation actually results in writing down the asset values.   5.____

6. If the closing merchandise inventory is understated, the profit for the period will be understated.   6.____

7. If accrued salaries during a period are not recorded, the profit for the period will be overstated.   7.____

8. If sales returns are understated during a fiscal period, the profit for that period will be understated.   8.____

9. Unpaid salaries should be added to the salaries for the period before the profit for the period is figured.   9.____

10. When posting the Sales Journal, each item is posted separately to the accounts receivable controlling account in the General Ledger.   10.____

11. A business is said to be solvent when it has a net profit for the period.   11.____

12. Accrued income is income earned but not received during a fiscal period.   12.____

Questions 13-30.

DIRECTIONS: Below is a list of terms with an accompanying list of definitions or explanations. In the space at the right, put the letter of the term in Column II which BEST explains the definition or explanation in Column I.

COLUMN I

13. Entries needed to bring accounts up to date at the end of an accounting period

14. An entry in a book of original entry that has more than one debit or credit

15. An account used to summarize the income and expense data at the close of the fiscal period

16. An account with a balance that is partly a balance sheet amount and partly an income statement amount

17. Discount granted to a customer for early payment of his account

18. A journal designed for recording a particular type of transaction only

19. A ledger used for recording the details of a single account

20. An account in the general ledger that is supported by a subsidiary ledger

21. A list of individual account balances in a subsidiary ledger

22. Expense items bought and paid for, but not entirely consumed during the fiscal period

23. Expenses incurred but not paid during a fiscal period

24. The decrease in the value of a fixed asset due to wear and tear

25. The amount of unsold merchandise on hand

COLUMN II

A. Abstract
B. Accrued expenses
C. Adjusting entries
D. Allowance for bad debts
E. Book value
F. Cash discount
G. Compound entry
H. Controlling account
I. Current asset
J. Depreciation
K. Fixed asset
L. General ledger
M. Income & expense summary
N. Merchandise inventory
O. Mixed account
P. Petty cash
Q. Prepaid expenses
R. Retail method
S. Special journal
T. Straight-line method
U. Subsidiary ledger
V. Voucher

13.____
14.____
15.____
16.____
17.____
18.____
19.____
20.____
21.____
22.____
23.____
24.____
25.____

3 (#4)

26. Assets of a more or less permanent nature used in the business   26.____

27. The amount of estimated uncollectible accounts receivable.   27.____

28. The most commonly used method of computing depreciation   28.____

29. The difference between the original cost of an asset and its valuation amount   29.____

30. A written authorization required for each expenditure   30.____

KEY (CORRECT ANSWERS)

1.	F	11.	F	21.	A
2.	F	12.	T	22.	Q
3.	T	13.	C	23.	B
4.	T	14.	G	24.	J
5.	F	15.	M	25.	N
6.	T	16.	O	26.	K
7.	T	17.	F	27.	D
8.	F	18.	S	28.	T
9.	T	19.	U	29.	E
10.	F	20.	H	30.	V

TEST 5

Questions 1-12.

DIRECTIONS: Questions 1 through 12 are to be answered by writing the CORRECT amount in the space at the right.

1. If the purchases for the month were $500, the beginning inventory was $1,500, the ending inventory was $1,000, and the gross profit was $2,000, what were the sales? 1.____

2. If the gross profit for the period was $750 and the net profit was $250, what was the amount of the expenses? 2.____

3. Determine the amount of the cost of goods sold if the purchases for the month were $10,000, the beginning inventory was $3,000, and the ending inventory was $5,000. 3.____

4. A typewriter was purchased for $300 with an estimated life of five years. What is the book value at the end of the third year? 4.____

5. A delivery truck costs $3,000. Its book value at the end of the third year was $2,100. What is the amount of depreciation each year? 5.____

6. The assets on a Balance Sheet are $7,500. The liabilities are $4,500. What is the capital? 6.____

7. A check was received for $242.50 in payment of a sale amounting to $250 less discount. What is the percent of discount allowed? 7.____

8. The capital at the close of the fiscal period was $10,000. The liabilities were $12,000. What are the TOTAL assets? 8.____

9. A note is dated March 1 and is due in 60 days. What is its due date? 9.____

10. A note is dated January 30. It is due in one month. What is its due date? 10.____

11. What is the interest on a note for $500 with interest at 6% for sixty days? 11.____

12. What is the interest on a note for $800 with interest at 6% for 45 days? 12.____

Questions 13-15

DIRECTIONS: Each of Questions 13 through 25 consists of a statement. You are to indicate whether the statement is TRUE (T) or FALSE (F). *PRINT THE LETTER OF THE CORRECT ANSWER IN THE SPACE AT THE RIGHT.*

13. To determine the value of the merchandise available for sale, the purchases are added to the beginning merchandise inventory. 13.____

14. The closing merchandise inventory is shown on both the Balance Sheet and the Income and Expense Statement.　　14._____

15. The allowance for bad debts account is closed into the income and expense summary account at the close of the fiscal period.　　15._____

16. The accounts payable account shows the total amount owed to creditors and also shows how much is owed to each creditor.　　16._____

17. Sales discount is usually subtracted from the sales in the Income and Expense Statement.　　17._____

18. The use of controlling accounts increases the possibility of errors in preparing the trial balance.　　18._____

19. The use of controlling accounts results in fewer accounts in the General Ledger.　　19._____

20. The total of the schedule of accounts receivable should equal the balance of the accounts receivable account in the General Ledger.　　20._____

21. Closing entries summarize in the income and expense summary account the income costs and expense for the fiscal period.　　21._____

22. The post-closing trial balance is made before the Balance Sheet has been made.　　22._____

23. The closing entries are recorded in the General Journal.　　23._____

24. The debit balance of the equipment account should show the book value of the equipment on hand.　　24._____

25. The balance of the allowance for depreciation of equipment account is shown on the Balance Sheet.　　25._____

3 (#5)

KEY (CORRECT ANSWERS)

1.	$3,000		11.	$5.00
2.	$500		12.	$6.00
3.	$8,000		13.	T
4.	$120		14.	T
5.	$300		15.	F
6.	$3,000		16.	F
7.	3%		17.	T
8.	$22,000		18.	F
9.	April 30		19.	T
10.	Feb. 28		20.	T

21. T
22. F
23. T
24. F
25. T

EXAMINATION SECTION
TEST 1

DIRECTIONS: Each question or incomplete statement is followed by several suggested answers or completions. Select the one that BEST answers the question or completes the statement. *PRINT THE LETTER OF THE CORRECT ANSWER IN THE SPACE AT THE RIGHT.*

Questions 1-5.

DIRECTIONS: Questions 1 through 5 are to be answered on the basis of the statement account shown below.

STATEMENT OF ACCOUNT

Regal Tools, Inc.
136 Culver Street
Cranston, R.I. 02910

TO: Vista, Inc.
572 No. Copeland Ave.
Pawtucket, R.I. 02800

DATE: March 31

DATE	ITEM	CHARGES	PAYMENTS AND CREDITS	BALANCE
	Previous Balance			785.35
March 8	Payment		785.35	----
12	Invoice 17-582	550 --		550.00
17	Invoice 17-692	700 --		1250.00
31	Payment		550.00	700.00

PAY LAST AMOUNT SHOWN IN BALANCE COLUMN

1. Which company is the customer? 1._____

2. What total amount was charged by the customer during March? 2._____

3. How much does the customer owe on March 31? 3._____

4. On which accounting schedule would Vista list Regal? 4._____

5. The terms on invoice 17-582 were 3/20, n/45.
   What was the CORRECT amount for which the check should have been written when payment was made? 5._____

6. Which item is NOT a source document? A(n)

   A. invoice
   B. magnetic tape
   C. punched card
   D. telephone conversation

7. What is double-entry accounting?

   A. Journalizing and posting
   B. Recording debit and credit parts for a transaction
   C. Using carbon paper when preparing a source document
   D. Posting a debit or credit and computing the new account balance

8. The balance in the asset account Supplies is $600. An ending inventory shows $200 of supplies on hand.
   The adjusting entry should be

   A. debit Supplies Expense for $200, credit Supplies for $200
   B. credit Supplies Expense for $200, debit Supplies for $200
   C. debit Supplies Expense for $400, credit Supplies for $400
   D. credit Supplies Expense for $400, debit Supplies for $400

9. What is the purpose of preparing an Income Statement? To

   A. report the net income or net loss
   B. show the owner's claims against the assets
   C. prove that the accounting equation is in balance
   D. prove that the total debits equal the total credits

10. Which account does NOT belong on the Income Statement?

    A. Salaries Payable
    B. Rental Revenue
    C. Advertising Expense
    D. Sales Returns and Allowances

11. The source document for entries made in a Purchases Journal is a purchase

    A. order   B. requisition   C. invoice   D. register

12. A business check guaranteed for payment by the bank is called a

    A. bank draft
    B. certified check
    C. cashier's check
    D. personal check

13. The entry that closes the Purchases Account contains a

    A. debit to Purchases
    B. debit to Purchases Returns and Allowances
    C. credit to Purchases
    D. credit to Income and Expense Summary

14. Which account would NOT appear on a Balance Sheet?

    A. Office Equipment
    B. Transportation In
    C. Mortgage Payable
    D. Supplies on Hand

15. Which entry is made at the end of the fiscal period for the purpose of updating the Prepaid Insurance Account?
    _____ entry.

    A. Correcting   B. Closing   C. Adjusting   D. Reversing

16. Which deduction from gross pay is NOT required by law?

    A. Hospitalization insurance
    B. FICA tax
    C. Federal income tax
    D. New York State income tax

17. What is the last date on which a 2 percent cash discount can be taken for an invoice dated October 15 with terms of 2/10, n/30?

    A. October 15
    B. October 17
    C. October 25
    D. November 14

18. Which item on the bank reconciliation statement would require the business to record a journal entry?
    A(n)

    A. deposit in transit
    B. outstanding check
    C. canceled check
    D. bank service charge

19. Which is NOT an essential component of a computer?
    A(n)

    A. input device
    B. central processor
    C. output device
    D. telecommunicator

20. Which group of accounts could appear on a post-closing trial balance?

    A. Petty Cash; Accounts Receivable; FICA Taxes Payable
    B. Office Furniture; Office Expense; Supplies on Hand
    C. Supplies Expense; Sales; Advertising Expense
    D. Sales Discount; Rent Expense; J. Smith, Drawing

21. The withdrawals of cash by the owner are recorded in the owner's drawing account as a(n)

    A. adjusting entry
    B. closing entry
    C. credit
    D. debit

22. An account in the General Ledger which shows a total of a related Subsidiary Ledger is referred to as a(n) _____ account.

    A. revenue
    B. controlling
    C. temporary
    D. owner's equity

23.

> *For Deposit Only*
> *Anthony Gill*

Which type of endorsement is shown above?

A. Restrictive B. Blank
C. Full D. Qualified

24. Which is a chronological record of all the transactions of a business?

A. Worksheet B. Income Statement
C. Journal D. Trial balance

25. Which error would NOT be revealed by the preparation of a trial balance?

A. Posting of an entire transaction more than once
B. Incorrectly pencil footing the balance of a general ledger account
C. Posting a debit of $320 as $230
D. Omitting an account with a balance

26. The Cash Receipts Journal is used to record the

A. purchase of merchandise for cash
B. purchase of merchandise on credit
C. sale of merchandise for cash
D. sale of merchandise on credit

27. On a systems flowchart, which symbol is commonly used to indicate the direction of the flow of work?
A(n)

A. arrow B. circle C. diamond D. rectangle

28. Which account balance would be eliminated by a closing entry at the end of the fiscal period?

A. Office Equipment B. Owner's Drawing
C. Owner's Capital D. Mortgage Payable

29. In a data processing system, the handling and manipulation of data according to precise procedures is called

A. input B. processing
C. storage D. output

30. Which financial statement reflects the cumulative financial position of the business?

A. Bank statement B. Income statement
C. Trial balance D. Balance sheet

31. Which account should be credited when recording a cash proof showing an overage? 31.____

    A. Sales
    B. Cash
    C. Cash Short and Over
    D. Sales Returns and Allowances

32. In which section of the income statement would the purchases account be shown? 32.____

    A. Cost of Goods Sold
    B. Income from Sales
    C. Operating Expenses
    D. Other Expenses

33. What is an invoice? 33.____
    A(n)

    A. order for the shipment of goods
    B. order for the purchase of goods
    C. receipt for goods purchased
    D. statement listing goods purchased

34. A business uses a Sales Journal, a Purchases Journal, a Cash Receipts Journal, a Cash Payments Journal, and a General Journal. 34.____
    In which journal would a credit memorandum received from a creditor be recorded?
    _____ Journal

    A. Sales
    B. Purchases
    C. General
    D. Cash Receipts

35. Which account is debited to record a weekly payroll? 35.____

    A. Employees Income Tax Payable
    B. FICA Taxes Payable
    C. General Expense
    D. Salaries Expense

KEY (CORRECT ANSWERS)

1. Vista, Inc.
2. $1,250
3. $700
4. Accts. Payable
5. $533.50

6. D
7. B
8. C
9. A
10. A

11. C
12. B
13. C
14. D
15. C

16. A
17. C
18. D
19. D
20. A

21. D
22. B
23. A
24. C
25. A

26. C
27. A
28. B
29. B
30. D

31. C
32. A
33. D
34. C
35. D

BOOKKEEPING PROBLEMS
EXAMINATION SECTION
TEST 1

DIRECTIONS: Each question or incomplete statement is followed by several suggested answers or completions. Select the one that BEST answers the question or completes the statement. *PRINT THE LETTER OF THE CORRECT ANSWER IN THE SPACE AT THE RIGHT.*

1. The accounts in a general ledger are BEST arranged

    A. in numerical order
    B. according to the frequency with which each account is used
    C. according to the order in which the headings of the columns in the cash journals are arranged
    D. according to the order in which they are used in preparing financial statements

2. A physical inventory is an inventory obtained by

    A. an actual count of the items on hand
    B. adding the totals of the stock record cards
    C. deducting the cost of goods sold from the purchases for the period
    D. deducting the purchases from the sales for the period

3. Modern accounting practice favors the valuation of the inventories of a going concern at

    A. current market prices, if higher than cost
    B. cost or market, whichever is lower
    C. estimated selling price
    D. probable value at forced sale

4. A subsidiary ledger contains accounts which show

    A. details of contingent liabilities of undetermined amount
    B. totals of all asset accounts in the general ledger
    C. totals of all liability accounts in the general ledger
    D. details of an account in the general ledger

5. A statement of the assets, liabilities, and net worth of a business is called a

    A. trial balance B. budget
    C. profit and loss statement D. balance sheet

6. The one of the following which is NEVER properly considered a negotiable instrument is a(n)

    A. invoice B. bond
    C. promissory note D. endorsed check

7. The term *current assets* USUALLY includes such things as

    A. notes payable B. machinery and equipment
    C. furniture and fixtures D. accounts receivable

8. An accounting system which records revenues as soon as they are earned and records liabilities as soon as they are incurred regardless of the date of payment is said to operate on a(n) _____ basis.   8.___

   A. accrual   B. budgetary   C. encumbrance   D. cash

9. A *trial balance* is a list of   9.___

   A. the credit balances in all accounts in a general ledger
   B. all general ledger accounts and their balances
   C. the asset accounts in a general ledger and their balances
   D. the liability accounts in a general ledger and their balances

10. A controlling account contains the totals of   10.___

    A. the accounts used in preparing the balance sheet at the end of the fiscal period
    B. the individual amounts entered in the accounts of a subsidiary ledger during the fiscal period
    C. all entries in the general journal during the fiscal period
    D. the accounts used in preparing the profit and loss statement for the fiscal period

11. The ESSENTIAL nature of an asset is that it(s)   11.___

    A. must be tangible
    B. must be easily converted into cash
    C. must have value
    D. cost must be included in the profit and loss statement

12. When an asset is depreciated on the straight-line basis, the amount charged off for depreciation   12.___

    A. is greater in the earlier years of the asset's life
    B. is greater in the later years of the asset's life
    C. varies each year according to the extent to which the asset is used during the year
    D. is equal each full year of the asset's life

Questions 13-27.

DIRECTIONS: Questions 13 to 27 consist of a list of some of the accounts in a general ledger. Indicate whether each account listed generally contains a debit or a credit balance by putting the letter D (for debit balance) or the letter C (for credit balance) in the correspondingly numbered space on the right for each account listed. For example, for the account Cash, which generally contains a debit balance, you would give the letter D as your answer.

13. Sales Taxes Collected   13.___

14. Social Security Taxes Paid by Employer   14.___

15. Deposits from Customers   15.___

16. Freight Inward   16.___

17. Sales Discount   17.___

18. Withholding Taxes Payable   18.____
19. L. Norton, Drawings   19.____
20. Office Salaries   20.____
21. Merchandise Inventory   21.____
22. L. Norton, Capital   22.____
23. Purchases Returns   23.____
24. Unearned Rent Income   24.____
25. Reserve for Bad Debts   25.____
26. Depreciation of Machinery   26.____
27. Insurance Prepaid   27.____

Questions 28-42.

DIRECTIONS: Questions 28 to 42 consist of a list of some of the accounts in a general ledger. For the purpose of preparing financial statements, each of these accounts is to be classified into one of the following five major classifications, lettered A to E, as follows:
A. Assets   B. Liabilities   C. Proprietorship
D. Income   E. Expense

You are to indicate the classification to which each account belongs by printing the correct letter, A, B, C, D, or E, in the correspondingly numbered space on the right. For example, for the account Furniture and Fixtures, which is an asset account, you would print the letter A.

28. Notes Receivable   28.____
29. Sales   29.____
30. Wages Payable   30.____
31. Office Salaries   31.____
32. Capital Stock Authorized   32.____
33. Goodwill   33.____
34. Capital Surplus   34.____
35. Office Supplies Used   35.____
36. Interest Payable   36.____
37. Prepaid Rent   37.____
38. Interest Cost   38.____
39. Accounts Payable   39.____

40. Prepaid Insurance   40.___

41. Merchandise Inventory   41.___

42. Interest Earned   42.___

43. A trial balance will NOT indicate that an error has been made in   43.___

    A. computing the balance of an account
    B. entering an amount in the wrong account
    C. carrying forward the balance of an account
    D. entering an amount on the wrong side of an account

44. Many business firms maintain a book of original entry in which all bills to be paid are recorded.   44.___
    This book is known as a

    A. purchase returns journal   B. subsidiary ledger
    C. voucher register   D. notes payable register

45. Many business firms provide a petty cash fund from which to pay for small items in order to avoid the issuing of many small checks.   45.___
    If this fund is replenished periodically to restore it to its original amount, the fund is called a(n) _____ fund.

    A. imprest   B. debenture
    C. adjustment   D. expense reserve

46. A firm which voluntarily terminates business, selling its assets and paying its liabilities, is said to be in   46.___

    A. receivership   B. liquidation
    C. depletion   D. amortization

47. The phrase *3%-10 days* on an invoice ORDINARILY means that   47.___

    A. 3% of the amount must be paid each 10 days
    B. the purchaser is entitled to only ten days credit
    C. a discount of 3% will be allowed for payment in 10 days
    D. the entire amount must be paid in 10 days or a penalty of 3% of the amount due will be added

48. The CHIEF disadvantage of *single-entry* bookkeeping is that it   48.___

    A. is too difficult to operate
    B. is illegal for income tax purposes
    C. provides no possibility of determining net profits
    D. furnishes an incomplete picture of the business

49. Sales *minus* cost of goods sold *equals*   49.___

    A. net profit   B. gross sales
    C. gross profit   D. net sales

50. The amounts of the transactions recorded in a journal are transferred to the general ledger accounts by a process known as   50.____

    A. auditing   B. balancing   C. posting   D. verifying

51. A merchant purchased a stock of goods and priced these goods so as to gain 40% on the cost to him.   51.____
    If the merchant sold these goods for $840, the COST of these goods to him was

    A. $556   B. $600   C. $348   D. $925

52. In the interest at 6% for one full year on a principal sum amounts to $12, the *principal sum* is   52.____

    A. $150   B. $96   C. $196   D. $200

53. On October 17, a business man discounted a customer's 90-day non-interest bearing note at his bank. The face of the note was $960, and it was dated September 28. The discount rate was 5%.   53.____
    Using a 360-day year, the amount in cash that the business man received from the bank was MOST NEARLY

    A. $899.33   B. $950.67   C. $967.50   D. $989.75

54. A certain correctly totaled cash receipts journal contained the following columns: Net Cash Debit, Accounts Receivable, Sales Discounts, and General.   54.____
    At the end of April, the totals of the columns were as follows: Net Cash Debit - $18,925.15, Accounts Receivable (not given), Sales Discounts - $379.65, General - $5,639.25.
    The TOTAL of the Accounts Receivable column was

    A. $11,194.50   B. $21,344.32   C. $7,621.19   D. $13,665.55

55. In its first year of operation, a retail store had cash sales of $49,000 and installment sales of $41,000.   55.____
    If 12% of the amount of these installment sales were collected in that year, the TOTAL amount of cash received from sales was

    A. $22,176   B. $34,987   C. $53,920   D. $55,650

56. I. Conklin and J. Ulster formed a partnership and agreed to share profits in proportion to their initial capital investments. I. Conklin invested $15,000 and J. Ulster invested $12,500.   56.____
    If the profits for the year were $16,500, J. Ulster's share of the profits was

    A. $6,750   B. $7,500   C. $8,100   D. $8,300

57. In a certain city, the tax rate on real estate one year was $48.75 per thousand dollars of assessed valuation. If an apartment house in that city was assessed for $185,000, the real estate tax payable by the owner of that house was MOST NEARLY   57.____

    A. $9,018.75   B. $9,009.75   C. $8,900.00   D. $8,905.25

58. A correctly totaled cash payments journal contained the following columns: Net Cash, Accounts Payable, Purchase Discounts, General.
At the end of April, the totals of the columns were as follows: Net Cash - $18,375.60, Accounts Payable - $16,981.19, Purchase Discounts (not given), General - $1,875.37.
The TOTAL of the Purchase Discounts column was

    A. $120.36   B. $239.87   C. $480.96   D. $670.51

59. On January 1, the credit balance of the Accounts Payable account in a general ledger was $9,139.87. For the month of January, the Purchase Journal total amounted to $3,467.81; the Accounts Payable column in the Cash Disbursements Journal amounted to $2,935.55; the total of the Returned Purchases Journal for January amounted to $173.15; and the Miscellaneous column in the Cash Disbursements Journal showed that $750 had been paid in January on notes given to creditors and entered in previous months.
The BALANCE in the Accounts Payable account at the end of January was

    A. $8,437.89   B. $9,498.98   C. $9,998.98   D. $10,132.68

60. The bank statement received from his bank by a business man showed a certain balance for the month of June. This bank statement showed a service charge of $5.19 for the month. He discovered that a check drawn by him in the amount of $83.75 and returned by the bank had been entered on the stub of his checkbook as $38.75. He also found that two checks which he had issued, #29 for $37.18 and #33 for $18.69, were not listed on the statement and had not been returned by the bank. The balance in his checkbook before he reconciled it with the balance shown on the bank statement was $8,917.91.
The BALANCE on the bank statement was

    A. $8,903.97   B. $8,923.59   C. $8,997.65   D. $9,303.95

KEY (CORRECT ANSWERS)

1.	D	16.	D	31.	E	46.	B		
2.	A	17.	D	32.	C	47.	C		
3.	B	18.	C	33.	A	48.	D		
4.	D	19.	D	34.	C	49.	C		
5.	D	20.	D	35.	E	50.	C		
6.	A	21.	D	36.	B	51.	B		
7.	D	22.	C	37.	A	52.	D		
8.	A	23.	C	38.	E	53.	B		
9.	B	24.	C	39.	B	54.	D		
10.	B	25.	C	40.	A	55.	C		
11.	C	26.	D	41.	A	56.	B		
12.	D	27.	D	42.	D	57.	A		
13.	C	28.	A	43.	B	58.	C		
14.	D	29.	D	44.	C	59.	B		
15.	C	30.	B	45.	A	60.	B		

TEST 2

Questions 1-25.

DIRECTIONS:
1. Below you will find the general ledger balances on February 28 in the books of C. Dutton.
2. On the following pages, you will find all the entries on the books of C. Dutton for the month of March.
3. In the appropriate spaces on the right, you are to supply the new balances for the accounts called for at the end of March.

The correct balances in the general ledger of C. Dutton on February 28 were as follows: (NOTE: The accounts below have not been arranged in the customary trial balance form.)

Cash	$4,336
Accounts Receivable	8,165
Notes Receivable	2,200
Furniture and Fixtures	9,000
Merchandise Inventory 1/1	4,175
Accounts Payable	5,560
Notes Payable	1,500
Reserve for Depreciation of Furniture and Fixtures	1,800
C. Dutton, Capital	14,162
C. Dutton, Drawing	900
Purchases	42,600
Freight In	36
Rent	1,750
Light	126
Telephone	63
Salaries	4,076
Shipping Expenses	368
Sales	53,200
Sales Biscount	637
Purchase Biscount	596
City Sales Tax Collected	804
Social Security Taxes Payable	96
Withholding Taxes Payable	714

CASH RECEIPTS

Date	Name	Net Cash	Accounts Receivable	Sales Disc.	Miscellaneous Acct.	Amount
3/1	T. Blint	6,027.00	6,150.00	123.00		
	K. Crowe	1,015.00			Notes Rec.	1,000.00
					Int. Income	15.00
3/10	N. Tandy	3,969.00	4,050.00	81.00		
3/17	Rebuilt Desk Co.	45.00			Furn. & Fixt.	45.00
3/24	J. Walter	2,910.00	3,000.00	90.00		
3/31	National Federal Bank	3,000.00			Notes Payable	3,000.00
		16,966.00	13,200.00	294.00		4,060.00

2 (#2)

CASH DISBURSEMENTS

Date		Net Cash	Accts. Pay.	Purch Disc.	Soc. Sec. Tax	With-hold Tax	Miscellaneous Acct.	Amount
3/1	Bliss Realty Co.	875.00					Rent	875.00
3/4	Con. Edison	54.00					Light	54.00
3/10	D. LaRue	2,891.00	2,950.00	59.00				
3/15	Payroll	747.00			26.00	175.	Sal.	948.00
3/19	Rebuilt Desk Co.	115.00					Furn/Fixt	115.00
3/26	Jiggs & Co.	3,686.00	3,800.00	114.00				
3/30	Nat'l Fed Bank	1,218.00					Notes Pay.	1200.00
							Int. Cost	18.00
3/31	Payroll	733.00			22.00	171.	Salary	926.00
3/31	C. Dutton	600.00					Draw	600.00
		10,919.00	6,750.00	173.00	48.00	346.00		4736.00

SALES BOOK

Date	Name	Accts. Rec.	Sales	City Sales Tax
3/3	K. Crowe	6,850.00	6,665.00	185.00
3/10	J. Walters	5,730.00	5,730.00	
3/16	N. Tandy	3,100.00	3,007.00	93.00
3/25	Willis & Co.	7,278.00	7,069.00	209.00
3/30	V. Clyburne	2,190.00	2,190.00	
		25,148.00	24,661.00	487.00

PURCHASE BOOK

Date		Accts. Pay.	Purchases	Freight In	Miscellaneous Acct.	Amount
3/4	Jiggs & Co.	5,212.00	5,070.00	142.00		
3/11	Barton & Co.	320.00			Ins. Prepd.	320.00
3/16	A. Field	6,368.00	6,179.00	189.00		
3/19	Smith Delivery	22.00			Ship. Exp.	22.00
3/23	N.Y. Telephone	29.00			Telephone	29.00
3/26	D. LaRue	3,000.00	3,000.00			
3/29	App & App	7,531.00	7,168.00	363.00		
		22,482.00	21,417.00	694.00		371.00

Supply the balances of the following accounts on March 31 after all posting has been done for March. Put answers in the appropriate spaces on the right. Give amounts only.

1. Cash   1._____

2. Accounts Receivable   2._____

3. Notes Receivable   3._____

4. Insurance Prepaid   4._____

5. Furniture and Fixtures   5._____

6. Accounts Payable   6._____

7. Notes Payable   7._____

8. Reserve for Depreciation of Furniture and Fixtures   8._____

9. C. Dutton, Capital   9._____

10. C. Dutton, Drawing   10._____

11. Purchases   11._____

12. Freight In   12._____

13. Rent   13._____

14. Light   14._____

15. Telephone   15._____

16. Salaries   16._____

17. Shipping Expenses   17._____

18. Sales   18._____

19. Sales Discount   19._____

20. Purchase Discount   20._____

21. City Sales Tax Collected   21._____

22. Social Security Taxes Payable   22._____

23. Withholding Taxes Payable   23._____

24. Interest Income   24._____

25. Interest Cost   25._____

Questions 26-35.

DIRECTIONS: Mr. Adams has a complete set of books - Cash Journals, Purchase and Sales Journals, and a General Journal. Below you will find the General Journal used by Mr. Adams. Under the heading of each money column, you will find a letter of the alphabet. Following the General Journal, there is a series of transactions. You are to determine the correct entry for each transaction and then show on the right in the appropriate space the columns to be used. For example, if a certain transaction results in an entry of $100 in the Notes Receiving Column (on the left side) and an entry of $100 in the General Ledger Column (on the right side), in the appropriate space on the right, you should write A, D. If the record of the transaction requires the use of more than two columns, your answer should contain more than two letters. DO NOT PUT THE AMOUNTS IN YOUR ANSWER SPACE. The LETTERS of the columns to be used are sufficient. If a transaction requires no entry in the General Journal, write *None* in the appropriate space in your answer space, even though a record would be made in some other journal.

4 (#2)

GENERAL JOURNAL

Notes Receivable	Accounts Payable	General Ledger	L. F.		General Ledger	Accounts Receivable	Notes Payable
A	B	C			D	E	F

26. We sent Tripp & Co. a 30-day trade acceptance for $500 for merchandise sold him today. They accepted it.   26.___

27. The proprietor, Mr. Adams, returned $100 in cash to be deposited, representing Traveling Expenses he had not used.   27.___

28. An entry in the purchase journal last month for a purchase invoice from V. Valides for $647 was erroneously entered in the purchase journal as $746 and posted as such.   28.___

29. A check for $200 received from Mr. Breen was erroneously credited to account of P. Ungar.   29.___

30. In posting the totals of the cash receipts journal last month, an item of bank discount of $30 on our note for $1500 discounted for 60 days was included in the total posted to the sales discount account.   30.___

31. M. Hogan paid his note of $600 and interest of $12 and his account was credited for $612.   31.___

32. Mr. Blow informed us he could not pay his invoice of $2000 due today. Instead, he sent us his 30-day note for $2000 for 30 days bearing interest at 6% per annum.   32.___

33. The proprietor, Mr. Adams, drew $75 to buy his daughter a U.S. Bond.   33.___

34. Mr. O'Brien wrote to us that we overcharged him on an invoice last week.   34.___

35. Returned $120 worth of merchandise to Pecora & Co. and received their credit memorandum.   35.___

Questions 36-50.

DIRECTIONS: In Questions 36 to 50, you will find a list of accounts with a number before each.

1. Cash
2. Accounts Receivable
3. Notes Receivable
4. Notes Receivable Discounted
5. Furniture and Fixtures
6. Delivery Equipment
7. Insurance Prepaid
8. Depreciation on Delivery Equipment
9. Bad Debts
10. Purchases
11. Discount on Purchases
12. Sales
13. Discount on Sales
14. Accounts Payable
15. Notes Payable
16. Interest Cost
17. Reserve for Depreciation on Delivery Equipment
18. Reserve for Bad Debts
19. Sales Taxes Collected
20. Ben Miller, Capital
21. Ben Miller, Drawing
22. Interest Income
23. Purchase Returns

5 (#2)

Using the number in front of each account title (using no accounts not listed), make journal entries for the transactions given below. Do not write the names of the accounts in your answer space. Simply indicate in the proper space on the right the numbers of the accounts to be debited or credited. Always give the number or numbers of the accounts to be debited first, then give the number or numbers of accounts to be credited. For example, if furniture and fixtures and delivery equipment are to be debited, and cash and notes payable are to be credited in a certain transaction, then write in your answer space 5, 6 - 1, 15 (use a dash to separate the debits from the credits).

36. F. Pierce, a customer, went into bankruptcy owing us $600. We received a check for $200.   36._____

37. Later in the month, we are informed that there is no possibility of collecting the balance from F. Pierce. There is a sufficient balance in the Reserve for Bad Debts to take care of the above.   37._____

38. Set up the Depreciation on the Delivery Equipment for the year amounting to $240.   38._____

39. Discounted M. Colby's note for $500 today and received $490 in proceeds.   39._____

40. Mr. Miller, the proprietor, invested $2000 in the business.   40._____

41. Paid our note due to Dillon & Co. today for $800 with interest of $16.   41._____

42. Accepted Finnegan's trade acceptance for $1500 for merchandise bought today.   42._____

43. Create a Reserve for Bad Debts of $2000 at the end of the year.   43._____

44. Returned to Dillon & Co. $30 worth of damaged merchandise for credit. They allowed it.   44._____

45. G. Garry claimed a discount of $12 which we had failed to allow him. He had already paid his bill. Sent him check for $12.   45._____

46. On one sale during the month, we had failed to collect the Sales Tax of $15. Wrote to the customer and he sent us a check for $15.   46._____

47. M. Colby paid his note due today which we had discounted two months ago.   47._____

48. Bought a new safe for $875 from Cramer & Co., terms 2/10, n/60 days. Agreed to pay them in 60 days.   48._____

49. Bought merchandise during the month amounting to $17,500 - all on account.   49._____

50. On December 31, paid for a Fire Insurance policy to run for three years from that date - premium was $480.   50._____

51. The following information was taken from the ledger of Peter Dolan on Dec. 31 after adjusting entries had been posted to the ledger.   51._____

Sales Income	$60,000
Sales Returns	3,500
Mdse. Purchases	42,000
Inventory of 1/1	9,400
Sales Taxes Payable	360
Freight Inward	225
Inventory 12/31	7,640
Insurance Unexpired	163

Find the gross profit on Sales for the year.

52. On March 31, your bank sent you a statement of account. You compared the canceled checks with the stubs in your checkbook and found the following:
    Check #34 - $56.00 had not been paid by the bank
           #44 - $38.00 had been paid by the bank as $38.89 because the amount on the check did not agree with your stub in the checkbook
           #52 - $76.50 had not been returned by the bank, though the check had been certified
           #57 - $127.42 had not been paid by the bank
    What total amount would you deduct from the balance on the bank's statement as checks outstanding?

53. On April 30, Mr. Jolley received his statement of account from the bank. A comparison of the bank statement and your checkbook revealed the following: Checkbook balance $5,640; this included a deposit of $325 on the last day of April which had not been entered on the bank statement.
    You also find the following:
    Check #69 - $89.00 had not been paid by the bank
           #70 - Paid by the bank as $47.55, had been entered in your checkbook as $45.57
           #76 - $114.30 had not been paid by the bank
    The bank statement included a debit memo of $4.00 for excessive activity during the month.
    What was the balance on the bank statement?

54. An invoice dated January 15 for merchandise you bought added up to $876.00. The terms were 3/10, n/60, F.O.B. DESTINATION. When the goods arrived, you paid freight amounting to $8.50. On January 20, you returned goods billed at $26 and received credit therefor. You paid the bill on January 24.
    What was the amount of your check?

55. Income taxes paid by residents of a certain state are based on the balance of taxable income at the following
    rates: 2% on first $1000 or less
             3% on 2nd and 3rd $1000
             4% on 4th and 5th $1000
             5% on 6th and 7th $1000
             6% on 8th and 9th $1000
             7% on all over $9000
    What would be the NORMAL income tax to be paid by a resident of that state whose taxable balance of income was $6,750?

56. A salesman's gross earnings for the year came to $8,820. His rate of Commission was 5% of his sales to customers after deducting returns by customers. During the year, his customers returned 10% of the goods they purchased. What were his total sales during the year before deducting returns?

57. On December 31, the insurance account contained a debit for $144 for a three-year fire insurance policy dated August 1. What amount should be listed on the balance sheet of December 31 of that year?

58. A partnership began business on January 1 with partners' investments of $26,000. During the year, the partners drew $18,500 for personal use. On December 31, the assets of the firm were $46,300, and the liabilities were $15,600. What was the firm's net profit for the year? (Write P or L before your answer.) 58.____

59. The rent income account of a real estate firm showed a total balance of $75,640 at the end of 1986. Of this amount, $3,545 represented prepaid 1987 rents. The account also included entries for 1986 rents due from tenants but not yet collected, amounting to $2,400.
What amount should be listed on the profit and loss statement as rent income for 1986? 59.____

60. You discounted a customer's note for $7,200 at your bank at the rate of 6% and received net proceeds of $7,182.
How many days did the note have to run from date of discount to date of maturity? (Use 360 days to the year.) 60.____

Questions 61-90.

DIRECTIONS: In Questions 61 to 90, you will find a list of ledger accounts. Indicate whether an account is generally listed in the Trial Balance as a DEBIT or as a CREDIT by putting the letter *D* or the letter *C* in the correct space on the right for each account listed.

61. Sales   61.____
62. Land   62.____
63. Notes Payable   63.____
64. Traveling Expenses   64.____
65. Purchases   65.____
66. Buildings   66.____
67. Merchandise Inventory   67.____
68. Machinery and Equipment   68.____
69. Notes Receivable   69.____
70. Bonds Payable   70.____
71. Advertising   71.____
72. Delivery Expense   72.____
73. Cash   73.____

74. Accounts Payable — 74.____
75. Interest on Bonds — 75.____
76. Real Estate Taxes — 76.____
77. Accounts Receivable — 77.____
78. Don Burch, Proprietor — 78.____
79. Sales Discount — 79.____
80. Withholding Taxes — 80.____
81. Depreciation — 81.____
82. Prepaid Insurance — 82.____
83. Reserve for Dep. on Buildings — 83.____
84. Rent Income — 84.____
85. Reserve for Bad Debts — 85.____
86. Don Burch, Drawing Account — 86.____
87. Sales Returns — 87.____
88. Bad Debts — 88.____
89. Purchase Discount — 89.____
90. Reserve for Dep. on Machinery & Equipment — 90.____

KEY (CORRECT ANSWERS)

1.	$ 10,383	31.	C,D,D	61.	C
2.	$ 20,113	32.	A,E	62.	D
3.	$ 1,200	33.	None	63.	C
4.	$ 320	34.	C,E	64.	D
5.	$ 9,070	35.	B,D	65.	D
6.	$ 21,292	36.	1-2	66.	D
7.	$ 3,300	37.	18-2	67.	D
8.	$ 1,800	38.	8-17	68.	D
9.	$ 14,162	39.	1,16-4	69.	D
10.	$ 1,500	40.	1-20	70.	C
11.	$ 64,017	41.	15,16-1	71.	D
12.	$ 730	42.	14-15	72.	D
13.	$ 2,625	43.	9-18	73.	D
14.	$ 180	44.	14-23	74.	C
15.	$ 92	45.	13-1	75.	D
16.	$ 5,950	46.	1-19	76.	D
17.	$ 390	47.	4-3	77.	D
18.	$ 77,861	48.	5-14	78.	C
19.	$ 931	49.	10-14	79.	D
20.	$ 769	50.	7-1	80.	C
21.	$ 1,291	51.	$12,515	81.	D
22.	$ 144	52.	$ 183.42	82.	D
23.	$ 1,060	53.	$ 5,512.32	83.	C
24.	$ 15	54.	$ 816	84.	C
25.	$ 18	55.	$ 247.50	85.	C
26.	A-E	56.	$196,000	86.	D
27.	None	57.	$ 124	87.	D
28.	B-D	58.	P $23,200	88.	D
29.	C,E	59.	$72,095	89.	C
30.	C,D	60.	15	90.	C

TEST 3

DIRECTIONS: Each question or incomplete statement is followed by several suggested answers or completions. Select the one that BEST answers the question or completes the statement. *PRINT THE LETTER OF THE CORRECT ANSWER IN THE SPACE AT THE RIGHT.*

1. Of the following taxes, the one which is levied MOST NEARLY in accordance with ability to pay is a(n) _____ tax.   1.___

   A. excise
   B. income
   C. general property
   D. sales

2. When a check has been lost, the bank on which it is drawn should ORDINARILY be notified and instructed to   2.___

   A. stop payment on the check
   B. issue a duplicate of the check
   C. charge the account of the drawer for the amount of the check
   D. certify the check

3. The profit and loss statement prepared for a retail store does NOT ordinarily show   3.___

   A. the cost of goods sold
   B. depreciation of fixtures and equipment
   C. expenditures for salaries of employees
   D. the net worth of the proprietor

4. When two business corporations join their assets and liabilities to form a new corporation, the procedures is called a(n)   4.___

   A. merger
   B. liquidation
   C. receivership
   D. exchange

5. The method of depreciation which deducts an equal amount each full year of an asset's life is called _____ depreciation.   5.___

   A. sum-of-years digits
   B. declining balance
   C. straight-line
   D. service-hours

6. A fixed asset is an asset that   6.___

   A. is held primarily for sale to customers
   B. is used in the conduct of the business until worn out or replaced
   C. is readily convertible into cash
   D. has no definite value

7. The gross profit on sales for a period is determined by   7.___

   A. subtracting the cost of goods sold from the sales
   B. subtracting the sales returns and the discounts on sales from the gross sales
   C. subtracting the sales from the purchases for the period
   D. finding the difference between the inventory of merchandise at the beginning of the period and the inventory of merchandise at the end of the period

8. The term *auditing* refers to the   8.____

   A. entering of amounts from the journals into the general ledger
   B. reconciliation of the accounts in a subsidiary ledger with the controlling account in the general ledger
   C. preparation of a trial balance of the accounts in the general ledger
   D. examination of the general ledger and other records of a concern to determine its true financial condition

9. A voucher register is a   9.____

   A. type of electric cash register
   B. list of customers whose accounts are past due
   C. list of the assets of a business
   D. book in which bills to be paid are recorded

10. The account DISCOUNT ON PURCHASES is *properly* closed directly to the _____ account.   10.____

    A. Accounts Payable   B. Sales
    C. Purchases   D. Fixtures

11. The account UNEARNED RENTAL INCOME is *usually* considered a(n) _____ account.   11.____

    A. asset   B. nominal   C. capital   D. liability

12. A controlling account is an account which contains   12.____

    A. the totals of *all* the expense accounts in the general ledger
    B. the total of the amounts entered in the accounts in a subsidiary ledger
    C. the total of the depreciation on fixtures claimed in *all* preceding years
    D. *all* totals of the income and expense accounts before closing to the Profit and Loss account

13. The purpose of the DRAWING account in the general ledger of an individual enterprise is to show the   13.____

    A. salaries paid to the employees
    B. amounts paid to independent contractors for services rendered
    C. amounts taken by the proprietor for his personal use
    D. total of payments made for general expenses of the business

14. The phrase *2%/10 net 30 days* on an invoice ORDINARILY means that   14.____

    A. 2% of the amount must be paid within 30 days
    B. the purchaser must add 2% to the amount of the invoice if he fails to pay within 30 days
    C. the entire amount must be paid within 30 days
    D. the purchaser may deduct 2% from the amount if he pays within 30 days

15. The ESSENTIAL characteristic of a C.O.D. sale of merchandise is that the   15.____

    A. purchaser pays for the merchandise upon its receipt by him
    B. seller guarantees the merchandise to be as specified by him
    C. merchandise is delivered by a common carrier
    D. purchaser is permitted to pay for the merchandise in convenient installments

16. If the drawer of a check makes an error in writing the amount of the check, he should

    A. erase the error and insert the correct amount
    B. cross out the error and insert the correct amount
    C. destroy the check and prepare another one
    D. write the correct amount directly above the incorrect one

17. States do NOT levy a(n) _____ tax.

    A. unemployment insurance   B. income
    C. corporation franchise   D. export

18. The cost of goods sold by a retail store is PROPERLY determined by

    A. *adding* the closing inventory to the total of the opening inventory and the purchases for the year
    B. *deducting* the closing inventory from the total of the opening inventory and the purchases for the year
    C. *deducting* the total of the opening and closing inventories from the purchases for the year
    D. *adding* the total of the opening and closing inventories

19. The PRIMARY purpose of a trial balance is to determine

    A. that all transactions have been entered in the journals
    B. the accuracy of the totals in the general ledger
    C. the correctness of the amounts entered in the journals
    D. that amounts have been posted to the proper accounts in the general ledger

20. The SURPLUS account of a corporation is *ordinarily* used to record

    A. the actual amount subscribed by stockholders
    B. the amount of profits earned by the corporation
    C. any excess of current assets over current liabilities
    D. the total of the fixed assets of the corporation

Questions 21-30.

DIRECTIONS: Each of Questions 21 to 30 consists of a typical transaction of Our Business followed by the debit and credit (amounts omitted) of the journal entry for that transaction. For each of these questions, the debit and credit given may be appropriately classified under one of the following categories:

    A. The debit of the journal entry is CORRECT but the credit is INCORRECT.
    B. The debit of the journal entry is INCORRECT but the credit is CORRECT.
    C. BOTH the debit and the credit of the journal entry are correct.
    D. BOTH the debit and the credit of the journal entry are incorrect.

Examine each question carefully. Then, in the correspondingly numbered space on the right, mark as your answer the letter preceding the category which is the BEST of the four suggested above.

SAMPLE QUESTION: We purchased a desk for cash.
    Debit: Office Equipment
    Credit: Accounts Payable

In this example, the debit is correct but the credit is incorrect. Therefore, you should mark A as your answer.

21. We sent a check for $500 to R. Thomas in payment for an invoice for that amount.
    Debit: Cash   Credit: Accounts Receivable

22. We took merchandise, amounting to $35, for our own use.
    Debit: Proprietor, Personal   Credit: Purchases

23. Arthur Townsend's 90-day note for $350, which was discounted by us at our bank last month, was paid by him today.
    Debit: Notes Receivable Discounted
    Credit: Accounts Receivable

24. We sold merchandise to T. Wilson on account of $275.
    Debit: Accounts Payable   Credit: Sales

25. We returned damaged merchandise to B. Lowell and received a credit memorandum from him for $28.
    Debit: Accounts Payable
    Credit: Sales Returns and Allowances

26. We paid our 30-day note given to Mr. Kane for $650 without interest.
    Debit: Notes Receivable   Credit: Cash

27. We sent Chet Carr a check for $10.50 for a discount he had forgotten to take when he paid us for merchandise this week.
    Debit: Sales Discounts   Credit: Cash

28. The bank loaned us $1000, and we invested it in the business.
    Debit: Cash   Credit: Loan Receivable

29. We recorded depreciation for the year on our office equipment.
    Debit: Reserve for Depreciation of Office Equipment
    Credit: Depreciation of Office Equipment

30. One of our customers, Allen Koren, was declared bankrupt and his debt of $25 to us was canceled.
    Debit: Reserve for Bad Debts   Credit: Accounts Receivable

Questions 31-45.

DIRECTIONS: Questions 31 to 45 consist of a list of some of the accounts in the general ledger of a corporation which operates a retail store. Indicate whether each account listed contains generally a debit or credit balance by marking the letter D (for debit balance) or the letter C (for credit balance) in the correspondingly numbered space on the right.
For example, for the account Cash, which generally contains a debit balance, you would mark the letter D as your answer.

31. Rent Expense 31.___
32. Allowance for Depreciation of Fixtures 32.___
33. Sales Returns and Allowances 33.___
34. Security Deposit for Electricity 34.___
35. Accrued Salaries Payable 35.___
36. Dividends Payable 36.___
37. Petty Cash Fund 37.___
38. Notes Receivable Discounted 38.___
39. Surplus 39.___
40. Capital Stock Authorized 40.___
41. Insurance Expense 41.___
42. Sales for Cash 42.___
43. Purchase Discounts 43.___
44. Automobile Delivery Equipment 44.___
45. Bad Debts Expense 45.___

Questions 46-60.

DIRECTIONS: Questions 46 to 60 consist of a list of some of the accounts in a general ledger. For the purpose of preparing financial statements, each of these accounts is to be classified into one of the following five major classifications, lettered A to E, as follows:
A. Assets   B. Liabilities   C. Income   D. Expense   E. Capital You are to indicate the classification to which each belongs by marking the appropriate letter, A, B, C, D or E. in the correspondingly numbered space on the right. For example, for the account MERCHANDISE INVENTORY, which is an asset account, you would mark the letter A as your answer.

46. Purchases 46.___
47. Prepaid Interest 47.___
48. Cash in Bank 48.___
49. Depreciation of Fixtures 49.___

50. Accounts Receivable   50._____
51. Mortgage Payable   51._____
52. Accrued Interest Receivable 52._____
53. Bad Debts   53._____
54. Insurance Expired   54._____
55. Treasury Stock   55._____
56. Investments   56._____
57. Loan to Partner   57._____
58. Unearned Rent Received   58._____
59. Petty Cash Fund   59._____
60. Loss on Sale of Equipment   60._____

KEY (CORRECT ANSWERS)

1. B	16. C	31. D	46. D
2. A	17. D	32. C	47. A
3. D	18. B	33. D	48. A
4. A	19. B	34. D	49. D
5. C	20. B	35. C	50. A
6. B	21. D	36. C	51. B
7. A	22. C	37. D	52. A
8. D	23. A	38. C	53. D
9. D	24. B	39. C	54. D
10. C	25. A	40. C	55. E
11. D	26. B	41. D	56. A
12. B	27. C	42. C	57. A
13. C	28. A	43. C	58. B
14. C	29. D	44. D	59. A
15. A	30. C	45. D	60. D

78

EXAMINATION SECTION
TEST 1

DIRECTIONS: Each question or incomplete statement is followed by several suggested answers or completions. Select the one that BEST answers the question or completes the statement. *PRINT THE LETTER OF THE CORRECT ANSWER IN THE SPACE AT THE RIGHT.*

1. A long-term liability of a corporation is represented by

    A. stock certificates issued
    B. stock subscriptions received
    C. the balance of a sinking fund
    D. bonds issued

2. Which is an advantage of incorporating?

    A. Establishing good will
    B. Acquiring treasury stock
    C. Limiting the liability of the owners
    D. Avoiding governmental control

3. Undistributed profits of a corporation are shown in the _____ account.

    A. earned surplus
    B. treasury stock
    C. capital stock
    D. bonds payable

4. The TOTAL amount of equity, or ownership, in a corporation is found by adding

    A. treasury stock and surplus
    B. capital stock and subscriptions
    C. capital stock and surplus
    D. capital stock and good will

5. On January 1, 2018, the earned surplus account of the Kalfur Corporation had a credit balance of $42,300. The net income for 2018 (after taxes) was $12,500. The dividends declared for 2018 amounted to $8,400.
The balance of the earned surplus account on December 31, 2018 after the books were closed was

    A. $4,100   B. $33,900   C. $38,200   D. $46,400

6. The State Disability Benefits Insurance law provides benefits for an employee or his family when the employee

    A. dies
    B. retires
    C. is temporarily unable to work because of an off-the-job accident
    D. is temporarily unable to work because of an on-the-job accident

7. Which account does NOT belong in the current liability section of a balance sheet? _____ payable.

    A. Interest   B. Notes   C. Accounts   D. Mortgage

8. If the merchandise inventory on hand at the end of 2018 was overstated, what would be the effect?

    A. Understatement of income for 2018
    B. Overstatement of income for 2018
    C. Understatement of assets at the end of 2018
    D. No effect on income or assets

9. The face value of a 45-day, 6% promissory note is $740. The maturity value of the note will be

    A. $734.45   B. $740.00   C. $745.55   D. $747.40

10. When cash is received as a result of sales, the PROPER business procedure is to

    A. put the cash in the petty cash box
    B. deposit the cash in a checking account at the end of the day
    C. deposit the cash in a savings account at the end of the day
    D. use the cash to pay current bills

11. Which item can be determined from information on the Income Statement (Profit and Loss Statement)?

    A. Working capital
    B. Rate of merchandise turnover
    C. Total liabilities
    D. Owner's worth

12. Which item belongs on the Income Statement for the year?

    A. B. Rand, Drawing
    B. Accrued Salaries, Payable
    C. Purchases Discount
    D. Allowance for Depreciation of Furniture and Fixtures

13. _____ tax is affected by the number of exemptions claimed.

    A. FICA
    B. State unemployment insurance
    C. State income tax
    D. Federal unemployment insurance

14. The source of an entry in the Cash Payments Journal is a

    A. sales invoice   B. checkbook stub
    C. petty cash voucher   D. general ledger

15. If a partnership agreement does not indicate how profits and losses are to be divided, then they will be distributed

    A. equally
    B. in proportion to investment
    C. according to duties and responsibilities
    D. by a court

16. The two parties on a promissory note are known as the _____ and _____.

    A. drawee; maker
    B. drawee; drawer
    C. payee; drawee
    D. payee; maker

17. In order to find the correct available cash balance when reconciling the checkbook balance with the bank balance, outstanding checks should be _____ balance.

    A. added to the checkbook
    B. subtracted from the checkbook
    C. added to the bank
    D. subtracted from the bank

18. A check drawn by a bank on funds that it has on deposit in another bank is known as a

    A. bank draft
    B. certified check
    C. cashier's check
    D. money order

19. _____ tax is contributed by the employee and matched by the employer.

    A. State unemployment insurance
    B. State income tax
    C. FICA
    D. Federal unemployment insurance

20. Which general ledger account would appear in a post-closing trial balance?

    A. Interest Income
    B. Notes Receivable
    C. Sales Discount
    D. Bad Debts Expense

21. A time draft frequently used in connection with a purchase of merchandise is a

    A. trade acceptance
    B. check
    C. cashier's check
    D. bank draft

22. A list of accounts and their balances prepared from a subsidiary ledger is called a

    A. statement of account
    B. trial balance
    C. balance sheet
    D. schedule

23. A time draft which states on its face that it resulted from the sale or purchase of merchandise is called a

    A. promissory note
    B. purchase order
    C. bank draft
    D. trade acceptance

24. A truck is purchased for $14,800. It is estimated that the truck will be used for four years. At the end of the four years, it is estimated that the truck will have a scrap value of $10,900.
    The amount of annual depreciation is

    A. $3,900   B. $1,425   C. $1,200   D. $975

25. The current ratio is found by

    A. *dividing* current assets by current liabilities
    B. *subtracting* current liabilities from current assets
    C. *subtracting* total liabilities from total assets
    D. *dividing* current assets by net income

KEY (CORRECT ANSWERS)

1. D
2. C
3. A
4. C
5. D

6. C
7. D
8. B
9. C
10. B

11. B
12. C
13. C
14. B
15. A

16. D
17. D
18. A
19. C
20. B

21. A
22. D
23. D
24. D
25. A

TEST 2

DIRECTIONS: Each question or incomplete statement is followed by several suggested answers or completions. Select the one that BEST answers the question or completes the statement. *PRINT THE LETTER OF THE CORRECT ANSWER IN THE SPACE AT THE RIGHT.*

1. The Federal individual income tax return must be filed by 1.____

   A. December 31 B. March 15
   C. April 15 D. June 30

2. When a firm discounts its own note at a bank, the account to be credited is 2.____

   A. Cash
   B. Notes Payable
   C. Notes Receivable Discounted
   D. Accounts Payable

3. Brooks and Carton are partners with an investment of $50,000 and $25,000, respectively. 3.____
   How much should be credited to Brooks as his share of a $60,000 profit if their agreement provides that the partners are to share profits and losses in proportion to their investments?

   A. $20,000 B. $30,000 C. $40,000 D. $50,000

4. At the end of the month, the total of the Schedule of Accounts Payable should equal the 4.____

   A. total of the Purchases column in the Purchases Journal
   B. total of the Accounts Payable column in the Cash Payments Journal
   C. balance of the Accounts Payable account in the General Ledger
   D. balance of the Purchases account in the General Ledger

5. When depreciation on a fixed asset is recorded, the effect of the entry on the fundamental bookkeeping equation is that the 5.____

   A. assets and capital remain unchanged
   B. assets increase; capital decreases
   C. assets decrease; capital decreases
   D. assets decrease; capital increases

6. The ORIGINAL source of an entry in the Purchases Journal is a 6.____

   A. purchase invoice B. stock inventory card
   C. purchase order D. creditor's account

7. The business form which is sent to each customer at the end of the month summarizing the transactions with him is called a 7.____

   A. schedule B. statement of account
   C. sales invoice D. voucher

8. When we receive a bank draft from a customer, our bookkeeper should debit 8.____

   A. Notes Payable B. Notes Receivable
   C. Accounts Receivable D. Cash

83

9. The gross sales of a business are $170,000 and Sales Returns and Allowances $450. It is estimated that an additional allowance of 1% of net sales will be required. The amount listed for Bad Debts Expense on the Income Statement should be

   A. $1,250   B. $1,695.50   C. $1,700   D. $1,704.50

10. Which group of accounts will appear on a post-closing trial balance?

    A. Assets, liabilities, and expenses
    B. Income and expenses
    C. Liabilities, capital, and income
    D. Assets, liabilities, and capital

Questions 11-16.

DIRECTIONS: Questions 11 through 16 are to be answered SOLELY on the basis of the last part of the bank statement below, mailed to Arthur Greene for the month of June.

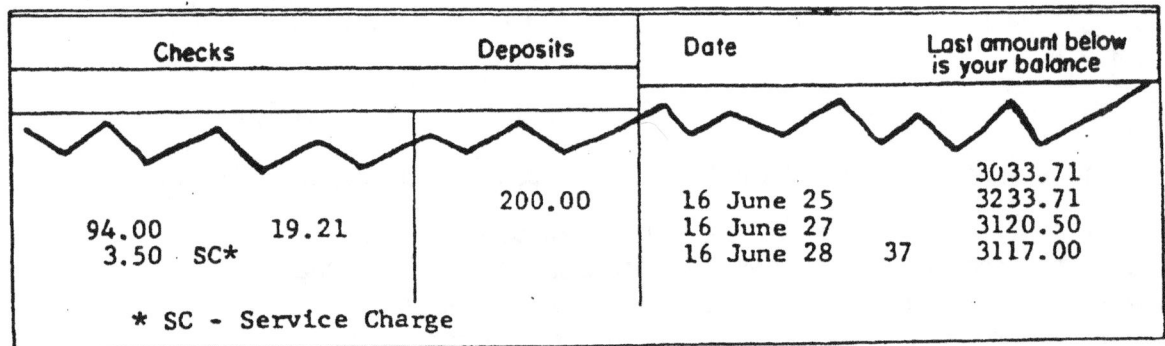

All the checks written have been paid except four. The last check written in June is No. 316. The stubs for the four outstanding checks are:

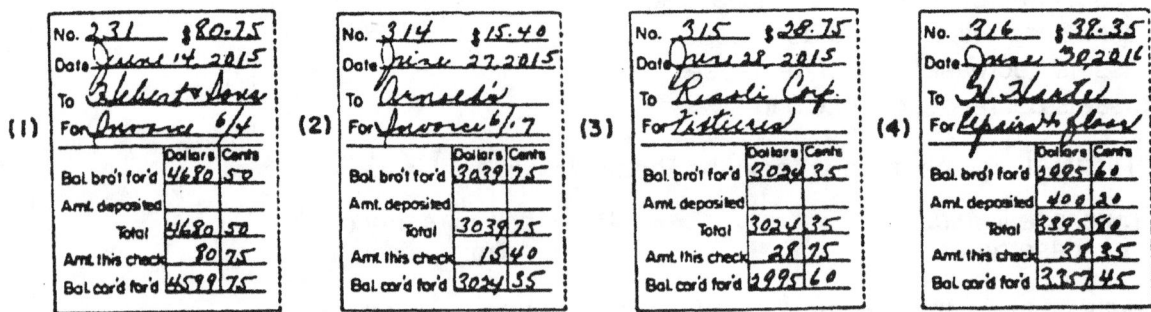

11. From the information available, what was Greene's corrected checkbook balance on June 30?

    A. $3,357.45   B. $3,117.00
    C. $3,353.95   D. $3,120.50

12. Which is the BEST reason that the deposit of $400.20, shown on Stub No. 316, does not appear on the bank statement?

    A. The bank has made an error.
    B. The bank has not credited his account.
    C. The withdrawals equal the deposits.
    D. The checks included in the deposit have not cleared the banks on which they were written.

13. When he examined the checks returned by his bank, Greene discovered that a check he had written for $44 had been incorrectly entered on the stub as $24.
    He should correct this error by

    A. adding $20 to his checkbook balance
    B. notifying his bank to add $20 to his account
    C. subtracting $20 from his checkbook balance
    D. subtracting $24 from his checkbook balance

14. On May 25, Greene wrote and had his bank certify a check for $150, which he mailed to Garcia, the payee. Garcia received the check on May 27 and deposited it in his bank on June 1. It was presented to Greene's bank and cleared for payment on June 2.
    On which date did Greene's bank deduct the $150 from his account?

    A. May 25   B. May 27   C. June 1   D. June 2

15. The journal entry to record the bank service charge shown on the bank statement should be made in the

    A. Petty Cashbook   B. General Journal
    C. Cash Receipts Journal   D. Cash Payments Journal

16. Greene's bookkeeper should prepare a bank reconciliation for June MAINLY to determine

    A. possible errors by comparing Greene's checkbook balance with the bank balance
    B. the total amount of checks written during the month
    C. which checks are still outstanding
    D. the total amount of cash deposited during the month

17. Which statement concerning a check is MOST accurate?

    A. A canceled check may be used to prove payment.
    B. Two signatures are required on each check drawn on a joint checking account.
    C. The corporation's name should be signed on the signature line of a check.
    D. Checks mailed for deposit should be endorsed by means of a blank endorsement.

18. If a check which has been certified is not used, which is the RECOMMENDED business practice?

    A. Mark the check *Void* and add the amount to the checkbook balance.
    B. Send a *stop payment* order to the bank.
    C. Deposit the check.
    D. Destroy the check.

19. Ames' bank returned a check which he had deposited, marked N.S.F. This notation indicates that the

    A. check has been improperly endorsed
    B. drawer has overdrawn his bank account
    C. drawer has stopped payment on the check
    D. signature on the check has been forged

20. In order to determine the correct available bank balance, the amount of a deposit made, but not yet recorded in an account, should be _____ balance.

    A. *added* to the checkbook
    B. *added* to the bank balance
    C. *subtracted* from the checkbook
    D. *subtracted* from the bank

Questions 21-25.

DIRECTIONS: Questions 21 through 25 are to be answered on the basis of the following depreciation record.

DEPRECIATION RECORD

Delivery Truck	Tractson	04387A	July 1, 2015
Asset	Make	Number	Acquired
$4,000	5 years	$500	straight-line
Cost	Estimated Life	Salvage Value	Meth. of Depr.

Year	1st quarter	2nd quarter	3rd quarter	4th quarter
1			$175	$175
2	...	...	$175	$175
3	$175	$175		
4	$175			
5				
6				

21. According to the record, the LAST adjusting entry had been made on or about

    A. June 1, 2015   B. June 1, 2016
    C. December 31, 2016   D. March 31, 2017

22. The book value on the date of the latest entry is

    A. $500   B. $2,275   C. $2,775   D. $3,500

23. The TOTAL amount of depreciation which would be recorded during the lifetime of the truck is

    A. $4,500   B. $4,000   C. $3,500   D. $500

24. What is the annual rate of depreciation for the truck?

    A. 17.5%   B. 2%   C. 20%   D. 5%

25. If a business uses the straight-line method of depreciation, which is CORRECT? 25.____
    A. All assets are depreciated at the same rate.
    B. The older the asset, the greater the amount of depreciation recorded each year.
    C. The rate of depreciation is the same each year for a particular asset.
    D. The salvage value will be the same for all fixed assets.

KEY (CORRECT ANSWERS)

1. C   11. C
2. B   12. B
3. C   13. C
4. C   14. A
5. C   15. D

6. A   16. A
7. B   17. A
8. D   18. C
9. B   19. B
10. D   20. B

21. D
22. C
23. C
24. A
25. C

TEST 3

DIRECTIONS: Each question or incomplete statement is followed by several suggested answers or completions. Select the one that BEST answers the question or completes the statement. *PRINT THE LETTER OF THE CORRECT ANSWER IN THE SPACE AT THE RIGHT.*

1. Entries in the Cash Payments Journal are USUALLY recorded from

    A. purchase invoices
    B. check stubs
    C. cancelled checks
    D. expense sheets

2. A bank draft received from a customer is recorded in the

    A. General Journal
    B. Note Register
    C. Sales Journal
    D. Cash Receipts Journal

3. When sales taxes are collected from cash customers, the account credited is

    A. Sales Tax Payable
    B. Sales Tax
    C. Cash
    D. Accounts Payable

4. One advantage of the corporate form of business is

    A. limited life
    B. limited capital
    C. limited liability
    D. dissolution on death of an officer

5. Current assets minus current liabilities equals

    A. current turnover
    B. current ratio
    C. asset ratio
    D. working capital

6. What is the LATEST date that an invoice dated October 15 with terms net 10 E.O.M. should be paid?

    A. October 25
    B. October 31
    C. November 10
    D. November 30

7. The deduction allowed to a customer for an early payment of his account is known as a

    A. cash discount
    B. mark down
    C. credit memorandum
    D. trade discount

8. In a C.O.D. freight shipment, the business form that the seller attaches to the bill of lading is a

    A. sight draft
    B. promissory note
    C. check
    D. time draft

9. The form prepared to test the equality of debits and credits in the General Ledger is called

    A. statement of account
    B. balance sheet
    C. trial balance
    D. income statement

10. If the depreciation of a truck is calculated by the straight-line method, which statement is CORRECT?

    A. As the truck becomes older, the rate of depreciation increases.
    B. The rate of depreciation is the same each year.
    C. The amount of annual depreciation is based on the truck's mileage.
    D. On a statement of profit and loss, the depreciation appears as a deferred expense.

11. A computer program used to create spreadsheets, graphs and charts, and maintain financial records is

    A. Quickbooks
    B. Adobe Reader
    C. Microsoft Powerpoint
    D. Microsoft Excel

12. An inventory of merchandise prepared from an actual count of stock items on hand is described as a(n) _____ inventory.

    A. perpetual   B. physical   C. estimated   D. fixed

13. Which is NOT classified as a current asset on the balance sheet?

    A. Petty Cash
    B. Notes Receivable
    C. Land
    D. Accounts Receivable

14. Which error will cause a trial balance to be out of balance?

    A. Failure to post the debit part of a journal entry
    B. Failure to record an entire journal entry
    C. Error in totaling the sales journal
    D. Posting a debit in the debit side of the wrong account

15. If a customer's check which you had deposited is returned to you by the bank labeled *dishonored,* what entry would be made?
    Debit

    A. Cash and credit customer's account
    B. Miscellaneous Expense and credit Cash
    C. customer's account and credit Capital
    D. customer's account and credit Cash

16. The total of the Purchases Journal for the month of May was incorrectly computed as $6,500. The correct amount was $5,500. The $6,500 was used to record and post the summary entry for the month.
    To correct the error, the bookkeeper should debit

    A. Merchandise Purchases and credit Accounts Payable $5,500
    B. Merchandise Purchases and credit Accounts Payable $1,000
    C. Accounts Payable and credit Merchandise Purchases $1,000
    D. Accounts Payable and credit Merchandise Purchases $6,500

17. Entries in the Purchases Journal are USUALLY recorded from

    A. purchase requisitions
    B. purchase invoices
    C. check stubs
    D. credit memorandums

18. Merchandise was sold on April 10, 2018 for $400 less a trade discount of 25%, terms 2/10, n/30.
    The amount required to settle the invoice on April 20 is

    A. $294   B. $300   C. $392   D. $400

19. When the books were closed at the end of the business fiscal year, there was a failure to record depreciation on Office Equipment for the year.
    This error had the effect of

    A. *understating* the book value of the asset Office Equipment
    B. *overstating* the book value of the asset Office Equipment
    C. *understating* the net income of the asset Office Equipment
    D. *overstating* operating expenses

Questions 20-25.

DIRECTIONS: Questions 20 through 25 are to be answered SOLELY on the basis of the following bank reconciliation statement.

CONDON, INC. Bank Reconciliation March 31.			
Checkbook balance	$3,148.70	Bank Balance	$3,830.65
Less: Service Charge	4.15	Add: Deposit in Transit	310.00
		Total	4,140.65
		Less: Outstanding Checks	
		No. 815 $470.20	
		817 525.90	996.10
		(No. 813 certified 920.00)	
Adjusted checkbook balance	$3,144.55	Available bank balance	$3,144.55

20. Which entry will be made on the books of Condon, Inc. to record the bank service charge?
    Debit

    A. Cash, credit Bank Charges
    B. Bank Charges, credit Accounts Payable
    C. Bank Charges, credit Cash
    D. Bank Account, credit Bank Charges

21. The deposit in transit of $310 will be listed on the

    A. bank statement for the month of March
    B. bank statement for the month of April
    C. bank statement for the month of February
    D. check stub record *only*

22. The bookkeeper determined which checks were outstanding by 22.____

    A. counting the cancelled checks
    B. examining the bank statement
    C. comparing the cancelled checks with the bank statement
    D. comparing the cancelled checks with the check stubs

23. The certified check of $920 was NOT deducted with the other outstanding checks because it 23.____

    A. was deducted from our bank balance at the time it was certified
    B. was not deducted from our checkbook balance when it was written
    C. will not be cashed by our bank
    D. will not be deducted from our bank balance until it clears our bank

24. The MAIN reason for preparing the bank reconciliation statement is to determine the 24.____

    A. total amount of cancelled checks
    B. total amount of outstanding checks
    C. total deposits with withdrawals for the month
    D. errors that might have been made

25. A trial balance is prepared to 25.____

    A. see if the totals agree with the subsidiary ledgers
    B. see if the total debit balances in the General Ledger agree with the total credit balances in the General Ledger
    C. show the worth of the business
    D. make up statements of customers' accounts

KEY (CORRECT ANSWERS)

1. B	11. D
2. D	12. B
3. A	13. C
4. C	14. A
5. D	15. D
6. C	16. C
7. A	17. B
8. A	18. A
9. C	19. B
10. B	20. C

21. B
22. D
23. A
24. D
25. B

TEST 4

DIRECTIONS: Each question or incomplete statement is followed by several suggested answers or completions. Select the one that BEST answers the question or completes the statement. *PRINT THE LETTER OF THE CORRECT ANSWER IN THE SPACE AT THE RIGHT.*

1. The due date of a 60-day promissory note dated June 15 is August 1.____
   A. 13 B. 14 C. 15 D. 16

2. Using the information that can be found in the Income Statement, one can find the 2.____
   A. current ratio
   B. merchandise turnover
   C. working capital
   D. rate of return on capital

3. Which of the following is NOT a computer program commonly used for accounting and finance purposes? 3.____
   A. QuarkXPress B. Peachtree
   C. Quicken D. Quickbooks

4. The ABC Corporation has 100,000 shares of stock outstanding. The Corporation decides to distribute to the stockholders a $200,000 profit. 4.____
   If a stockholder owns 100 shares of stock, he will receive a TOTAL dividend of
   A. $50.00 B. $2.00 C. $200.00 D. $.50

5. A transaction that will cause a DECREASE in capital is a 5.____
   A. purchase of office equipment on credit
   B. payment of a creditor's account less a cash discount
   C. payment of an interest-bearing note
   D. prepayment of freight for a customer, to be charged to the customer's account

6. Mr. Davis is married and has three children who go to school. His oldest son, age 17, earned $900 during the year working parttime. 6.____
   On his joint Federal income tax return, Mr. Davis may claim a MAXIMUM of _____ exemptions.
   A. five B. two C. three D. four

7. If the total of the Schedule of Accounts Receivable does not agree with the balance in the Accounts Receivable Controlling account, the difference may have been caused by 7.____
   A. adding the Sales Journal incorrectly
   B. failing to enter a sale in the Sales Journal
   C. posting a sale to the wrong customer's account
   D. failing to record a check received from a customer

8. An entry in the general journal is USUALLY made from the 8.____
   A. sales invoice B. purchase invoice
   C. credit memorandum D. incoming check

9. An example of a tax collected by the Federal government is the

   A. sales tax
   B. real estate tax
   C. automobile registration fee
   D. social security tax

10. The adjusting entry at the end of the year to record the estimated depreciation for the year results in a(n)

    A. *increase* in liabilities and a decrease in capital
    B. *decrease* in assets and an increase in assets
    C. *decrease* in assets and a decrease in capital
    D. *decrease* in assets and an increase in capital

11. On December 28, the total in the Salaries Expense Account was $59,500. On December 31, the bookkeeper recorded accrued salaries of $600.
    The entry to close the Salaries Expense Account on December 31 should be debit the _____ and credit the _____.

    A. Income and Expense Summary Account for $59,500; Salaries Expense Account for $59,500
    B. Income and Expense Summary Account for $60,100; Salaries Expense Account for $60,100
    C. Income and Expense Summary Account for $58,900; Salaries Expense Account for $58,900
    D. Salaries Expense Account for $59,500; Income and Expense Summary Account for $59,500

12. The tax paid by the employee to provide benefits upon his retirement is the

    A. FICA tax
    B. State Disability Benefits
    C. Federal withholding tax
    D. workmen's compensation insurance

13. The Federal income tax form that is given to the employee to show his total salary for the year and the amount of withholding tax for the year is called Form

    A. 941   B. W-4   C. 1099   D. W-2

14. An error that would cause the trial balance to be out of balance would be INCORRECTLY adding

    A. the Purchase Journal
    B. the cash column in the Cash Receipts Journal
    C. the Schedule of Accounts Receivable
    D. extensions on an invoice

15. An account that would be shown in a post-closing trial balance is

    A. Notes Receivable   B. Sales Income
    C. Discount on Purchases   D. Freight Out

16. You have just posted an entry from the Sales Journal to the customer's account. The correct amount in the Sales Journal is $125, but you posted $12.50.
To correct the error, you should

   A. draw a single line through the $12.50 in the account and write $125 above it
   B. debit in the General Journal the customer's account for $112.50 and credit the Sales Income Account for $112.50
   C. credit in the General Journal the customer's account for $12.50 and debit the Sales Income Account for $12.50
   D. debit in the Sales Journal the customer's account for $112.50 and credit the Sales Income Account for $112.50

16.____

17. When the bookkeeper added the trial balance, she found that it did not balance. To find the reason, a logical FIRST step would be to

   A. check the pencil footings in ledger accounts
   B. add the trial balance a second time
   C. check whether figures were copied correctly from the ledger to the trial balance
   D. check postings from the journals

17.____

18. A column or group of columns containing data of a specific nature on a punched card is called a

   A. zone   B. field   C. row   D. file

18.____

19. *Allowance for Doubtful Accounts* is BEST described as a(n) _____ account.

   A. contingent liability   B. capital
   C. expense   D. asset valuation

19.____

20. A sales invoice to Judy Burns for $50 was entered in the Sales Journal as $150. Which would occur as a result of this error?
The

   A. trial balance will not balance at the end of the month
   B. balance of the monthly statement to Judy Burns will be overstated
   C. check received from Judy Burns in payment of her account will be larger than the correct amount
   D. Accounts Receivable controlling account will not agree with the Schedule of Accounts Receivable at the end of the month

20.____

21. Sales taxes which are collected from customers and which will subsequently be remitted to the State Tax Bureau are recorded by the retailer as a(n)

   A. operating expense in the Income Statement
   B. addition to sales in the Income Statement
   C. current asset in the Balance Sheet
   D. current liability in the Balance Sheet

21.____

22. When the payee of a check writes as an endorsement *Pay to the order of (name of the firm)* before his signature, he has used a _____ endorsement.

   A. blank   B. qualified
   C. restrictive   D. full

22.____

23. Entries in the Purchases Journal are USUALLY made from which source document?

   A. Purchase order
   B. Purchase requisition
   C. Incoming invoice
   D. Outgoing invoice

24. Which is shown on the bank statement sent by the bank each month?

   A. Outstanding checks
   B. Deposits in transit
   C. Checks paid by the bank during the month
   D. The amount of interest earned during the month

25. The authorization by the State of New York which permits a group of persons to do business as a corporation is called the

   A. charter
   B. by-laws
   C. trade acceptance
   D. articles of copartnership

KEY (CORRECT ANSWERS)

1. B	11. B
2. B	12. A
3. A	13. D
4. C	14. B
5. C	15. A
6. A	16. A
7. A	17. B
8. C	18. B
9. D	19. D
10. C	20. B

21. D
22. D
23. C
24. C
25. A

EXAMINATION SECTION
TEST 1

DIRECTIONS: Each question or incomplete statement is followed by several suggested answers or completions. Select the one that BEST answers the question or completes the statement. *PRINT THE LETTER OF THE CORRECT ANSWER IN THE SPACE AT THE RIGHT.*

Questions 1-5.

DIRECTIONS: Questions 1 through 5 are to be answered on the basis of the following information.

The balance on our bank statement is $6,842.50. The bank had made a service charge of $4.50. Our check stubs reveal a final balance of $5,747.50. A comparison of the check stubs with the bank statement indicated that a deposit we had mailed on the 29th for $585 had not been recorded by the monthly closing. Four checks which we had made out ($1,001, $645, $38.50, and a certified check for $1,200) had not been cleared by the monthly closing.

1. The effect of the deposit in transit is to _____ balance.   1._____

    A. *increase* the final check stub
    B. *decrease* the final check stub
    C. *increase* the bank
    D. *decrease* the bank

2. The effect of the bank service charge is to _____ balance.   2._____

    A. *increase* the final check stub
    B. *decrease* the final check stub
    C. *increase* the bank
    D. *decrease* the bank

3. The CORRECTED check stub balance after reconciliation is   3._____
    A. $5,743   B. $5,752   C. $6,337   D. $6,843

4. The TOTAL of the outstanding checks to be subtracted from the bank balance is   4._____
    A. $484.50   B. $1,684.50   C. $2,269.50   D. $2,885.50

5. The CORRECTED bank balance after reconciliation is   5._____
    A. $5,743   B. $5,789   C. $6,843   D. $7,428

Questions 6-8.

DIRECTIONS: Questions 6 through 8 are to be answered on the basis of the worksheet below, which is for the first quarter of the Argo Taxi Company.

2 (#1)

[Worksheet image: ARGC TAXI CO., INC WORKSHEET FOR QUARTER ENDED 3/31/-- with Trial Balance, Adjustments, Income Statement, and Balance Sheet columns]

6. The balance of the Automobiles account after the June adjustment is 6.___

   A. $8,750   B. $23,000   C. $31,750   D. $105,000

7. The book value of the asset Maintenance Equipment, after adjusting entries, is 7.___

   A. $7,500   B. $12,500   C. $13,000   D. $20,000

8. Assuming that the entire net profit after taxes was transferred to Retained Earnings, the balance of the Retained Earnings account would be 8.___

   A. $10,252.50
   C. $23,452.50
   B. $13,200
   D. $36,652.50

9. The TOTAL operating expenses for the quarter were 9.___

   A. $13,530   B. $48,730   C. $121,450   D. $192,200

10. Closing entries are prepared from _____ columns. 10.___

    A. Trial Balance   B. Adjustment
    C. Income Statement   D. Balance Sheet

11. When sales taxes are collected from cash customers, the account credited is 11.___

    A. Sales Taxes Payable   B. Sales Taxes
    C. Cash   D. Accounts Payable

12. What type of data processing equipment would arrange punched cards alphabetically? 12.___

    A. Card punch   B. Card verifier
    C. Sorter   D. Tabulator

13. _____ tax is affected by the number of exemptions claimed by the employee. 13.___

    A. State Unemployment Insurance   B. Federal Unemployment Insurance
    C. FICA   D. Federal income

14. The merchandise turnover is found by dividing _____ merchandise inventory.   14._____

    A. net sales by ending
    B. net sales by average
    C. cost of goods sold by average
    D. cost of goods sold by ending

15. The process of summarizing the income and expense accounts and transferring the net   15._____
    result to the Retained Earnings account is known as

    A. adjusting the accounts
    B. reversing the accounts
    C. closing the ledger
    D. preparing a post-closing trial balance

16. An example of a fixed asset is   16._____

    A. equipment
    C. cash
    B. merchandise inventory
    D. prepaid insurance

17. Determining that the amount of cash on hand agrees with the balance of the cash   17._____
    account is known as

    A. recording
    B. proving cash
    C. reconciling the bank statement
    D. establishing the petty cash fund

18. The balance in the Accounts Receivable controlling account on December 31 is $20,500.   18._____
    The balance in the Allowance for Bad Debts account is $750 after adjustments.
    The amount believed to be collectible from customers is

    A. $750   B. $19,750   C. $20,500   D. $21,250

19. The FIRST record of any transaction of a business is made in the   19._____

    A. ledger
    C. journal
    B. account
    D. balance sheet

20. A decrease in owner's capital that results from a business transaction is called   20._____

    A. income   B. expense   C. asset   D. liability

21. The difference between the sales and the cost of goods sold is called   21._____

    A. net sales
    C. gross profit on sales
    B. sales returns
    D. sales discount

22. A customer sent a check for $50 in partial payment of her account.   22._____
    What would be the effect of erroneously posting the check as a debit to the customer's
    account?

    A. *Overstatement* of the total of the Schedule of Accounts Receivable
    B. *Understatement* of the Accounts Receivable controlling account
    C. *Overstatement* of the Accounts Receivable controlling account
    D. *Understatement* of the total of the Schedule of Accounts Receivable

23. In the absence of any statement in the partnership agreement as to the manner of sharing profits and losses, such profits and losses will be shared

   A. equally
   B. according to investments
   C. according to work performed
   D. according to sales

24. At the end of the year, which account should be closed into the Income and Expense Summary account?

   A. Petty Cash
   B. Depreciation of Furniture and Fixtures
   C. Allowance for Bad Debts
   D. Notes Payable

25. On an Income Statement, losses from bad debts will appear as a(n)

   A. operating expense
   B. deduction from Accounts Receivable
   C. addition to the cost of goods sold
   D. deduction from the cost of goods sold

KEY (CORRECT ANSWERS)

1.	C	11.	A
2.	B	12.	C
3.	A	13.	D
4.	B	14.	C
5.	A	15.	C
6.	D	16.	A
7.	B	17.	B
8.	D	18.	B
9.	B	19.	C
10.	C	20.	B

21. C
22. A
23. A
24. B
25. A

TEST 2

DIRECTIONS: Each question or incomplete statement is followed by several suggested answers or completions. Select the one that BEST answers the question or completes the statement. *PRINT THE LETTER OF THE CORRECT ANSWER IN THE SPACE AT THE RIGHT.*

1. A bookkeeping worksheet is prepared　　　　　　　　　　　　　　　　　　1.____

    A. to be used as a source document
    B. to distribute to the stockholders at the end of the year
    C. as an aid in the preparation of financial statements
    D. to be used as a financial statement

2. When a set of books for a partnership is opened, the CORRECT procedure is to set up　　2.____

    A. a capital account for each partner
    B. a capital account for each partner except *silent* partners
    C. one capital account that would show the combined investment of the partners
    D. an account showing stock already subscribed

3. At the end of the fiscal period, it is determined that the interest owed and not paid on the mortgage amounts to $420. This amount will be debited to　　3.____

    A. Interest Expense   B. Mortgage Payable
    C. Interest Receivable   D. Interest Income

4. Income that has been earned but not yet received is referred to as _____ income.　　4.____

    A. deferred   B. accrued   C. unearned   D. prepaid

5. The account Mortgage Payable is a(n)　　5.____

    A. current liability   B. prepaid expense
    C. accrued expense   D. fixed liability

6. Under the cash basis of keeping books, all items of income are recorded when　　6.____

    A. paid   B. billed   C. received   D. ordered

7. A financial statement prepared by a data processing system is an example of　　7.____

    A. a source document   B. output
    C. a flowchart   D. input

8. On an income statement, net sales minus cost of goods sold is the　　8.____

    A. gross profit
    B. merchandise available for sale
    C. net operating profit
    D. net profit before taxes

9. Allowance for Depreciation of Delivery Equipment is a(n) _____ account.　　9.____

    A. liability   B. expense   C. accrual   D. valuation

10. When the totals of the two columns of a Trial Balance are equal, it proves that
    A. all debits and credits have been posted to the proper accounts
    B. there have been no offsetting errors
    C. no entries have been omitted
    D. equal amounts of debits and credits have been posted

11. The TOTAL of the Sales Journal is posted as a debit to
    A. Accounts Receivable   B. Accounts Payable
    C. Sales   D. Cash

12. Unexpired insurance is recorded as a debit to
    A. Insurance Receivable   B. Prepaid Insurance
    C. Insurance Payable   D. Insurance Expense

13. The cost price of a fixed asset minus the Allowance for Depreciation is known as its _____ value.
    A. cash   B. par   C. market   D. book

14. The payment in cash by The Lake Corporation on April 1, 2008 of a dividend declared and recorded on March 10, 2008 results in
    A. a decrease in assets and a decrease in capital
    B. both an increase and a decrease in assets
    C. a decrease in assets and a decrease in liabilities
    D. a decrease in liabilities and an increase in capital

15. Current assets minus current liabilities equals
    A. current ratio   B. current turnover
    C. merchandise turnover   D. working capital

16. The proprietor withdrew cash for his personal use. The effect on the fundamental bookkeeping equation is to
    A. *increase* assets and decrease owner's worth
    B. *increase* assets and increase owner's worth
    C. *decrease* assets and decrease liabilities
    D. *decrease* assets and decrease owner's worth

17. A payment for gasoline and oil was incorrectly debited to the Delivery Equipment account instead of to the Delivery Expense account.
    This error, if not corrected, would result in
    A. understatement of the total assets
    B. no effect on the net profit
    C. an understatement of the net profit
    D. an overstatement of the net profit

18. A bookkeeper made an entry debiting the Bad Debts Expense account and crediting the Allowance for Bad Debts account. The credit represents a(n)
    A. *increase* in the liabilities
    B. *increase* in the net worth

C. *decrease* in the value of the assets
D. *decrease* in the liabilities

19. Adjusting entries are NORMALLY made

   A. before the Trial Balance is taken
   B. whenever price changes occur in inventory costs
   C. at the beginning of each fiscal period
   D. at the end of the current fiscal period

19.____

20. The declaration of a cash dividend by the Yule Corporation will result in a(n)

   A. *increase* in assets and an increase in liabilities
   B. *increase* in liabilities and a decrease in capital
   C. *decrease* in assets and a decrease in liabilities
   D. *decrease* in assets and a decrease in capital

20.____

21.

Accounts Payable

May	31	CP6	178	00	May	31		P3	320	00
	31	J4	80	00						
June	2	J5	75	00						

21.____

The above account was taken from the General Ledger of Clarke & Scott. The above account is classified as a

   A. fixed liability   B. contingent asset
   C. deferred asset   D. current liability

22. When a corporation declares a dividend on its stock, the account debited is

   A. Dividends Payable   B. Retained Earnings
   C. Capital Stock   D. Stock Subscriptions

22.____

23. The payroll tax for the State unemployment insurance is paid by

   A. the employee *only*
   B. both the employee and the employer
   C. the employer *only*
   D. the insurance company

23.____

24. Which computer application would MOST likely be used for accounting purposes?

   A. Microsoft Powerpoint   B. Adobe Reader
   C. Internet Explorer   D. Microsoft Excel

24.____

25. A diagram of a bookkeeping operation through a computerized system is called a

   A. floor plan   B. worksheet
   C. flowchart   D. CPU

25.____

KEY (CORRECT ANSWERS)

1. C
2. A
3. A
4. B
5. D

6. C
7. B
8. A
9. D
10. D

11. A
12. B
13. D
14. C
15. D

16. D
17. D
18. C
19. D
20. B

21. D
22. B
23. C
24. D
25. C

TEST 3

DIRECTIONS: Each question or incomplete statement is followed by several suggested answers or completions. Select the one that BEST answers the question or completes the statement. *PRINT THE LETTER OF THE CORRECT ANSWER IN THE SPACE AT THE RIGHT.*

1. The process of transferring information from the journal to the ledger is called 1.____
    - A. journalizing
    - B. posting
    - C. closing
    - D. balancing

2. Which is NOT an asset account? 2.____
    - A. Supplies on Hand
    - B. Prepaid Insurance
    - C. Office Equipment
    - D. Sales

3. Which journal entries are used at the end of each accounting period to clear the balances from the temporary accounts so that these accounts may be used in accumulating data for preparing the next period's statement. _____ entries. 3.____
    - A. Correcting
    - B. Closing
    - C. Adjusting
    - D. Opening

4. The verification of the equality of debits and credits in the General Ledger is called a 4.____
    - A. trial balance
    - B. schedule
    - C. statement
    - D. worksheet

5. Which account would NOT be listed on the Balance Sheet as a current liability? 5.____
    - A. Accounts Payable
    - B. Sales Taxes Payable
    - C. Mortgage Payable
    - D. FICA Taxes Payable

6. Debts owed by a business enterprise are referred to as 6.____
    - A. capital
    - B. income
    - C. assets
    - D. liabilities

7. If insurance premiums were recorded as an asset when paid, the adjusting entry needed to record the expired insurance would require a debit to which account? 7.____
    - A. Miscellaneous Expense
    - B. Prepaid Insurance
    - C. Insurance Expense
    - D. John Green, Capital

8. A diagram showing the sequence of steps involved in an automated data processing procedure is called a 8.____
    - A. flowchart
    - B. source document
    - C. coding sheet
    - D. spreadsheet

9. If a business enterprise paid $3,000 to its creditors on account, what was the effect of the transaction on the accounting equation? A(n)

   A. *increase* in an asset, an increase in a liability
   B. *decrease* in an asset, a decrease in a liability
   C. *increase* in an asset, an increase in capital
   D. *increase* in one asset, a decrease in another asset

10. Which three steps of an automated data processing system are listed in the PROPER order?

    A. Input, storage, process
    B. Process, data origination, output
    C. Output, input, storage
    D. Input, process, output

11. The Merchandise Inventory account is GENERALLY adjusted

    A. when inventory is purchased
    B. when inventory is sold
    C. at the end of the accounting period
    D. at the beginning of each month

12. Which transaction is recorded in the Sales Journal? The sale of

    A. merchandise for cash
    B. merchandise on account
    C. vacant land (plant asset) for cash
    D. vacant land (plant asset) on account

13. Which is an example of a transposition error? Recording $450 as

    A. $540   B. $4,500.00   C. $455   D. $4.50

14. The accounting equation is CORRECTLY stated as

    A. Owner's Equity = Assets + Liabilities
    B. Owner's Equity - Assets = Liabilities
    C. Owner's Equity = Liabilities - Assets
    D. Assets = Liabilities + Owner's Equity

15. The Wage and Tax statement, Form W-2, is a form which shows

    A. a listing of deductions taken from an employee's salary
    B. an end-of-year listing of total wages and income tax and FICA withholdings
    C. the bonds purchased for an employee by an employer
    D. the marital status of an employee and the number of allowances claimed

16. A set of instructions which guides the processing of data by an electronic computer is called a

    A. file   B. diagram   C. program   D. record

17. An invoice is dated June 3. Terms of the sale are n/45. What is the LAST date for payment?

    A. June 30 B. July 17 C. July 18 D. July 19

18. The accounting equation is summarized in the

    A. Balance Sheet
    B. Trial Balance
    C. Income Statement
    D. Schedule of Accounts Payable

19. The Accounts Payable Subsidiary Ledger contains the amounts

    A. owed to the business by charge customers
    B. owed by the business to creditors
    C. of all cash purchases of merchandise
    D. of all sales discounts

20. Which procedure is followed in a journalless accounting system for handling accounts receivable?

    A. A trial balance must be prepared daily.
    B. Debits do not equal credits at the end of the accounting period when all postings have been made.
    C. Individual sales are recorded in a multicolumn Sales Journal instead of in a one-column Sales Journal.
    D. Posting to customers' accounts is made directly from the sales invoices.

21. _____ is a voluntary payroll deduction.

    A. FICA tax   B. Credit union savings
    C. Federal withholding tax   D. State income tax

22. On a worksheet, if the Trial Balance debit column is larger than the Trial Balance credit column, it indicates a(n)

    A. net income   B. net loss
    C. error   D. decrease in capital

23. In the General Ledger, the controlling account that summarizes the activities in the Customer's Ledger is called

    A. Accounts Receivable   B. Accounts Payable
    C. Purchases   D. Sales

24. The balance of the Insurance Expense account in the Income Statement debit column on the worksheet represents the

    A. insurance expired during the fiscal period
    B. face value of all insurance policies
    C. value of the prepaid insurance at the end of the fiscal period
    D. cash value of all insurance policies

25. A fee paid to the bank when securing a cashier's check should be recorded by a debit to _____ and a credit to _____. 25._____
    A. Petty Cash; Cash
    B. Miscellaneous Expense; Bank Charges
    C. Accounts Receivable; Cash
    D. Miscellaneous Expense; Cash

KEY (CORRECT ANSWERS)

1.	B	11.	C
2.	D	12.	B
3.	B	13.	A
4.	A	14.	D
5.	C	15.	B
6.	D	16.	C
7.	C	17.	C
8.	A	18.	A
9.	B	19.	B
10.	D	20.	D

21. B
22. C
23. A
24. A
25. D

TEST 4

DIRECTIONS: Each question or incomplete statement is followed by several suggested answers or completions. Select the one that BEST answers the question or completes the statement. *PRINT THE LETTER OF THE CORRECT ANSWER IN THE SPACE AT THE RIGHT.*

1. A 60-day promissory note dated April 12 will be due on June

    A. 11   B. 12   C. 13   D. 14

2. Failure to set up an allowance for doubtful accounts at the end of 2012 will result in an _____ 2012.

    A. *understatement* of net profit for
    B. *overstatement* of net profit for
    C. *understatement* of assets at the end of
    D. *overstatement* of liabilities at the end of

3. Which error will cause the trial balance to be out of balance?

    A. Forgetting to post from the Sales Journal to the H. Allen account in the Accounts Receivable Ledger
    B. Failing to record the purchase of a desk
    C. Incorrectly totaling the Purchase Journal
    D. Posting the $1,250 total of the accounts receivable column in the Cash Receipts Journal as $1,520

4. The checkbook balance on May 2, at the start of the day, was $1,500. During the day, a deposit of $75 was made, and checks for $100 and $50 were written.
What was the checkbook balance at the end of the day?

    A. $1,275   B. $1,425   C. $1,575   D. $1,725

5. Data about Accounts Receivable to be fed into an automatic data processing system is often recorded in the form of

    A. statements of account
    B. punched cards
    C. schedule of accounts receivable
    D. sales journals

6. A purchase of merchandise on credit results in a(n) _____ in assets and a(n) _____ in liabilities.

    A. increase; increase   B. increase; decrease
    C. decrease; decrease   D. decrease; increase

7. During her vacation, Harriet Miller, age 45, was injured while driving her own car. For part of the 5 weeks she was unable to work, cash benefits MOST likely would be paid to her under

    A. Workers' Compensation
    B. the Social Security Administration

C. State Disability Benefits Insurance
D. Unemployment Insurance

8. The book value of a share of stock of a corporation may be found by

   A. dividing the net worth of the corporation by the number of shares of stock
   B. dividing the total amount of stock of the corporation by the number of shares of stock
   C. looking at the amount shown on the stock certificate
   D. looking at the price of the stock on the stock exchange page of the daily newspaper

9. In a business, which are MOST likely to be prepared by automatic data processing?

   A. Sales invoices
   B. Inspection reports by the night watchman
   C. Business correspondence (letters)
   D. Applications for employment

10. The entry recording the estimated depreciation for the year results in a(n) _____ in capital.

    A. increase in liabilities and a decrease
    B. decrease in liabilities and an increase
    C. increase in assets and an increase
    D. decrease in assets and a decrease

11. The balance of the Accounts Receivable controlling account would be different from the total of the Accounts Receivable Schedule if the bookkeeper

    A. made an error in totaling the Sales Journal and posted the incorrect total
    B. failed to record a sale made to S. Charles
    C. recorded the receipt of a check from a customer but neglected to record the cash discount
    D. added an invoice incorrectly and entered the incorrect total in the Sales Journal

12. Credits in the Notes Payable account USUALLY originate in the _____ Journal.

    A. Purchase   B. Cash Receipts
    C. Cash Payments   D. General

13. On the books of the seller, the deduction granted to a customer for early payment of the invoice is called a _____ discount.

    A. retail   B. purchase   C. trade   D. sales

14. A firm started the year with $25 worth of office supplies. During the year, the firm purchased $65 worth of office supplies. A count of the office supplies at the end of the year showed that $20 worth was still on hand.
    What was the TOTAL cost of the office supplies which the firm must have used during the year?

    A. $45   B. $60   C. $70   D. $110

15. A payroll check prepared by a computer is an example of _____ data processing _____.

    A. electronic; input
    B. electronic; output
    C. manual; output
    D. manual; input

16. A sale of $250 was made subject to a 7% sales tax.
    To record the sale CORRECTLY, the credits should be Sales Income

    A. $250, Sales Taxes $17.50
    B. $250, Sales Taxes Payable $17.50
    C. $267.50, Sales Taxes $17.50
    D. $267.50, Sales Taxes Payable $17.50

17. In order to determine which checks are outstanding, the bookkeeper should compare the

    A. cancelled checks with the stubs in the checkbook
    B. cancelled checks with the checks listed in the bank statement
    C. check stubs with entries made in the Cash Payments Journal
    D. checkbook deposits with entries made in the Cash Receipts Journal

18. In a sale on credit to B. Benson, the bookkeeper, by mistake, posted to the B. Boyers account.
    The error will PROBABLY be discovered when

    A. the schedule of the subsidiary ledger does not agree with the controlling account
    B. the trial balance does not balance
    C. B. Boyers receives his monthly statement
    D. the bookkeeper receives monthly statements from creditors

19. Which does a person receive as evidence of part ownership in a corporation? A

    A. certificate of incorporation
    B. stock certificate
    C. bond
    D. charter

20. The count of merchandise inventory on hand at the end of the year was overstated.
    This error will result in an _____ the year.

    A. *overstatement* of profit for
    B. *understatement* of profit for
    C. *overstatement* of liabilities at the end of
    D. *understatement* of assets at the end of

21. The Accounts Receivable account is an example of a _____ account.

    A. subsidiary
    B. controlling
    C. fixed asset
    D. valuation

22. The _____ check provides space for stating the purpose for which the check is written.

    A. cashier's   B. certified   C. preferred   D. voucher

23. If the assets of a firm at the end of the year were greater than the assets at the beginning of the year, then which statement would be CORRECT?   23.____

    A. The firm made a profit for the year.
    B. The firm was well managed for the year.
    C. The capital of the firm was greater at the end of the year.
    D. More information is needed before arriving at a conclusion.

24. Which is a legal characteristic of a general partnership? _____ liability.   24.____

    A. Long-term   B. Unlimited
    C. Contingent   D. Deferred

25. The term *double entry bookkeeping* means that, for each transaction, an entry is made   25.____

    A. in the journal and also in the ledger
    B. in the general ledger and also in a subsidiary ledger
    C. on the debit side of one account and on the credit side of another account
    D. on a business paper and also in the books

KEY (CORRECT ANSWERS)

1.	A	11.	A
2.	B	12.	D
3.	D	13.	D
4.	B	14.	C
5.	B	15.	B
6.	A	16.	B
7.	C	17.	A
8.	A	18.	C
9.	A	19.	B
10.	D	20.	A

21. B
22. D
23. D
24. B
25. C

EXAMINATION SECTION
TEST 1

DIRECTIONS: Each question or incomplete statement is followed by several suggested answers or completions. Select the one that BEST answers the question or completes the statement. *PRINT THE LETTER OF THE CORRECT ANSWER IN THE SPACE AT THE RIGHT.*

1. In the preparation of a balance sheet, failure to consider the inventory of office supplies will result in _____ assets and _____.

    A. overstating; overstating liabilities
    B. understating; overstating capital
    C. understating; understating capital
    D. overstating; understating liabilities

    1._____

2. The annual federal unemployment tax is paid by the

    A. employer *only*
    B. employee *only*
    C. employer and the employee equally
    D. employee, up to a maximum of 30 cents per week, and the balance is paid by the employer

    2._____

3. Which are NORMALLY considered as current assets?

    A. Bank overdrafts
    B. Prepaid expenses
    C. Accrued expenses
    D. Payroll taxes

    3._____

4. What type of ledger account is a summary of a number of accounts in another ledger? The _____ account.

    A. controlling
    B. subsidiary
    C. asset
    D. proprietorship

    4._____

5. The PRIMARY purpose of a petty cash fund is to

    A. provide a fund for paying all miscellaneous expenses
    B. take the place of the cash account
    C. provide a common drawing fund for the owners of the business
    D. avoid entering a number of small amounts in the Cash Payments Journal

    5._____

6. In the absence of a written agreement, profits in a partnership would be divided

    A. in proportion to the investment of the partners
    B. on an equitable basis depending on the time and effort spent by the partners
    C. equally
    D. on a ratio of investment basis, giving the senior partner preference

    6._____

7. Which account represents a subtraction or decrease to an income account?

    A. Purchase Returns & Allowances
    B. Sales Returns & Allowances
    C. Freight In
    D. Prepaid Rent

    7._____

8. If the Interest Expense account showed a debit balance of $210 as of December 31, and $40 of this amount was prepaid on Notes Payable, which statement is CORRECT as of December 31?

   A. Prepaid Interest of $170 should be shown as a deferred expense in the balance sheet.
   B. Interest Expense should be shown in the Income Statement as $210.
   C. Prepaid Interest of $40 should be listed as a deferred credit to income in the balance sheet.
   D. Interest Expense should be shown in the Income Statement as $170.

9. When prices are rising, which inventory-valuation method results in the LOWEST inventory value?

   A. FIFO
   B. LIFO
   C. Average cost
   D. Declining balance

10. Which of the following is a CORRECT procedure in preparing a bank reconciliation?

    A. Deposits in transit should be added to the cash balance on the books, and outstanding checks should be deducted from the cash balance on the bank statement.
    B. The cash balance on the bank statement and the cash balance on the books should be equal if there are deposits in transit and outstanding checks.
    C. Outstanding checks should be deducted from the cash balance on the books.
    D. Any service charge should be deducted from the check stub balance.

11. Which ratio indicates that there may NOT be enough on hand to meet current obligations?

    A. $\dfrac{\text{fixed assets}}{\text{fixed liabilities}} = \dfrac{2}{3}$
    B. $\dfrac{\text{total assets}}{\text{total obligations}} = \dfrac{3}{5}$
    C. $\dfrac{\text{current assets}}{\text{current liabilities}} = \dfrac{1}{3}$
    D. $\dfrac{\text{current assets}}{\text{fixed liabilities}} = \dfrac{1}{2}$

12. Which asset is NOT subject to depreciation?

    A. Factory equipment
    B. Land
    C. Buildings
    D. Machinery

13. Which form is prepared to verify that the total of the account balances in the Customers Ledger agrees with the balance in the controlling account in the General Ledger?

    A. Worksheet
    B. Schedule of accounts payable
    C. Schedule of accounts receivable
    D. Trial balance

14. If the merchandise inventory on hand at the end of the year was overstated, what will be the result of this error?

    A. *Understatement* of income for the year
    B. *Overstatement* of income for the year
    C. *Understatement* of assets at the end of the year
    D. No effect on income or assets

15. Working capital is found by subtracting the total current liabilities from the total

    A. fixed liabilities
    B. fixed assets
    C. current income
    D. current assets

16. Which is the CORRECT procedure for calculating the rate of merchandise turnover?

    A. Gross Sales divided by Net Sales
    B. Cost of Sales divided by Average Inventory
    C. Net Purchases divided by Average Inventory
    D. Gross Purchases divided by Net Purchases

17. The books of the Atlas Cement Corporation show a net profit of $142,000. To close the Profit and Loss account of the corporation at the end of the year, the account CREDITED should be

    A. Earned Surplus
    B. Capital Stock
    C. C. Atlas, Capital
    D. C. Atlas, Personal

18. The bank statement at the end of the month indicated a bank charge for printing a new checkbook.
    How is this information recorded?
    Debit

    A. Cash and credit Office Supplies
    B. Office Supplies and credit the Bank Charges
    C. the Bank Charges and credit Office Supplies
    D. Miscellaneous Expense and credit Cash

19. The Allowance for Doubtful Accounts appears on the balance sheet as a deduction from

    A. Accounts Receivable
    B. Notes Receivable
    C. Accounts Payable
    D. Notes Payable

20. The Tucker Equipment Corporation had a $45,000 profit for the year ended December 31.
    Which would be the PROPER entry to close the Income and Expense account at the end of the year?
    Debit Income and Expense Summary; credit

    A. Tucker, Capital
    B. Tucker, Drawing
    C. Retained Earnings
    D. Capital Stock

21. A failure to record a purchases invoice would be discovered when the

    A. monthly statement of account is sent to the customer
    B. check is received from the customer
    C. check is sent to the creditor
    D. statement of account is received from the creditor

22. Which General Ledger account would appear in a post-closing trial balance?

    A. Notes Receivable   B. Bad Debts Expense
    C. Sales Discount   D. Fee Income

23. Which deduction is affected by the number of exemptions claimed?

    A. State Disability   B. State income tax
    C. FICA tax   D. Workers' Compensation

24. The face value of a 60-day, 12% promissory note is $900.
    The maturity value of this note will be

    A. $909   B. $900   C. $918   D. $1,008

25. An invoice dated March 10, terms 2/10, n/30, should be paid no later than

    A. March 20   B. March 31   C. April 9   D. April 10

KEY (CORRECT ANSWERS)

1. C
2. A
3. B
4. A
5. D

6. C
7. B
8. D
9. B
10. D

11. C
12. B
13. C
14. B
15. D

16. B
17. A
18. D
19. A
20. C

21. D
22. A
23. B
24. C
25. C

TEST 2

DIRECTIONS: Each question or incomplete statement is followed by several suggested answers or completions. Select the one that BEST answers the question or completes the statement. *PRINT THE LETTER OF THE CORRECT ANSWER IN THE SPACE AT THE RIGHT.*

1. Which is NOT an essential element of a computer system? 1.____

   A. Input
   C. Verifier
   B. Central processing unit
   D. Output

2. The general ledger account that would NOT appear in a post-closing trial balance would be 2.____

   A. Cash
   C. Furniture and Fixtures
   B. Accounts Payable
   D. Sales Income

3. Ralph Hanley, age 45, supports his wife and three children. Mr. Hanley is the only member of the family required to file an income tax return. What is the MAXIMUM number of exemptions he can claim? 3.____

   A. One B. Five C. Three D. Four

4. The cost of a fixed asset minus the allowance for depreciation (accumulated depreciation) is the _____ value. 4.____

   A. market B. cost C. liquidation D. book

5. The form used by a bookkeeper in summarizing adjustments and information which will be used in preparing statements is called a 5.____

   A. journal
   C. ledger
   B. balance sheet
   D. worksheet

6. When a large number of transactions of a particular kind are to be entered in bookkeeping records, it is USUALLY advisable to use 6.____

   A. cash records
   C. special journals
   B. controlling accounts
   D. special ledgers

7. The petty cash book shows a petty cash balance of $9.80 on May 31. The petty cash box contains only $9.10. What account will be debited to record the $.70 difference? 7.____

   A. Cash
   C. Cash Short and Over
   B. Petty Cash
   D. Petty Cash Expense

8. The ONLY difference between the books of a partnership and those of a sole proprietorship appears in the _____ accounts. 8.____

   A. proprietorship
   C. asset
   B. liability
   D. expense

9. The earnings of a corporation are FIRST recorded as a credit to an account called 9.____

   A. Dividends Payable
   C. Retained Earnings
   B. Capital Stock Authorized
   D. Profit and Loss Summary

10. A firm purchased a new delivery truck for $2,900 and sold it four years later for $500. The Allowance for Depreciation of Delivery Equipment account was credited for $580 at the end of each of the four years.
    When the machine was sold, there was a

    A. loss of $80
    B. loss of $1,820
    C. loss of $2,400
    D. gain of $80

11. FICA taxes are paid by

    A. employees *only*
    B. employers *only*
    C. both employees and employers
    D. neither employees nor employers

12. Which phase of the data processing cycle is the SAME as calculating net pay in a manual system?

    A. Input   B. Processing   C. Storing   D. Output

13. Which error will cause the trial balance to be out of balance?

    A. A sales invoice for $60 was entered in the Sales Journal for $600.
    B. A credit to office furniture in the journal was posted as a credit to office machines in the ledger.
    C. A debit to advertising expense in the journal was posted as a debit to miscellaneous expense in the ledger.
    D. A debit to office equipment in the journal was posted as a credit to office equipment in the ledger.

14. The collection of a bad debt previously written off will result in a(n)

    A. *decrease* in assets
    B. *decrease* in capital
    C. *increase* in assets
    D. *increase* in liabilities

15. Which account does NOT belong in the group?

    A. Notes Receivable
    B. Building
    C. Office Equipment
    D. Delivery Truck

16. The adjusting entry to record the estimated bad debts is debit _____ and credit _____.

    A. Allowance for Bad Debts; Bad Debts Expense
    B. Bad Debts Expense; Allowance for Bad Debts
    C. Allowance for Bad Debts; Accounts Receivable
    D. Bad Debts Expense; Accounts Receivable

17. At the end of the year, which account should be closed into the income and expense summary?

    A. Freight In
    B. Allowance for Doubtful Accounts
    C. Notes Receivable
    D. Petty Cash

18. Which form is prepared to aid in verifying that the customer's account balances in the customer's ledger agree with the balance in the Accounts Receivable account in the general ledger?

    A. Worksheet
    B. Schedule of Accounts Payable
    C. Schedule of Accounts Receivable
    D. Trial Balance

19. In the preparation of an income statement, failure to consider accrued wages will result in

    A. *overstating* operating expense and understating net profit
    B. *overstating* net profit *only*
    C. *understating* operating expense and overstating net profit
    D. *understating* operating expense *only*

20. The CORRECT formula for determining the rate of merchandise turnover is

    A. cost of goods sold divided by average inventory
    B. net sales divided by net purchases
    C. gross sales divided by ending inventory
    D. average inventory divided by cost of goods sold

21. A legal characteristic of a corporation is _____ liability.

    A. contingent   B. limited
    C. unlimited   D. deferred

22. A customer's check you had deposited is returned to you by the bank labeled *Dishonored*.
    What entries would be made as a result of this action? Debit _____ and credit _____.

    A. cash; customer's account
    B. miscellaneous expense; cash
    C. customer's account; capital
    D. customer's account; cash

23. The TOTAL capital of a corporation may be found by adding

    A. assets and liabilities
    B. assets and capital stock
    C. liabilities and capital stock
    D. earned surplus and capital stock

24. The source of an entry made in the Petty Cash book is the

    A. general ledger   B. voucher
    C. register   D. general journal

25. Which account is debited to record interest earned but not yet due?

    A. Deferred Interest
    B. Interest Receivable
    C. Interest Income
    D. Income and Expense Summary

KEY (CORRECT ANSWERS)

1. C
2. D
3. B
4. D
5. D

6. C
7. C
8. A
9. C
10. A

11. C
12. B
13. D
14. C
15. A

16. B
17. A
18. C
19. C
20. A

21. B
22. D
23. D
24. B
25. B

TEST 3

DIRECTIONS: Each question or incomplete statement is followed by several suggested answers or completions. Select the one that BEST answers the question or completes the statement. *PRINT THE LETTER OF THE CORRECT ANSWER IN THE SPACE AT THE RIGHT.*

1. Which reason should NOT generally be used by an employer when making a hiring decision? An applicant('s)

    A. resume reveals a lack of job-related skills
    B. attendance record on a previous job is poor
    C. has improperly prepared the job application
    D. is married

    1.____

2. Graves, Owens, and Smith formed a partnership and invested $15,000 each. If the firm made a profit of $18,000 last year and profits and losses were shared equally, what was Owens' share of the net profit?

    A. $1,000   B. $5,000   C. $6,000   D. $9,000

    2.____

3. The bank statement balance of the Bedford Co. on May 31 was $3,263.28. The checkbook balance was $3,119.06. A reconciliation showed that the outstanding checks totaled $147.22 and that there was a bank service charge of $3.00. The CORRECT checkbook balance should be

    A. $3,260.28   B. $3,122.06   C. $3,116.06   D. $3,266.28

    3.____

4. Which account is shown in a post-closing trial balance?

    A. Prepaid Insurance   B. Fees Income
    C. Purchases   D. Freight In

    4.____

5. A check endorsed *For deposit only (signed) Samuel Jones* is an example of a _____ endorsement.

    A. full   B. blank   C. complete   D. restrictive

    5.____

6. The selling price of a share of stock as published in a daily newspaper is called the _____ value.

    A. book   B. face   C. par   D. market

    6.____

7. Which is obtained by dividing the cost of goods sold by the average inventory?

    A. Current ratio
    B. Merchandise inventory turnover
    C. Average rate of mark-up
    D. Acid-test ratio

    7.____

8. A Suzuki truck costing $39,000 is expected to have a useful life of six years and a salvage value of $3,000.
If $6,000 is debited to the depreciation expense account each year for six years, what method of depreciation is used?

    A. Units of production   B. Straight line
    C. Declining balance   D. Sum of the years digits

    8.____

9. Which form is prepared to aid in verifying that the customer's account balances in the customer's ledger agree with the balance in the Accounts Receivable account in the General Ledger?

   A. Worksheet
   B. Schedule of Accounts Payable
   C. Schedule of Accounts Receivable
   D. Trial Balance

10. In the preparation of a balance sheet, failure to consider commissions owed to salespersons will result in _____ liabilities and _____ capital.

    A. understating; overstating
    B. understating; understating
    C. overstating; overstating
    D. overstating; understating

11. A financial statement generated by a computer is an example of a(n)

    A. audit trail   B. output
    C. input   D. program

12. Merchandise was sold for $150 cash plus a 3% sales tax. The CORRECT credit(s) should be

    A. Sales Income $150, Sales Taxes Payable $4.50
    B. Sales Income $154.50
    C. Merchandise $150, Sales Taxes Payable $4.50
    D. Sales Income $150

13. The bookkeeper should prepare a bank reconciliation MAINLY to determine

    A. which checks are outstanding
    B. whether the checkbook balance and the bank statement balance are in agreement
    C. the total amount of checks written during the month
    D. the total amount of cash deposited during the month

14. Which is the CORRECT procedure for calculating the rate of merchandise turnover?

    A. Gross Sales divided by Net Sales
    B. Cost of Goods Sold divided by Average Inventory
    C. Net Purchases divided by Average Inventory
    D. Gross Purchases divided by Net Purchases

15. Which previous job should be listed FIRST on a job application form? The

    A. least recent job   B. most recent job
    C. job you liked best   D. job which paid the most

16. Failure to record cash sales will result in

    A. *overstatement* of profit
    B. *understatement* of profit
    C. *understatement* of liabilities
    D. *overstatement* of capital

17. When a fixed asset is repaired, the cost of the repairs should be _____ account.

    A. *debited* to the asset
    B. *debited* to the expense
    C. *credited* to the proprietor's capital
    D. *credited* to the asset

18. The form used by a bookkeeper to summarize information which will be used in preparing financial statements is called a

    A. journal
    B. balance sheet
    C. ledger
    D. worksheet

19. Which type of ledger account is a summary of a number of accounts in another ledger? _____ account.

    A. Controlling
    B. Subsidiary
    C. Asset
    D. Proprietorship

20. What is the summary entry on the Purchases Journal?
    Debit _____ and credit _____.

    A. Accounts Payable; Merchandise Purchases
    B. Accounts Receivable; Merchandise Purchases
    C. Merchandise Purchases; Accounts Receivable
    D. Merchandise Purchases; Accounts Payable

21. The source document for entries made in the Sales Journal is a(n)

    A. credit memo
    B. statement of accounts
    C. invoice
    D. bill of lading

22. A Trial Balance which is in balance would NOT reveal the

    A. omission of the credit part of an entry
    B. posting of the same debit twice
    C. omission of an entire transaction
    D. omission of an account with a balance

23. A financial statement prepared by a computerized accounting system is an example of

    A. input
    B. output
    C. flowcharting
    D. programming

24. The form which the payroll clerk gives to each employee to show gross earnings and taxes withheld for the year is a

    A. W-2   B. W-3   C. W-4   D. 1040

25. Who would be the LEAST appropriate reference on an application for a job?
    A

    A. relative
    B. guidance counselor
    C. former employer
    D. prominent member of the community

KEY (CORRECT ANSWERS)

1.	D	11.	B
2.	C	12.	A
3.	C	13.	B
4.	A	14.	B
5.	D	15.	B
6.	D	16.	B
7.	B	17.	B
8.	B	18.	D
9.	C	19.	A
10.	A	20.	D

21. C
22. C
23. B
24. A
25. A

EXAMINATION SECTION
TEST 1

DIRECTIONS: Each question or incomplete statement is followed by several suggested answers or completions. Select the one that BEST answers the question or completes the statement. *PRINT THE LETTER OF THE CORRECT ANSWER IN THE SPACE AT THE RIGHT.*

1. A line of a Federal Income Tax Rate Schedule reads:
   over   but not over   your tax is:
   $6,000 $8,000 $1,130 plus 25% of excess over $6,000.
   The income tax due on taxable income of $7,200 is

   A. $1,130 B. $1,430 C. $1,630 D. $1,800

2. We discounted at our bank a customer's promissory note for $3,000. The proceeds were $2,985.
   The CORRECT credit part of the entry to record this transaction is

   A. Notes Payable, $3,000
   B. Notes Receivable Discounted, $3,000
   C. Notes Payable, $2,985
   D. Notes Receivable Discounted, $2,985

3. A payment for gasoline and oil was incorrectly debited to the Delivery Equipment account instead of to the Delivery Expense account.
   This error, if not corrected, would result in

   A. an overstatement of the net profit
   B. an understatement of the net profit
   C. no change in the net profit
   D. no change in the total assets

4. A federal depository receipt is issued when a firm

   A. reports to an employee the amount of federal taxes withheld from his wages during the year
   B. purchases United States government bonds
   C. deposits its surplus cash in a bank
   D. deposits in a bank FICA taxes and federal withholding taxes

5. As evidence of part ownership in a corporation, a person receives a

   A. certificate of incorporation
   B. stock certificate
   C. bond
   D. charter

6. One advantage resulting from the use of controlling accounts in the general ledger is that fewer

   A. bookkeepers are needed to do the work
   B. pages are needed in each journal

C. accounts are needed in the subsidiary ledgers
D. postings are required in the general ledger

7. The proprietor took home an office desk from the business for his personal use. The effect on the fundamental bookkeeping equation is to

A. *increase* assets, decrease owner's worth
B. *increase* assets, increase liabilities
C. *increase* assets, increase owner's worth
D. *decrease* owner's worth, decrease assets

7._____

8. Which can be determined from information found on the Balance Sheet?

A. Current ratio
B. Ratio of net profit to sales
C. Total operating expenses
D. Total income

8._____

9. In recording the amount of State sales tax collected on cash sales, the amount to be credited is

A. Sales
B. Sales Taxes Payable
C. Sales Taxes Receivable
D. Sales Taxes Expense

9._____

10. The rate of return on capital investment is found by dividing the amount of investment into

A. total sales
B. proprietor's drawings
C. net income
D. total current assets

10._____

Questions 11-15.

DIRECTIONS: Questions 11 through 15 are to be answered on the basis of the following account.

Name Grey-Jackson, Inc.   Terms: 2/10, N/30
Address 75 E. 43, New York, N.Y.   10017

DATE	EXPLANATION	POST. REF.	DEBIT	CREDIT	BALANCE
May 3		J 21	630 00		630 00
7		Ma 11		25 00	605 00
10		CR 34		605 00	
June 13		J 32	230 00		230 00
15		Jg 27		15 00	215 00

11. This account will be found in

A. Accounts Receivable Subsidiary
B. Accounts Payable Subsidiary
C. General
D. Sales

11._____

12. From which business paper did the entry on May 3 originate? 12._____
    A

    A. purchases invoice
    B. shipping memo
    C. sales invoice
    D. statement of account

13. The MOST probable reason for the entry on May 7 is that 13._____

    A. a partial payment was made
    B. merchandise was returned
    C. a cash discount on the transaction of May 3 was allowed
    D. shipping charges were prepaid

14. In order to obtain more information regarding the entry of May 7, the bookkeeper should refer to 14._____

    A. invoice number 11
    B. page 11 of the Grey-Jackson, Inc. file
    C. the 11th entry in the General Journal
    D. page 11 of the General Journal

15. If the debit on June 15 represents a freight charge, how much should be paid on June 22? 15._____

    A. $245.00   B. $240.40   C. $240.10   D. $230.00

16. Which error will cause the Trial Balance to be out of balance? 16._____
    The

    A. bookkeeper charged an item to Miscellaneous Expense instead of to Advertising Expense
    B. bookkeeper failed to post an entire entry from the General Journal
    C. bookkeeper incorrectly entered the amount of a purchase into the Purchases Journal
    D. Petty Cash account was omitted from the Trial Balance

17. On October 14, the bookkeeper received in the mail a customer's check for $500. The identical amount, $500, is also due to a creditor on October 14. 17._____
    Which is the recommended bookkeeping procedure?

    A. Endorse the check to the creditor, and mail it to him.
    B. Request your firm's bank to certify the customer's check, and mail it to your creditor.
    C. Deposit the customer's check, and mail a separate check to the creditor.
    D. Return the customer's check to him, and request him to mail it to the creditor.

18. A sale is made on June 16, terms 2/10, EOM. 18._____
    In order for the discount to be allowed, payment must be made no later than

    A. June 26   B. June 30   C. July 2   D. July 10

19. When a petty cash fund is established, the effect on the fundamental accounting equation is that total assets 19._____

    A. and total liabilities remain unchanged
    B. decrease; total liabilities increase

C. decrease; proprietorship decreases
D. increase; proprietorship increases

20. One of the reasons for preparing a Schedule of Accounts Receivable is to

   A. make up statements of customers accounts
   B. determine if the subsidiary ledger agrees with the controlling account
   C. determine the worth of the business
   D. determine the total sales for the fiscal period

21. The current price of a share of stock traded on the stock exchange is called the _____ value.

   A. market   B. par   C. book   D. face

22. In a certain industry, firm A had a current ratio of 4:1; while firm B had a current ratio of 1:1.
   A logical conclusion would be that firm A

   A. had a higher merchandise turnover than firm B
   B. had more cash than firm B
   C. had more assets than firm B
   D. was better able to pay its current debts than firm B

23. When a bank certifies a $100 check for the person who wrote the check, it

   A. pays $100 to the person who wrote the check
   B. tells the depositor that he should remember this check so as to avoid overdrawing his account
   C. immediately deducts the $100 from the balance of the account
   D. asks the depositor for $100 to cover the check

24. A 90-day, 6% interest-bearing note for $340 was paid on the due date.
   The amount of the check was

   A. $345.10   B. $343.40   C. $340.00   D. $334.90

25. The declaration by a corporation of dividend to be paid at a future date results in a decrease in

   A. assets and a decrease in net worth
   B. assets and an increase in liabilities
   C. liabilities and a decrease in net worth
   D. net worth and an increase in liabilities

KEY (CORRECT ANSWERS)

1.	B	11.	A
2.	B	12.	D
3.	A	13.	B
4.	D	14.	D
5.	B	15.	B
6.	D	16.	D
7.	D	17.	B
8.	A	18.	D
9.	B	19.	A
10.	C	20.	B

21. A
22. D
23. C
24. A
25. D

TEST 2

DIRECTIONS: Each question or incomplete statement is followed by several suggested answers or completions. Select the one that BEST answers the question or completes the statement. *PRINT THE LETTER OF THE CORRECT ANSWER IN THE SPACE AT THE RIGHT.*

1. Which can be determined from information found on the Balance Sheet? 1._____

    A. Current ratio
    B. Rate of net profit based on sales
    C. Merchandise turnover
    D. Total operating expenses

2. Which statement BEST describes the function of a source document in an automatic data processing system? 2._____

    A. Input is recorded on it.
    B. Output is recorded on it.
    C. Raw data is obtained from it.
    D. It manipulates the central processing unit.

3. Postings to the debit side of Accounts Payable in the General Ledger USUALLY come from the _____ Journal. 3._____

    A. Cash Payments   B. Sales
    C. Purchases   D. Cash Receipts

4. The PRIMARY purpose of a trial balance is to 4._____

    A. check the accuracy of control accounts
    B. locate errors in posting
    C. assure the accuracy of financial reports
    D. determine if the general ledger is in balance

5. An outstanding check is a check that has 5._____

    A. been voided   B. been deposited
    C. not been written   D. not been paid

6. If the total of the credit column on the Income Statement of the worksheet is larger than the total of the debit column, the difference is called net 6._____

    A. income   B. loss   C. worth   D. value

7. Which is NOT an input device in an electronic data processing system? A(n) 7._____

    A. optical scanner   B. magnetic tape unit
    C. printer   D. console keyboard

8. After all closing entries are recorded and posted, the _____ account would still have a balance. 8._____

    A. Income and Expense Summary   B. Purchases
    C. Owner's Drawing   D. Owner's Capital

9. Failure to replenish Petty Cash at the end of the fiscal period will result in

    A. *understatement* of Net Income
    B. *overstatement* of Net Income
    C. *understatement* of Petty Cash
    D. *overstatement* of Expenses

10. Which item should NOT appear on a job application form?

    A. Current address
    B. Social security number
    C. Religion
    D. Education

11. If a person holds a civil service job, he or she is employed by

    A. the government
    B. a private accounting firm
    C. a large engineering firm
    D. a nonprofit charitable organization

12. Which is NOT given by an employer to an employee as a fringe benefit?

    A. Paid vacation days
    B. Paid sick leave
    C. Group life insurance coverage
    D. Payment of federal income taxes

13. A source of current job openings is(are)

    A. DICTIONARY OF OCCUPATIONAL TITLES
    B. CAREER INFORMATION HANDBOOK
    C. classified advertisements in a newspaper
    D. OCCUPATIONAL OUTLOOK HANDBOOK

14. Which reason should NOT generally be used by an employer when making a hiring decision?
    An applicant('s)

    A. resume reveals a lack of job-related skills
    B. attendance record on a previous job is poor
    C. has improperly prepared the job application
    D. is married

15. When listing previous jobs on an employment application, the prospective employer should list his/her _____ job first.

    A. least recent
    B. most recent
    C. favorite
    D. highest salaried

16. The LEAST appropriate reference on an application for a job would be a

    A. relative
    B. guidance counselor
    C. former employer
    D. prominent member of the community

17. Receipt of a $300 check from a customer in payment of his $300 account results in   17.____

    A. an increase in total value of assets
    B. a decrease in total value of assets
    C. no change in total value of assets
    D. an increase in net worth

18. The monthly report sent to each customer to remind him of the amount he owes is called a(n)   18.____

    A. invoice
    B. statement of account
    C. bank statement
    D. credit memorandum

19. Entries in the Cash Payments Journal are USUALLY made from   19.____

    A. Sales Invoices
    B. Petty Cash Vouchers
    C. Checkbook stubs
    D. Purchase orders

20. The Petty Cash book shows a petty cash balance of $10 on June 30. An actual count of the petty cash on hand on June 30 shows $9.00 in the petty cash box.   20.____
    The account to be debited to record the difference between the book balance and the petty cash on hand would be

    A. Petty Cash
    B. Cash
    C. Cash Short and Over
    D. Petty Cash Expense

KEY (CORRECT ANSWERS)

1. A
2. C
3. A
4. D
5. D

6. A
7. C
8. D
9. B
10. C

11. A
12. D
13. C
14. D
15. B

16. A
17. C
18. B
19. C
20. C

TEST 3

DIRECTIONS: Each question or incomplete statement is followed by several suggested answers or completions. Select the one that BEST answers the question or completes the statement. *PRINT THE LETTER OF THE CORRECT ANSWER IN THE SPACE AT THE RIGHT.*

1. Information prepared in machine-readable form for processing by automatic data processing equipment is commonly referred to as

    A. output
    B. business data
    C. input
    D. financial data

2. Mr. H. Brown, the owner of a small business, withdrew money for his own use. The bookkeeper debited the H. Brown Capital account and credited the Cash account. To correct this error, the bookkeeper should debit the _____ account and credit the _____ account.

    A. H. Brown Personal; H. Brown Capital
    B. H. Brown Personal; Cash
    C. Cash; H. Brown Personal
    D. H. Brown Capital; H. Brown Personal

3. The Dale Corporation earned a net profit of $50,000 for the year. Before closing the books, the Capital Stock account showed a balance of $300,000, and the Retained Earnings account had a balance of $40,000.
The net worth of the firm on December 31 was

    A. $340,000   B. $350,000   C. $390,000   D. $310,000

4. Of the following examples of computer programs, the one most commonly associated with standard bookkeeping procedures is

    A. Microsoft Word
    B. Adobe Acrobat Pro
    C. Microsoft PowerPoint
    D. Microsoft Excel

5. The receipt of a check in settlement of an interest-bearing note will result in an increase in assets(,)

    A. and a decrease in assets
    B. a decrease in assets, and an increase in capital
    C. a decrease in assets, and a decrease in capital
    D. a decrease in liabilities, and an increase in capital

6. A sale on credit to George Rogers for $200 was incorrectly posted to his account as $20. This error would mean that the

    A. Schedule of Accounts Receivable would be understated
    B. Accounts Receivable controlling account would be overstated
    C. Schedule of Accounts Receivable would be overstated
    D. trial balance would not balance

7. A cash sale of $250 worth of merchandise subject to a 6% sales tax should be recorded as a debit to the Cash account for

   A. $250 and a credit to the Sales Income account for $250
   B. $265 and a credit to the Sales Income account for $265
   C. $250, a debit to the Sales Tax Expense account for $15, and a credit to the Sales Income account for $265
   D. a credit to the Sales Income account for $250, and a credit to the Sales Taxes Payable account for $15

8. To determine which checks are outstanding at the end of each month, the bookkeeper should

   A. ask the bank to send a list of these outstanding checks
   B. find the necessary information in the bank statement
   C. compare the cancelled checks with the bank statement
   D. compare the cancelled checks with the checkbook stubs

9. An error was made in writing the amount of a check. The BEST business procedure to be followed is to

   A. cross off the incorrect amount on the check and neatly write the correct amount above the incorrect figure
   B. erase the incorrect amount on the check and neatly fill in the correct amount
   C. write *void* across the check and the stub and write a new check
   D. tear up the check and write a new check

10. When a posting machine is used, Accounts Receivable and Accounts Payable are USUALLY kept in a

    A. bound ledger with money columns for debit and credit
    B. looseleaf ledger with money columns for debit and credit
    C. card ledger with money columns for debit, credit, and balance
    D. bound ledger with money columns for debit, credit, and balance

11. The federal individual income tax return MUST be filed by

    A. December 31   B. March 15
    C. April 15   D. June 30

12. When cash is received as a result of sales, the PROPER business procedure is to

    A. put the cash in the petty cash box
    B. deposit the cash in a checking account at the end of the day
    C. deposit the cash in a savings account at the end of the day
    D. use the cash to pay current bills

13. Which of the following is computer software used for bookkeeping purposes?

    A. Adobe InDesign   B. Microsoft Outlook
    C. Adobe Dreamweaver D. Sage 50

14. The bookkeeper failed to record depreciation for the year. As a result, the   14.____

    A. assets will be understated
    B. profit will be understated
    C. profit will be overstated
    D. liabilities will be overstated

15. The TOTAL of the Schedule of Accounts Receivable should agree with the   15.____

    A. total of the Accounts Receivable column in the cash receipts journal
    B. total of the Accounts Receivable column in the general journal
    C. balance of the Accounts Receivable controlling account
    D. balance in the Sales account

16. Which error would cause the trial balance to be out of balance?   16.____

    A. Incorrectly totaling the Sales Journal
    B. Failing to post to a customer's account from the Sales Journal
    C. Incorrectly debiting the Office Expense account instead of the Furniture and Fixtures account
    D. Incorrectly adding the debits in the Notes Payable account

17. The business paper which is used as a source for an entry in the Petty Cash book is a   17.____

    A. voucher   B. purchase order
    C. check stub   D. credit memorandum

18. On December 31, the Capital Stock account of the Rogers Corporation showed a balance of $75,000, and the Retained Earnings account showed a balance of $15,000. If 1,000 shares of stock were in the hands of stockholders, the book value of each share of stock was   18.____

    A. $90   B. $75   C. $60   D. 15

19. A 60-day promissory note dated July 7 will be due on   19.____

    A. August 6   B. September 5
    C. September 6   D. September 7

20. A bank reconciliation showed a deposit in transit, a bank charge, outstanding checks, and a certified outstanding check.   20.____
    On the basis of this information, the bookkeeper should make an entry to record the

    A. deposit in transit   B. bank charge
    C. outstanding checks   D. certified outstanding check

21. Merchandise was sold on February 8 for $175 less a trade discount of 20%, terms 2/10, n/30.   21.____
    The amount of the check received on March 9 should be

    A. $137.20   B. $140.00   C. $171.50   D. $175.00

22. The monthly report sent by a bank to a depositor showing his balance in the bank, deposits made during the month, and checks paid during the month is called a   22.____

    A. bank reconciliation   B. monthly report
    C. bank statement   D. balance sheet

23. A $200 check received from John Howard, a customer, in payment of his $200 promissory note was entered incorrectly by debiting the Cash account and crediting the John Howard account.
The CORRECTING entry should debit the _____ account and credit the _____ account.

   A. Cash; Notes Receivable
   B. Notes Receivable; John Howard
   C. John Howard; Notes Receivable
   D. Cash; John Howard

24. Bond holders of a corporation are _____ of the corporation.

   A. owners   B. creditors   C. customers   D. directors

25. Which error will cause the trial balance to be out of balance?

   A. Posting to the wrong side of a customer's account in the Accounts Receivable Ledger
   B. Failure to record a sale in the Sales Journal
   C. Totaling the Purchase Journal incorrectly
   D. Posting a $1,450 debit to the Accounts Payable controlling account as $1,540

KEY (CORRECT ANSWERS)

1. C		11. C	
2. A		12. B	
3. C		13. D	
4. D		14. C	
5. B		15. C	
6. A		16. D	
7. D		17. A	
8. D		18. A	
9. C		19. B	
10. C		20. B	

21. B
22. C
23. C
24. B
25. D

REPORT WRITING
EXAMINATION SECTION
TEST 1

DIRECTIONS: Each question or incomplete statement is followed by several suggested answers or completions. Select the one that BEST answers the question or completes the statement. *PRINT THE LETTER OF THE CORRECT ANSWER IN THE SPACE AT THE RIGHT.*

Questions 1-4.

DIRECTIONS: Answer Questions 1 through 4 on the basis of the following report which was prepared by a supervisor for inclusion in his agency's annual report.

Line #
1 On Oct. 13, I was assigned to study the salaries paid.
2 to clerical employees in various titles by the city and by
3 private industry in the area.
4 In order to get the data I needed, I called Mr. Johnson at
5 the Bureau of the Budget and the payroll officers at X Corp.—
6 a brokerage house, Y Co. —an insurance company, and Z Inc. —
7 a publishing firm. None of them was available and I had to call
8 all of them again the next day.
9 When I finally got the information I needed, I drew up a
10 chart, which is attached. Note that not all of the companies I
11 contacted employed people at all the different levels used in the
12 city service.
13 The conclusions I draw from analyzing this information is
14 as follows: The city's entry-level salary is about average for
15 the region; middle-level salaries are generally higher in the
16 city government plan than in private industry; but salaries at the
17 highest levels in private industry are better than city em-
18 ployees' pay.

1. Which of the following criticisms about the style in which this report is written is MOST valid?
   A. It is too informal.
   B. It is too concise.
   C. It is too choppy.
   D. The syntax is too complex.

   1._____

2. Judging from the statements made in the report, the method followed by this employee in performing his research was
   A. *good*; he contacted a representative sample of businesses in the area
   B. *poor*; he should have drawn more definite conclusions
   C. *good*; he was persistent in collecting information
   D. *poor*; he did not make a thorough study

   2._____

137

3. One sentence in this report contains a grammatical error. This sentence begins on line number
   A. 4   B. 7   C. 10   D. 14

4. The type of information given in this report which should be presented in footnotes or in an appendix is the
   A. purpose of the study
   B. specifics about the businesses contacted
   C. reference to the chart
   D. conclusions drawn by the author

5. The use of a graph to show statistical data in a report is SUPERIOR to a table because it
   A. features approximations
   B. emphasizes facts and relationships more dramatically
   C. presents data more accurately
   D. is easily understood by the average reader

6. Of the following, the degree of formality required of a written report in tone is MOST likely to depend on the
   A. subject matter of the report
   B. frequency of its occurrence
   C. amount of time available for its preparation
   D. audience for whom the report is intended

7. Of the following, a distinguishing characteristic of a written report intended for the head of your agency as compared to a report prepared for a lower-echelon staff member is that the report for the agency head should USUALLY include
   A. considerably more detail, especially statistical data
   B. the essential details in an abbreviated form
   C. all available source material
   D. an annotated bibliography

8. Assume that you are asked to write a lengthy report for use by the administrator of your agency, the subject of which is "The Impact of Proposed New Data Processing Operation on Line Personnel" in your agency. You decide that the *most* appropriate type of report for you to prepare is an analytical report, including recommendations.
   The MAIN reason for your decision is that
   A. the subject of the report is extremely complex
   B. large sums of money are involved
   C. the report is being prepared for the administrator
   D. you intend to include charts and graphs

9. Assume that you are preparing a report based on a survey dealing with the attitudes of employees in Division X regarding proposed new changes in compensating employees for working overtime. Three percent of the respondents to the survey voluntarily offer an unfavorable opinion on the method of assigning overtime work, a question not specifically asked of the employees.
On the basis of this information, the MOST appropriate and significant of the following comments for you to make in the report with regard to employees' attitudes on assigning overtime work is that
   A. an insignificant percentage of employees dislike the method of assigning overtime work
   B. three percent of the employees in Division X dislike the method of assigning overtime work
   C. three percent of the sample selected for the survey voiced an unfavorable opinion on the method of assigning overtime work
   D. some employees voluntarily voiced negative feelings about the method of assigning overtime work, making it impossible to determine the extent of this attitude

9.____

10. A supervisor should be able to prepare a report that is well-written and unambiguous.
Of the following sentences that might appear in a report, select the one which communicates MOST clearly the intent of its author.
   A. When your subordinates speak to a group of people, they should be well-informed.
   B. When he asked him to leave, SanMan King told him that he would refuse the request.
   C. Because he is a good worker, Foreman Jefferson assigned Assistant Foreman D'Agostino to replace him.
   D. Each of us is responsible for the actions of our subordinates.

10.____

11. In some reports, especially longer ones, a list of the resources (books, papers, magazines, etc.) used to prepare it is included. This list is called the
   A. accreditation   B. bibliography
   C. summary   D. glossary

11.____

12. Reports are usually divided into several sections, some of which are more necessary than others.
Of the following, the section which is ABSOLUTELY necessary to include in a report is
   A. a table of contents   B. the body
   C. an index   D. a bibliography

12.____

13. Suppose you are writing a report on an interview you have just completed with a particularly hostile applicant.
    Which of the following BEST describes what you should include in this report?
    A. What you think caused the applicant's hostile attitude during the interview
    B. Specific examples of the applicant's hostile remarks and behavior
    C. The relevant information uncovered during the interview
    D. A recommendation that the applicant's request be denied because of his hostility

14. When including recommendations in a report to your supervisor, which of the following is MOST important for you to do?
    A. Provide several alternative courses of action for each recommendation
    B. First present the supporting evidence, then the recommendations
    C. First present the recommendations, then the supporting evidence
    D. Make sure the recommendations arise logically out of the information in the report

15. It is often necessary that the writer of a report present facts and sufficient arguments to gain acceptance of the points, conclusions, or recommendations set forth in the report.
    Of the following, the LEAST advisable step to take in organizing a report, when such argumentation is the important factor, is a(n)
    A. elaborate expression of personal belief
    B. businesslike discussion of the problem as a whole
    C. orderly arrangement of convincing data
    D. reasonable explanation of the primary issues

16. In some types of reports, visual aids add interest, meaning, and support. They also provide an essential means of effectively communicating the message of the report.
    Of the following, the selection of the suitable visual aids to use with a report is LEAST dependent on the
    A. nature and scope of the report
    B. way in which the aid is to be used
    C. aid used in other reports
    D. prospective readers of the report

17. Visual aids used in a report may be placed either in the text material or in the appendix.
    Deciding where to put a chart, table, or any such aid should depend on the
    A. title of the report   B. purpose of the visual aid
    C. title of the visual aid   D. length of the report

18. A report is often revised several times before final preparation and distribution in an effort to make certain the report meets the needs of the situation for which it is designed.
    Which of the following is the BEST way for the author to be sure that a report covers the areas he intended?

A. Obtain a coworker's opinion
B. Compare it with a content checklist
C. Test it on a subordinate
D. Check his bibliography

19. In which of the following situations is an oral report preferable to a written report? When a(n)
    A. recommendation is being made for a future plan of action
    B. department head requests immediate information
    C. long-standing policy change is made
    D. analysis of complicated statistical data is involved

19.____

20. When an applicant is approved, the supervisor must fill in standard forms with certain information.
    The GREATEST advantage of using standard forms in this situation rather than having the supervisor write the report as he sees fit is that
    A. the report can be acted on quickly
    B. the report can be written without directions from a supervisor
    C. needed information is less likely to be left out of the report
    D. information that is written up this way is more likely to be verified

20.____

21. Assume that it is part of your job to prepare a monthly report for your unit head that eventually goes to the director. The report contains information on the number of applicants you have interviewed that have been approved and the number of applicants you have interviewed that have been turned down.
    Errors on such reports are serious because
    A. you are expected to be able to prove how many applicants you have interviewed each month
    B. accurate statistics are needed for effective management of the department
    C. they may not be discovered before the report is transmitted to the director
    D. they may result in loss to the applicants left out of the report

21.____

22. The frequency with which job reports are submitted should depend MAINLY on
    A. how comprehensive the report has to be
    B. the amount of information in the report
    C. the availability of an experienced man to write the report
    D. the importance of changes in the information included in the report

22.____

23. The CHIEF purpose in preparing an outline for a report is usually to insure that
    A. the report will be grammatically correct
    B. every point will be given equal emphasis
    C. principal and secondary points will be properly integrated
    D. the language of the report will be of the same level and include the same technical terms

23.____

24. The MAIN reason for requiring written job reports is to
    A. avoid the necessity of oral orders
    B. develop better methods of doing the work
    C. provide a permanent record of what was done
    D. increase the amount of work that can be done

25. Assume you are recommending in a report to your supervisor that a radical change in a standard maintenance procedure should be adopted.
    Of the following, the MOST important information to be included in this report is
    A. a list of the reasons for making this change
    B. the names of others who favor the change
    C. a complete description of the present procedure
    D. amount of training time needed for the new procedure

KEY (CORRECT ANSWERS)

1.	A	11.	B
2.	D	12.	B
3.	D	13.	C
4.	B	14.	D
5.	B	15.	A
6.	D	16.	C
7.	B	17.	B
8.	A	18.	B
9.	D	19.	B
10.	D	20.	C

21.	B
22.	D
23.	C
24.	C
25.	A

TEST 2

DIRECTIONS: Each question or incomplete statement is followed by several suggested answers or completions. Select the one that BEST answers the question or completes the statement. *PRINT THE LETTER OF THE CORRECT ANSWER IN THE SPACE AT THE RIGHT.*

1. It is often necessary that the writer of a report present facts and sufficient arguments to gain acceptance of the points, conclusions, or recommendations set forth in the report.
   Of the following, the LEAST advisable step to take in organizing a report, when such argumentation is the important factor, is a(n)
   A. elaborate expression of personal belief
   B. businesslike discussion of the problem as a whole
   C. orderly arrangement of convincing data
   D. reasonable explanation of the primary issues

1._____

2. Of the following, the factor which is generally considered to be LEAST characteristic of a good control report is that it
   A. stresses performance that adheres to standard rather than emphasizing the exception
   B. supplies information intended to serve as the basis for corrective action
   C. provides feedback for the planning process
   D. includes data that reflect trends as well as current status

2._____

3. An administrative assistant has been asked by his superior to write a concise, factual report with objective conclusions and recommendations based on facts assembled by other researchers.
   Of the following factors, the administrative assistant should give LEAST consideration to
   A. the educational level of the person or persons for whom the report is being prepared
   B. the use to be made of the report
   C. the complexity of the problem
   D. his own feelings about the importance of the problem

3._____

4. When making a written report, it is often recommended that the findings or conclusions be presented near the beginning of the report.
   Of the following, the MOST important reason for doing this is that it
   A. facilitates organizing the material clearly
   B. assures that all the topics will be covered
   C. avoids unnecessary repetition of ideas
   D. prepares the reader for the facts that will follow

4._____

143

5. You have been asked to write a report on methods of hiring and training new employees. Your report is going to be about ten pages long.
   For the convenience of your readers, a brief summary of your findings should
   A. appear at the beginning of your report
   B. be appended to the report as a postscript
   C. be circulated in a separate memo
   D. be inserted in tabular form in the middle of your report

   5.____

6. In preparing a report, the MAIN reason for writing an outline is usually to
   A. help organize thoughts in a logical sequence
   B. provide a guide for the typing of the report
   C. allow the ultimate user to review the report in advance
   D. ensure that the report is being prepared on schedule

   6.____

7. The one of the following which is MOST appropriate as a reason for including footnotes in a report is to
   A. correct capitalization   B. delete passages
   C. improve punctuation   D. cite references

   7.____

8. A completed formal report may contain all of the following EXCEPT
   A. a synopsis   B. a preface
   C. marginal notes   D. bibliographical references

   8.____

9. Of the following, the MAIN use of proofreaders' marks is to
   A. explain corrections to be made
   B. indicate that a manuscript has been read and approved
   C. let the reader know who proofread the report
   D. indicate the format of the report

   9.____

10. Informative, readable, and concise reports have been found to observe the following rules:
    Rule I.   Keep the report short and easy to understand
    Rule II. Vary the length of sentences.
    Rule III. Vary the style of sentences so that, for example, they are not all just subject-verb, subject-verb.
    Consider this hospital laboratory report: The experiment was started in January. The apparatus was put together in six weeks. At that time, the synthesizing process was begun. The synthetic chemicals were separated. Then they were used in tests on patients.
    Which one of the following choices MOST accurately classifies the above rules into those which are violated by this report ad those which are not?
    A. II is violated, but I and III are not.
    B. III is violated, but I and II are not.
    C. II and III are violated, but I is not.
    D. I, II, and III are violated,

    10.____

Questions 11-13.

DIRECTIONS: Questions 11 through 13 are based on the following example of a report. The report consists of eight numbered sentences, some of which are not consistent with the principles of good report writing.

(1) I interviewed Mrs. Loretta Crawford in Room 424 of County Hospital. (2) She had collapsed on the street and been brought into emergency. (3) She is an attractive woman with many friends judging by the cards she had received. (4) She did not know what her husband's last job had been, or what their present income was. (5) The first thing that Mrs. Crawford said was that she had never worked and that her husband was presently unemployed. (6) She did not know if they had any medical coverage or if they could pay the bill. (7) She said that her husband could not be reached by telephone but that he would be in to see her that afternoon. (8) I left word at the nursing station to be called when he arrived.

11. A good report should be arranged in logical order.
    Which of the following sentences from the report does NOT appear in its proper sequence in the report?
    A. 1   B. 4   C. 7   D. 8

12. Only material that is relevant to the main thought of a report should be included.
    Which of the following sentences from the report contains material which is LEAST relevant to this report? Sentence
    A. 3   B. 4   C. 6   D. 8

13. Reports should include all essential information.
    Of the following, the MOST important fact that is missing from this report is:
    A. Who was involved in the interview
    B. What was discovered at the interview
    C. When the interview took place
    D. Where the interview took place

Questions 14-15.

DIRECTIONS: Each of Questions 14 and 15 consists of four numbered sentences which constitute a paragraph in a report. They are not in the right order. Choose the numbered arrangement appearing after letter A, B, C, or D which is MOST logical and which BEST expresses the thought of the paragraph.

14. I. Congress made the commitment explicit in the Housing Act of 1949, establishing as a national goal the realization of a decent home and suitable environment for every American family.
    II. The result has been that the goal of decent home and suitable environment is still as far distant as ever for the disadvantaged urban family
    III. In spite of this action by Congress, federal housing programs have continued to be fragmented and grossly under-funded.
    IV. The passage of the National Housing Act signaled a new federal commitment to provide housing for the nation's citizens.

The CORRECT answer is:
A. I, IV, III, II   B. IV, I, III, II   C. IV, I, III, II   D. II, IV, I, III

15. I. The greater expense does not necessarily involve "exploitation," but it is often perceived as exploitative and unfair by those who are aware of the price differences involved, but unaware of operating costs.
    II. Ghetto residents believe they are "exploited" by local merchants, and evidence substantiates some of these beliefs.
    III. However, stores in low-income areas were more likely to be small independents, which could not achieve the economies available to supermarket chains and were, therefore, more likely to charge higher prices, and the customers were more likely to buy smaller-sized packages which are more expensive per unit of measure.
    IV. A study conducted in one city showed that distinctly higher prices were charged for goods sold in ghetto stores than in other areas.

    The CORRECT answer is:
    A. IV, II, I, III   B. IV, I, III, II   C. II, IV, III, I   D. II, III, IV, I

16. In organizing data to be presented in a formal report, the FIRST of the following steps should be
    A. determining the conclusions to be drawn
    B. establishing the time sequence of the data
    C. sorting and arranging like data into groups
    D. evaluating how consistently the data support the recommendations

17. All reports should be prepared with at least one copy so that
    A. there is one copy for your file
    B. there is a copy for your supervisor
    C. the report can be sent to more than one person
    D. the person getting the report can forward a copy to someone else

18. Before turning in a report of an investigation he has made, a supervisor discovers some additional information he did not include in this report. Whether he rewrites this report to include this additional information should PRIMARILY depend on the
    A. importance of the report itself
    B. number of people who will eventually review this report
    C. established policy covering the subject matter of the report
    D. bearing this new information has on the conclusions of the report

KEY (CORRECT ANSWERS)

1. A
2. A
3. D
4. D
5. A

6. A
7. D
8. C
9. A
10. C

11. B
12. A
13. C
14. B
15. C

16. C
17. A
18. D

EXAMINATION SECTION

TEST 1

DIRECTIONS: Each question or incomplete statement is followed by several suggested answers or completions. Select the one that BEST answers the question or completes the statement. *PRINT THE LETTER OF THE CORRECT ANSWER IN THE SPACE AT THE RIGHT.*

1. Which one of the following generalizations is MOST likely to be INACCURATE and lead to judgmental errors in communication?
   A. A supervisor must be able to read with understanding.
   B. Misunderstanding may lead to dislike.
   C. Anyone can listen to another person and understand what he means.
   D. It is usually desirable to let a speaker talk until he is finished.

1.____

2. Assume that, as a supervisor, you have been directed to inform your subordinates about the implementation of a new procedure which will affect their work.
   While communicating this information, you should do all of the following EXCEPT
   A. obtain the approval of your subordinates regarding the new procedure
   B. explain the reason for implementing the new procedure
   C. hold a staff meeting at a time convenient to most of your subordinates
   D. encourage a productive discussion of the new procedure

2.____

3. Assume that you are in charge of a section that handles requests for information on matters received from the public. One day, you observe that a clerk under your supervision is using a method to log-in requests for information that is different from the one specified by you in the past. Upon questioning the clerk, you discover that instructions changing the old procedure were delivered orally by your supervisor on a day on which you were absent from the office.
   Of the following, the MOST appropriate action for you to take is to
   A. tell the clerk to revert to the old procedure at once
   B. ask your supervisor for information about the change
   C. call your staff together and tell them that no existing procedure is to be changed unless you direct that it be done
   D. write a memo to your supervisor suggesting that all future changes in procedure are to be in writing and that they be directed to you

3.____

4. At the first meeting with your staff after appointment as a supervisor, you find considerable indifference and some hostility among the participants.
   Of the following, the MOST appropriate way to handle this situation is to
   A. disregard the attitudes displayed and continue to make your presentation until you have completed it
   B. discontinue your presentation but continue the meeting and attempt to find out the reasons for their attitudes

4.____

149

C. warm up your audience with some good-natured statements and anecdotes and then proceed with your presentation
D. discontinue the meeting and set up personal interviews with the staff members to try to find out the reason for their attitude

5. In order to start the training of a new employee, it has been a standard practice to have him read a manual of instructions or procedures.
This method is currently being replaced by the _____ method.
   A. audio-visual
   B. conference
   C. lecture
   D. programmed instruction

6. Of the following subjects, the one that can usually be successfully taught by a first-line supervisor who is training his subordinates is:
   A. theory and philosophy of management
   B. human relations
   C. responsibilities of a supervisor
   D. job skills

7. Assume that as supervisor you are training a clerk who is experiencing difficulty learning a new task.
Which of the following would be the LEAST effective approach to take when trying to solve this problem? To
   A. ask questions which will reveal the clerk's understanding of the task
   B. take a different approach in explaining the task
   C. give the clerk an opportunity to ask questions about the task
   D. make sure the clerk knows you are watching his work closely

8. One school of management and supervision involves participation by employees in the setting of group goals and in the sharing of responsibility for the operation of the unit.
If this philosophy were applied to a unit consisting of professional and clerical personnel, one should expect
   A. the professional and clerical personnel to participate with equal effectiveness in operating areas and policy areas
   B. the professional personnel to participate with greater effectiveness than the clerical personnel in policy areas
   C. the clerical personnel to participate with greater effectiveness than the professional personnel in operating areas
   D. greater participation by clerical personnel but with less responsibility for their actions

9. With regard to productivity, high morale among employees generally indicates a
   A. history of high productivity
   B. nearly absolute positive correlation with high productivity
   C. predisposition to be productive under facilitating leadership and circumstances
   D. complacency which has little effect on productivity

10. Assume that you are going to organize the professionals and clerks under your supervision into work groups or team of two or three employees.
Of the following, the step which is LEAST likely to foster the successful development of each group is to
    A. allow friends to work together in the group
    B. provide special help and attention to employees with no friends in their group
    C. frequently switch employees from group to group
    D. rotate jobs within the group in order to strengthen group identification

11. Following are four statements which might be made by an employee to his supervisor during a performance evaluation interview.
Which of the statements BEST provides a basis for developing a plan to improve the employee's performance?
    A. *I understand that you are dissatisfied with my work and I will try harder in the future.*
    B. *I feel that I've been making too many careless clerical errors recently.*
    C. *I am aware that I will be subject to disciplinary action if my work does not improve within one month.*
    D. *I understand that this interview is simply a requirement of your job and not a personal attack on me.*

12. Three months ago, Mr. Smith and his supervisor, Mrs. Jones, developed a plan which was intended to correct Mr. Smith's inadequate job performance. Now, during a follow-up interview, Mr. Smith, who thought his performance had satisfactorily improved, has been informed that Mrs. Jones is still dissatisfied with his work.
Of the following, it is MOST likely that the disagreement occurred because, when formulating the plan, they did NOT
    A. set realistic goals for Mr. Smith's performance
    B. set a reasonable time limit for Mr. Smith to effect his improvement in performance
    C. provide for adequate training to improve Mr. Smith's skills
    D. establish performance standards for measuring Mr. Smith's progress

13. When a supervisor delegates authority to subordinates, there are usually many problems to overcome, such as inadequately trained subordinates and poor planning.
All of the following are means of increasing the effectiveness of delegation EXCEPT:
    A. Defining assignments in the light of results expected
    B. Maintaining open lines of communication
    C. Establishing tight controls so that subordinates will stay within the bounds of the area of delegation
    D. Providing rewards for successful assumption of authority by a subordinate

14. Assume that one of your subordinates has arrived late for work several times during the current month. The last time he was late you had warned him that another unexcused lateness would result informal disciplinary action.
If the employee arrives late for work again during this month, the FIRST action you should take is to
    A. give the employee a chance to explain this lateness
    B. give the employee a written copy of your warning
    C. tell the employee that you are recommending formal disciplinary action
    D. tell the employee that you will give him only one more chance before recommending formal disciplinary action

15. In trying to decide how many subordinates a manager can control directly, one of the determinants is how much the manager can reduce the frequency and time consumed in contacts with his subordinates.
Of the following, the factor which LEAST influences the number and direction of these contacts is:
    A. How well the manager delegates authority
    B. The rate at which the organization is changing
    C. The control techniques used by the manager
    D. Whether the activity is line or staff

16. Systematic rotation of employees through lateral transfer within a government organization to provide for managerial development is
    A. *good*, because systematic rotation develops specialists who learn to do many jobs well
    B. *bad*, because the outsider upsets the status quo of the existing organization
    C. *good*, because rotation provides challenge and organizational flexibility
    D. *bad*, because it is upsetting to employees to be transferred within a service

17. Assume that you are required to provide an evaluation of the performance of your subordinates.
Of the following factors, it is MOST important that the performance evaluation include a rating of each employee's
    A. initiative   B. productivity   C. intelligence   D. personality

18. When preparing performance evaluations of your subordinates, one way to help assure that you are rating each employee fairly is to
    A. prepare a list of all employees and all the rating factors and rate all employees on one rating factor before going on to the next factor
    B. prepare a list of all your employees and all the rating factors and rate each employee on all factors before going on to the next employee
    C. discuss all the ratings you anticipate giving with another supervisor in order to obtain an unbiased opinion
    D. discuss each employee with his co-workers in order to obtain peer judgment of worth before doing any rating

19. A managerial plan which would include the GREATEST control is a plan which is 19._____
    A. spontaneous and geared to each new job that is received
    B. detailed and covering an extended time period
    C. long-range and generalized, allowing for various interpretations
    D. specific and prepared daily

20. Assume that you are preparing a report which includes statistical data covering 20._____
    increases in budget allocations of four agencies for the past ten years.
    For you to represent the statistical data pictorially or graphically within the report is a
    A. *poor* idea, because you should be able to make statistical data understandable through the use of words
    B. *good* idea, because it is easier for the reader to understand pictorial representation rather than quantities of words conveying statistical data
    C. *poor* idea, because using pictorial representation in a report may make the report too expensive to print
    D. *good* idea, because a pictorial representation makes the report appear more attractive than the use of many words to convey the statistical data

KEY (CORRECT ANSWERS)

1.	C	11.	A
2.	A	12.	B
3.	B	13.	C
4.	D	14.	A
5.	D	15.	D
6.	D	16.	C
7.	D	17.	B
8.	B	18.	A
9.	C	19.	B
10.	C	20.	B

TEST 2

DIRECTIONS: Each question or incomplete statement is followed by several suggested answers or completions. Select the one that BEST answers the question or completes the statement. *PRINT THE LETTER OF THE CORRECT ANSWER IN THE SPACE AT THE RIGHT.*

1. Research studies have shown that supervisors of groups with high production records USUALLY
   A. give detailed instructions, constantly check on progress, and insist on approval of all decisions before implementation
   B. do considerable paperwork and other work similar to that performed by subordinates
   C. think of themselves as team members on the same level as others in the work group
   D. perform tasks traditionally associated with managerial functions

   1.____

2. Mr. Smith, a bureau chief, is summoned by his agency's head in a conference to discuss Mr. Jones, an accountant who works in one of the divisions of his bureau. Mr. Jones has committed an error of such magnitude as to arouse the agency head's concern.
   After agreeing with the other conferees that a severe reprimand would be the appropriate punishment, Mr. Smith SHOULD
   A. arrange for Mr. Jones to explain the reasons for his error to the agency head
   B. send a memorandum to Mr. Jones, being careful that the language emphasizes the nature of the error rather than Mr. Jones' personal faults
   C. inform Mr. Jones' immediate supervisor of the conclusion reached at the conference, and let the supervisor take the necessary action
   D. suggest to the agency head that no additional action be taken against Mr. Jones because no further damage will be caused by the error

   2.____

3. Assume that Ms. Thomson, a unit chief, has determined that the findings of an internal audit have been seriously distorted as a result of careless errors. The audit had been performed by a group of auditors in her unit and the errors were overlooked by the associate accountant in charge of the audit. Ms. Thomson has decided to delay discussing the matter with the associate accountant and the staff who performed the audit until she verifies certain details, which may require prolonged investigation.
   Mrs. Thomson's method of handling this situation is
   A. *appropriate*; employees should not be accused of wrongdoing until all the facts have been determined
   B. *inappropriate*; the employees involved may assume that the errors were considered unimportant
   C. *appropriate*; employees are more likely to change their behavior as a result of disciplinary action taken after a *cooling off* period
   D. *inappropriate*; the employees involved may have forgotten the details and become emotionally upset when confronted with the facts

   3.____

4. After studying the financial situation in his agency, an administrative accountant decides to recommend centralization of certain accounting functions which are being performed in three different bureaus of the organization
The one of the following which is MOST likely to be a DISADVANTAE if this recommendation is implemented is that
   A. there may be less coordination of the accounting procedure because central direction is not so close to the day-to-day problems as the personnel handling them in each specialized accounting unit
   B. the higher management levels would not be able to make emergency decisions in as timely a manner as the more involved, lower-level administrators who are closer to the problem
   C. it is more difficult to focus the attention of the top management in order to resolve accounting problems because of the many other activities top management is involved in at the same time
   D. the accuracy of upward and inter-unit communication may be reduced because centralization may require insertion of more levels of administration in the chain of command

4.____

5. Of the following assumptions about the role of conflict in an organization, the one which is the MOST accurate statement of the approach of modern management theorists is that conflict
   A. can usually be avoided or controlled
   B. serves as a vital element in organizational change
   C. works against attainment of organizational goals
   D. provides a constructive outlet for problem employees

5.____

6. Which of the following is generally regarded as the BEST approach for a supervisor to follow in handling grievances brought by subordinates?
   A. Avoid becoming involved personally
   B. Involve the union representative in the first stage of discussion
   C. Settle the grievance as soon as possible
   D. Arrange for arbitration by a third party

6.____

7. Assume that supervisors of similar-sized accounting units in city, state, and federal offices were interviewed and observed at their work. It was found that the ways they acted in and viewed their roles tended to be very similar, regardless of who employed them.
Which of the following is the BEST explanation of this similarity
   A. A supervisor will ordinarily behave in conformance to his own self-image.
   B. Each role in an organization, including the supervisory role, calls for a distinct type of personality.
   C. The supervisor role reflects an exceptionally complex pattern of human response.
   D. The general nature of the duties and responsibilities of the supervisory position determines the role.

7.____

8. Which of the following is NOT consistent with the findings of recent research about the characteristics of successful top managers?
   A. They are *inner-directed* and not overly concerned with pleasing others.
   B. They are challenged by situations filled with high risk and ambiguity.
   C. They tend to stay on the same job for long periods of time.
   D. They consider it more important to handle critical assignments successfully than to do routine work well.

9. As a supervisor, you have to give subordinates operational guidelines.
   Of the following, the BEST reason for providing them with information about the overall objectives within which their operations fit is that the subordinates will
   A. be more likely to carry out the operation according to your expectations
   B. know that there is a legitimate reason for carrying out the operation in the way you have prescribed
   C. be more likely to handle unanticipated problems that may arise without having to take up your time
   D. more likely to transmit the operating instructions correctly to their subordinates

10. A supervisor holds frequent meetings with his staff.
    Of the following, the BEST approach he can take in order to elicit productive discussions at these meetings is for him to
    A. ask questions of those who attend
    B. include several levels of supervisors at the meetings
    C. hold the meetings at a specified time each week
    D. begin each meeting with a statement that discussion is welcomed

11. Of the following, the MOST important action that a supervisor can take to increase the productivity of a subordinate is to
    A. increase his uninterrupted work time
    B. increase the number of reproducing machines available in the office
    C. provide clerical assistance whenever he requests it
    D. reduce the number of his assigned tasks

12. Assume that, as a supervisor, you find out that you often must countermand or modify your original staff memos.
    If this practice continues, which one of the following situations is MOST likely to occur? The
    A. staff will not bother to read your memos
    B. office files will become cluttered
    C. staff will delay acting on your memos
    D. memos will be treated routinely

13. In making management decisions, the committee approach is often used by managers.
    Of the following, the BEST reason for using this approach is to
    A. prevent any one individual from assuming too much authority
    B. allow the manager to bring a wider range of experience and judgment to bear on the problem

C. allow the participation of all staff members, which will make them feel more committed to the decisions reached
D. permit the rapid transmission of information about decisions reached to the staff members concerned

14. In establishing standards for the measurement of the performance of a management project team, it is MOST important for the project manager to
    A. identify and define the objectives of the project
    B. determine the number of people who will be assigned to the project team
    C. evaluate the skills of the staff who will be assigned to the project team
    D. estimate fairly accurately the length of time required to complete each phase of the project

14.____

15. It is virtually impossible to tell an employee either that he is not good as another employee or that he does not measure up to a desirable level of performance, without having him feel threatened, rejected, and discouraged.
    In accordance with the foregoing observation, a supervisor who is concerned about the performance of the less efficient members of his staff should realize that
    A. he might obtain better results by not discussing the quality and quantity of their work with them, but by relying instead on the written evaluation of their performance to motivate their improvement
    B. since he is required to discuss their performance with them, he should do so in words of encouragement and in so friendly a manner as to not destroy their morale
    C. he might discuss their work in a general way, without mentioning any of the specifics about the quality of their performance, with the expectation that they would understand the full implications of his talk
    D. he should make it a point, while telling them of their poor performance, to mention that their work is as good as that of some of the other employees in the unit

15.____

16. Some advocates of management-by-objectives procedures in public agencies have been urging that this method of operations be expanded to encompass all agencies of the government, for one or more of the following reasons, not all of which may be correct:
    I. The MBO method is likely to succeed because it embraces the practice of setting near-term goals for the subordinate manager, reviewing accomplishments at an appropriate time, and repeating this process indefinitely
    II. Provision for authority to perform the tasks assigned as goals in the MBO method is normally not needed because targets are set in quantitative or qualitative terms and specific times for accomplishment are arranged in short-term, repetitive intervals
    III. Many other appraisal-of-performance programs failed because both supervisors and subordinates resisted them, while the MBO approach is not instituted until there is an organizational commitment to it
    IV. Personal accountability is clearly established through the MBO approach because verifiable results are set up in the process of formulating the targets

16.____

Which of the choices below includes ALL of the foregoing statements that are CORRECT?
A. I, III   B. II, IV   C. I, II, III, IV   D. I, III, IV

17. In preparing an organizational structure, the PRINCIPAL guideline for locating staff units is to place them
    A. all under a common supervisor
    B. as close as possible to the activities they serve
    C. as close to the chief executive as possible without over-extending his span of control
    D. at the lowest operational level

17.____

18. The relative importance of any unit in a department can be LEAST reliably judged by the
    A. amount of office space allocated to the unit
    B. number of employees in the unit
    C. rank of the individual who heads the unit
    D. rank of the individual to whom the unit head reports directly

18.____

19. Those who favor Planning-Programming-Budgeting Systems (PPBS) as a new method of governmental financial administration emphasize that PPBS
    A. applies statistical measurements which correlate highly with criteria
    B. makes possible economic systems analysis, including an explicit examination of alternatives
    C. makes available scarce government resources which can be coordinated on a government-wide basis and shared between local units of government
    D. shifts the emphasis in budgeting methods to an automated system of data processing

19.____

20. The term applied to computer processing which processes data concurrently with a given activity and provides results soon enough to influence the selection of a course of action is _____ processing.
    A. realtime   B. batch
    C. random access   D. integrated data

20.____

KEY (CORRECT ANSWERS)

1.	D	11.	A
2.	C	12.	C
3.	B	13.	B
4.	D	14.	A
5.	B	15.	B
6.	C	16.	D
7.	D	17.	B
8.	C	18.	B
9.	C	19.	B
10.	A	20.	A

EXAMINATION SECTION
TEST 1

DIRECTIONS: Each question or incomplete statement is followed by several suggested answers or completions. Select the one that BEST answers the question or completes the statement. *PRINT THE LETTER OF THE CORRECT ANSWER IN THE SPACE AT THE RIGHT.*

1. From time to time, your subordinates are assigned to other units to do reception work and other duties. You receive a note from Mr. Jones, the head of one of these other units, stating that the work of Miss Smith, one of your subordinates, was unsatisfactory when she worked for him, and asking you not to assign her to him again. Although Miss Smith has worked in your unit for a long time, this is the first time that anyone has complained about her work.
   The one of the following actions that you should take FIRST in this situation is to ask
   A. the heads of the other units for whom Miss Smith has worked whether or not her work has been satisfactory
   B. Mr. Jones in what way Miss Smith's work has been unsatisfactory
   C. Miss Smith to explain in what way her work for Mr. Jones was unsatisfactory
   D. Mr. Jones which of your subordinates he would prefer to have assigned to him

   1.____

2. Suppose that you are the supervisor of a small unit in a city agency. You have given one of your subordinates, Mr. Smith, an assignment which must be completed by the end of the day. Because he is unfamiliar with the assignment, Mr. Smith will be unable to complete it on time. Your other subordinates are too busy to help Mr. Smith, but you have the time to help him complete the assignment.
   For you to help Mr. Smith complete the assignment would be
   A. *desirable*; because a supervisor is expected to be familiar with his subordinates' work
   B. *undesirable*; because Mr. Smith will come to depend on you to help him do his work
   C. *desirable*; because Mr. Smith is likely to appreciate your help and give you his cooperation when you need it
   D. *undesirable*; because a supervisor should not perform the same type of work as his subordinates do

   2.____

3. For a supervisor to listen to the personal problems which his subordinates bring to him is GENERALLY
   A. *desirable*; it is likely that the supervisor has broader experience in solving personal problems than do his subordinates
   B. *undesirable*; the supervisor may be unable to solve such problems

   3.____

C. *desirable*; the supervisor can better understand his subordinates' behavior on the job
D. *undesirable*; permitting a subordinate to talk about his personal problems may only make them seem worse

4. A generally accepted concept of management is that the authority given to a person should be commensurate with his
   A. responsibility
   B. ability
   C. seniority
   D. dependability

5. It has been said that the best supervisor is the one who gives the fewest orders. The one of the following supervisor practices that would be MOT likely to increase the number of orders that a supervisor must give to get out the work is to
   A. set general goals for his subordinates and give them the authority for reaching the goals
   B. train subordinates to make decisions for themselves
   C. establish routines for his subordinates' jobs
   D. introduce frequent changes in the work methods his subordinates are using

6. The one of the following supervisory practices that would be MOST likely to give subordinates a feeling of satisfaction in their work is to
   A. establish work goals that take a long time to achieve
   B. show the subordinates how their work goals are related to the goals of the agency
   C. set work goals higher than the subordinates can achieve
   D. refrain from telling the subordinates that they are failing to meet their work goals

7. You are about to design a system for measuring the quantity of work produced by your subordinates.
   The one of the following which is the FIRST step that you should take in designing this system is to
   A. establish the units of work measurement to be used in the system
   B. determine the actual advantages and disadvantages of the system
   C. determine the abilities of each of your subordinates
   D. ascertain the types of work done in the unit

8. One of your subordinates tells you that he is dissatisfied with his work assignment and that he wishes to discuss the matter with you.   The employee is obviously very angry and upset.
   Of the following, the course of action that you should take FIRST in this situation is to
   A. postpone discussion of the employee's complaint, explaining to him that the matter can be settled more satisfactorily if it is discussed calmly
   B. have the employee describe his complaint, correcting him whenever he makes what seems to be an erroneous charge against you

C. permit the employee to present his complaint in full, withholding your comments until he has finished describing his complaint
D. promise the employee that you will review all the work assignments in the unit to determine whether or not any changes should be made

9. Assume that you are the supervisor of a unit in a city agency. One of your subordinates has violated an important rule of the agency. For such a violation, you are required to impose discipline in the form of a reprimand given in private.
Of the following, the MOST important reason for disciplining the employee for violating the rule is to
   A. obtain his compliance with the rule
   B. punish him for his action in an impartial manner
   C. establish your authority to administer discipline
   D. impress upon all the employees in the unit the need for observing the rule

10. You are the newly appointed supervisor of a small unit in a city agency. One of your subordinates, Mr. Smith, a competent employee, has resented your appointment as his supervisor and has not been as cooperative toward you as you have wanted him to be. One day, Mr. Smith fails to observe an important rule of the agency. You are required to reprimand any employee who fails to observe the rule.
The one of the following courses of action you should take in this situation is to
   A. attempt to overcome Mr. Smith's resentment by explaining to him that although you should reprimand him, you will not do so
   B. reprimand Mr. Smith after pointing out to him that he failed to observe the rule
   C. tell Mr. Smith that if he becomes more cooperative, you will overlook his failure to observe the rule
   D. tell Mr. Smith that although you did not originate the rule, nevertheless you are required to reprimand him

11. Suppose that a clerk who has injured himself on the job because of his carelessness informs his supervisor of the accident. The supervisor has been newly appointed to his job and is anxious to keep accidents at a minimum. The action taken by the supervisor is to criticize the subordinate for his carelessness and to tell him that he is holding him responsible for the accident. Of the following, it would be MOST reasonable to conclude that, as a result of the supervisor's action, his subordinates may
   A. tend to withhold information from him about future accidents
   B. be critical of him, in turn, if he himself is injured on the job
   C. expect him to supervise them more closely in the future
   D. attempt to correct hazardous job conditions without his knowledge

12. The one of the following which is GENERALLY the basic reason for using standard procedures in an agency is to
   A. provide sequences of steps for handling recurring activities
   B. facilitate periodic review of standard practices

C. train new employees in the agency's policies and objectives
D. serve as a basis for formulating agency policies

13. Assume that the operations of a certain unit in an agency enable the supervisor to allow each of his subordinates wide discretion in selecting the kind and amount of work he chooses to do. However, in evaluating the work of his subordinates, the supervisor places more emphasis on some area of work than on others. Factors such as number of applications processed and number of letters written are given great weight in evaluation, while factors such as number of papers filed and number of forms checked are given little weight. Hence, a subordinate who processes a large number of applications would receive a high evaluation even if he checked very few forms.
The supervisor's method of evaluation would MOST likely result in a(n)
    A. increase in the amount of time spent on processing each application
    B. backlog of papers waiting to be filed
    C. improvement in the quality of letters written
    D. decline in output in all areas of work

14. Some management authorities propose that work assignments be made by assigning a varied set of tasks to a group of employees and then allowing the group to decide for itself how to organize the work to be done. This method of assigning work is called *job enlargement*.
The one of the following which is considered to be the CHIEF advantage of job enlargement is that it
    A. encourages employees to specialize in the work they are assigned to do
    B. reduces the amount of control that employees have over their work
    C. increases the employees' job satisfaction
    D. reduces the number of skills that each employee is required to learn

15. In conducting a meeting to pass along information to his subordinates, a supervisor may talk to his subordinates without giving them the opportunity to interrupt him. This method is called one-way communication. On the other hand, the supervisor may talk to his subordinates and give them the opportunity to ask questions or make comments while he is speaking. This method is called two-way communication.
It would be MORE desirable for the supervisor to use two-way communication rather than one-way communication at a meeting when his primary purpose is to
    A. avoid, during the meeting, open criticism of any mistakes he may make
    B. conduct the meeting in an orderly fashion
    C. pass along information quickly
    D. transmit information which must be clearly understood

16. Assume that you are the leader of a training conference on supervisory techniques and problems. One of the participants in the conference proposes what you consider to be an unsatisfactory technique for handling the problem under discussion.

The one of the following courses of action which you should take in this situation is to
- A. explain to the participants why the proposed technique is unsatisfactory
- B. stimulate the other participants to discuss the appropriateness of the proposed technique
- C. proceed immediately to another problem without discussing the proposed technique
- D. end further discussion of the problem but explain to the participant in private, after the conference is over, why he proposed technique is unsatisfactory

17. In measuring the work of his subordinates, the supervisor of a unit performing routine filing began by observing his subordinates at work. If a subordinate seemed to be busy, then the supervisor concluded that the subordinate was producing a great deal of work. On the other hand, the supervisor concluded that a subordinate was not producing much work if he did not seem to be busy. The supervisor's work measurement method was faulted CHIEFLY because
    - A. it did not use a standard against which a subordinate's work could be measured
    - B. the type of work performed by his subordinates did not lend itself to accurate measurement
    - C. his subordinates may not have worked at their normal rates if they were aware that their work was being observed
    - D. the supervisor may not have observed a subordinate's work for a long enough period of time

18. Assume that a system of statistical reports designed to provide information about employee work performance is put into effect in a unit of a city agency. There is some evidence that the employees of this unit are working below their capacities. The information obtained from the system is to be used by management to improve employee work and performance and to evaluate such performance. The employees whose work is to be recorded by the reports resent them. Nevertheless, the employees' work performance improves substantially after the reporting system is put into effect, and before management has put the information to use.
    The one of the following which is the MOST accurate conclusion to be drawn from this situation is that
    - A. a statistical reporting system may fail to provide the information it is designed to provide
    - B. low employee morale may have been the cause of the employees' former level of work performance
    - C. a statistical reporting system designed only to provide information about problems may also help to solve the problems
    - D. willing employee cooperation is essential to the success of a system of statistical reports

19. In setting the work standard for a certain task, a unit supervisor took the total output of all the employees in the unit and divided it by the number of employees. He thus established the average output as the work standard for the task.
The method that the supervisor used to establish the work standard is GENERALLY considered to be
    A. *proper,* since the method takes into account the output of the outstanding, as well as of the less productive, employees
    B. *improper,* since the average output may not be what could reasonably be expected of a competent, satisfactory employee
    C. *proper,* since the standard is based on the actual output of the employees who are to be evaluated
    D. *improper,* since all the employees in the unit may be successful in meeting the work standard

20. There are disadvantages as well as advantages in using statistical controls to measure specific aspects of subordinates' jobs.
The one of the following which can LEAST be considered to be an advantage of statistical controls to a supervisor is that such controls may
    A. reduce the need for close, detailed supervision
    B. give the supervisor information that he needs for making decisions
    C. stimulate subordinates whose work is measured by statistical controls to improve their performance
    D. encourage subordinates to emphasize aspects being measured rather than their jobs as a whole

21. Mr. Stone, who has been recently placed in charge of a clerical unit staffed with ten employees, plans to institute several radical changes in the procedures of his unit.
Of the following actions he may take before adopting any of the revisions, the MOST desirable one is for Mr. Stone to
    A. distribute to each staff member a memorandum describing the revised procedures and requesting the staff's cooperation in giving the revised procedures a fair trial
    B. issue to each staff member a memorandum describing the proposed changes and inviting him to submit his written criticism of these proposed changes
    C. issue to each staff member a memorandum describing the proposed changes and notifying him of the time and date of a staff conference to be held on the merits
    D. of the proposed changes discuss the proposed changes with each staff member independently and obtain his opinion of the proposed changes

22. An assignment completed by Frank King is returned to him by his unit supervisor for certain changes. Frank King objects to making these changes.
Of the following, the MOST appropriate action for the unit supervisor to take FIRST is to
    A. permit Frank King to present his arguments against making these changes

B. inform Frank King that he is free to take the matter up with a higher authority
C. reprimand Frank King for objecting and assign another employee to make these changes
D. state briefly that his decision is final and indicate by his manner that further discussion would be useless

23. Of the following, it is LEAST essential for a supervisor, in assigning work to a subordinate, to issue written instructions when the
    A. supervisor will be on hand to check the work
    B. instructions are to be passed on to other employees
    C. assignment involves many details
    D. subordinate is to be held strictly accountable for the work performed

23._____

24. Assume that you have been placed in charge of a unit where the quality of the work performed is poor. You plan to discuss the matter of improving the quality of the wok at a staff meeting of the unit.
    Of the following courses of action which you might take at this meeting, the BEST one is to
    A. describe a few cases of exceptionally poor work performance; then have the employees performing this work explain why their work was done poorly
    B. inform the staff that you will be criticized by your own superior if the quality of the unit's work does not improve; then discuss, in general terms, the problem of improving the quality of the work
    C. discuss the problem of improving the quality of the unit's work; then call upon each employee by name for his suggestions for improving the work he performs
    D. present the problem to the staff; then indicate and discuss specific methods for improving the quality of the work

24._____

25. Suppose that certain office responsibilities require you to be frequently absent from the unit you supervise. You have, therefore, decided to designate one of your staff members to act as unit head in your absence.
    Of the following factors, the one which is MOST important in selecting the employee best fitted for this assignment is his
    A. manner and personal appearance
    B. estimated ability to perform work of a supervisory nature
    C. ability to perform his present duties
    D. relative seniority in the service

25._____

KEY (CORRECT ANSWERS)

1.	B	11.	A
2.	C	12.	A
3.	C	13.	B
4.	A	14.	C
5.	D	15.	D
6.	B	16.	B
7.	D	17.	A
8.	C	18.	C
9.	A	19.	B
10.	B	20.	D

21.	C
22.	A
23.	A
24.	D
25.	B

TEST 2

DIRECTIONS: Each question or incomplete statement is followed by several suggested answers or completions. Select the one that BEST answers the question or completes the statement. *PRINT THE LETTER OF THE CORRECT ANSWER IN THE SPACE AT THE RIGHT.*

1. Assume that your supervisor has placed you in complete charge of an important project and that several clerks have been assigned to assist you. You have been given authority to establish any new procedures or revise existing procedures in order to complete the project as soon as possible. Just before you begin work on the project, one of the clerks suggests a change in the procedure which you realize at once would result in completion of the project in about half the time you expected to spend on it.
Of the following, the MOST effective course of action for you to take is to
   A. adopt the suggestion immediately to expedite the completion of the project
   B. discuss the suggestion with your superior to obtain his consent to the change
   C. point out to the clerk that an adequate procedure has already been established, but that his suggestion may be used in future projects of this type
   D. encourage the other clerks to make further suggestions

2. A supervisor of a unit may safely delegate certain of his functions to his subordinates.
Of the following, the function which can MOST safely be delegated is the
   A. settlement of employee grievances
   B. planning and scheduling of the production of the unit
   C. improvement of production methods of the unit
   D. maintenance of records of the work output of the unit

3. Some organizations now question the effectiveness of extreme job specialization. It is felt that in some instances it may be more advantageous to enlarge the scope of individual jobs, thus providing the employee with a greater variety of tasks.
Of the following, the one which is LEAST likely to be a result of enlarging the scope of jobs is a(n)
   A. increase in the employee's job responsibilities
   B. decrease in the number of job titles in the organization
   C. increase in the number of tasks performed by an employee
   D. decrease in employee flexibility

4. A manual that is essentially designed to present detailed procedures and policies is not necessarily a good training medium, nor is a manual designed for high-level administrators likely to be satisfactory for use at lower levels.
The MOST valid implication of this quotation is that
   A. a manual, to be effective, should be flexible enough to apply to any working level in an organization

B. the uses to which a manual will be put and the people who will use it should be carefully determined before it is prepared
C. the more detailed procedures a manual contains, the more effective it will be for the use of administrators
D. the degree of difficulty encountered in the preparation of a manual varies with the purpose for which it is designed and the people for whom it is written

5. In assigning a complicated task to a group of subordinates, Mr. Jones, a unit supervisor, neither indicates the specific steps to be followed in performing the assignment nor designates the subordinate to be responsible for seeing that the task is done on time.
This supervisor's method of assigning the task is MOST likely to result in
   A. the loss of skills previously acquired by his subordinates
   B. assumption of authority by the most capable subordinates
   C. friction and misunderstanding among subordinates with consequent delays in work
   D. greater individual effort and self-reliance on the part of his subordinates

6. Assume that the head of your agency has appointed you to a committee that has been assigned the task of reviewing the clerical procedures used in a large bureau of the agency and of recommending appropriate changes in the procedures where necessary.
Of the following, the FIRST step that should be taken by the committee in carrying out its assignment is to
   A. survey the most efficient procedures used in comparable agencies
   B. study the organization of the bureau and the work it is required to do
   C. evaluate the possible effects of proposed revisions in the procedures
   D. determine the effectiveness of existing procedures

7. A recently developed practice in administration favors reducing the number of levels of authority in an organization, increasing the number of subordinates reporting to a superior, and also increasing the authority delegated to the subordinates.
This practice would MOST likely result in a(n)
   A. increase in the span of control exercised by superiors
   B. increase in detailed information that flows to a superior from each subordinate
   C. decrease in the responsibility exercised by the subordinates
   D. decrease in the number of functions performed by the subordinates

8. As an organization grows larger, the amount of personal contact between the top administrative officials and the rank and file employees diminishes. Consequently, management comes to rely more heavily upon written reports and records for securing information and exercising control.
The MOST valid implication of this quotation is that, as an organization grows larger,
   A. evaluation of the work of rank and file employees becomes more objective because of greater reliance upon written reports and records

B. relations between first-line supervisors and their subordinates grow more impersonal
C. top administrative officials depend upon less direct methods for controlling the work of their subordinates
D. it becomes more difficult for top administrative officials to maintain high morale among rank and file employees

9. A supervisor whose unit has a good production record is usually found to be more occupied with the functions associated with leadership than with the performance of the same functions as his subordinates.
The MOST valid implication of this quotation is that
   A. a supervisor whose unit has a good production record usually is not as competent in performing routine tasks as are his subordinates
   B. ability to lead and competence in performing the day-to-day tasks of his subordinates are the requirements of a successful supervisor
   C. a supervisor who spends more time on planning and organizing the work of his unit than on performing the routine tasks of his subordinates will find that a his unit's production record will be good
   D. a supervisor whose unit has a good production record usually places less emphasis on performing the day-to-day tasks of his subordinates than on planning the work of his unit

10. To delegate work is one of the main functions of the supervisor. In delegating work, the supervisor should remember that even though an assignment is delegated to a subordinate, the supervisor ultimately is responsible for seeing that the work is done.
The MOST valid implication of this quotation for a supervisor is that he should
   A. delegate as few difficult tasks as possible so as to minimize the consequences of inadequate performance by his subordinates
   B. delegate to his subordinates those tasks which he considers difficult or time-consuming
   C. check the progress of delegated assignments periodically to make certain that the work is being done properly
   D. assign work to a subordinate without holding him directly accountable for carrying it out

11. A supervisor should select and develop an understudy to take charge of the unit in the supervisor's absence and to assist the supervisor whenever necessary.
Of the following, the technique that would be LEAST effective in developing an understudy is for the supervisor to
   A. permit him to exercise complete supervision over certain parts of the work
   B. assign him to work in which there is little likelihood of his making mistakes, so as to increase his self-confidence
   C. accustom him to making reports on the progress of work he is supervising
   D. give him responsibility gradually so that he will have time to absorb each new responsibility

12. A procedure manual of an agency is potentially more usable than are files of individual messages or bulletins, but usability and usefulness are not routine by-products of the manual form.
    The MOST valid implication of this is that
    A. the purpose of a manual should not be confined to an explanation of routine procedures
    B. a manual may prove to be unsuitable for some of its anticipated uses
    C. individual messages or bulletins are more likely to be of use than are manuals
    D. a manual suffers from certain limitations that are not found in individual messages or bulletins

13. As the supervisor of a unit in an agency, you have just been instructed to put into effect a new procedure which you know will be disliked by your subordinates.
    Of the following, the MOST important reason for calling a meeting of your staff before putting the new procedure into effect is to
    A. help you to determine which workers will be reluctant to cooperate in carrying out the new procedure
    B. allow you to announce that the new procedure must be put into effect despite any objections which might be raised
    C. enable you to explain that you don't approve of the new procedure and to give the reasons why it must nevertheless be put into effect
    D. permit you to discuss the purpose of the new procedure and to present the reasons for its adoption

14. Assume that you are a training conference leader and that you have just begun a series of conferences on supervisory techniques for new supervisors. Each conference is scheduled to last for three hours. A thorough discussion of all the material planned for the first session, which you had estimated would last until 4 P.M., is completed by 3:30 P.M.
    For you to summarize the points that have been made and close the meeting would be
    A. *advisable*; the participants will lose interest in the conference if it is permitted to continue merely to occupy the remaining time
    B. *inadvisable*; the participants should be asked if there are any other topics that they would like to discuss
    C. *advisable*; the participants in a training conference should not be kept from their regular work for long periods of time
    D. *inadvisable*; material scheduled for discussion at future sessions should be used for the remainder of this session

15. In any agency, the top administrative officials are concerned largely with the work of overall creative planning with respect to the anticipated progress of the agency. The first-line supervisors, on the other hand, are concerned largely with the control of current action for the execution of current jobs.
    On the basis of this quotation, a first-line supervisor would be CHIEFLY responsible for

A. increasing or decreasing the responsibilities of his unit to reflect changes in the policies of the agency
B. modifying the work assignments of his present staff to handle a seasonal variation in the activities of the unit
C. revising the procedure that is used for transmitting instructions from the head of the agency to the unit heads
D. raising and lowering the production goals of his unit as often as necessary to adjust them to the abilities of his subordinates

16. The control of clerical work in an agency appears impossible if the clerical work is regarded merely as a series of duties unrelated to the functions of the agency. However, this control becomes feasible when it is realized that clerical work links and coordinates the functions of the agency.
On the basis of this quotation, the MOST accurate of the following statements is that the
    A. complexity of clerical work may not be fully understood by those assigned to control it
    B. clerical work can be readily controlled if it is coordinated by other work of the agency
    C. number of clerical tasks may be reduced by regarding coordination as the function of clerical work
    D. purposes of clerical work must be understood to make possible its proper control

16._____

17. Assume that as supervisor of a unit you are to prepare a vacation schedule for the employees in your unit.
Of the following, the factor which is LEAST important for you to consider in setting up this schedule is
    A. the vacation preferences of each employee in the unit
    B. the anticipated workload in the unit during the vacation period
    C. how well each employee has performed his work
    D. how essential a specific employee's services will be during the vacation period

17._____

18. In order to promote efficiency and economy in an agency, it is advisable for the management systematize and standardize procedures and relationships insofar as this can be done; however, excessive routinizing which does not permit individual contributions or achievements should be avoided.
On the basis of this quotation, it is MOST accurate to state that
    A. systematized procedures should be designed mainly to encourage individual achievements
    B. standardized procedures should allow for individual accomplishments
    C. systematization of procedures may not be possible in organizations which have a large variety of functions
    D. individual employees of an organization must fully accept standardized procedures if the procedures are to be effective

18._____

19. Trained employees work most efficiently and with a minimum expenditure of time and energy. Suitable equipment and definite, well-developed procedures are effective only when employees know how to use the equipment and procedures.
    This quotation means MOST NEARLY that
    A. employees can be trained most efficiently when suitable equipment and definite procedures are used
    B. training of employees is a costly but worthwhile investment
    C. suitable equipment and definite procedures are of greatest value when employees have been properly traced to use them
    D. the cost of suitable equipment and definite procedures is negligible when the saving in time and energy that they bring is considered

20. Assume that your supervisor has asked you to present to him comprehensive, periodic reports on the progress that your unit is making in meeting its work goals.
    For you to give your superior oral reports rather than written ones is
    A. *desirable*; it will be easier for him to transmit your oral reports to his superiors
    B. *undesirable*; the oral reports will provide no permanent record to which he may refer
    C. *undesirable*; there will be less opportunity for you to discuss the oral reports with him than the written ones
    D. *desirable*; the oral reports will require little time and effort to prepare

21. Assume that an employee under your supervision complains to you that your evaluation of his work is too low.
    The MOST appropriate action for you to take FIRST is to
    A. explain how you arrived at the evaluation of his work
    B. encourage him to improve the quality of his work by pointing out specifically how he can do so
    C. suggest that he appeal to an impartial higher authority if he disagrees with your evaluation
    D. point out to him specific instances in which his work has been unsatisfactory

22. The nature of the experience and education that are made a prerequisite to employment determines in large degree the training job to be done after employment begins.
    On the basis of this quotation, it is MOST accurate to state that
    A. the more comprehensive the experience and education required for employment, the more extensive the training that is usually given after appointment
    B. the training that is given to employees depends upon the experience and education required of them before appointment
    C. employees who possess the experience and education required for employment should need little additional training after appointment
    D. the nature of the work that employees are expected to perform determines the training that they will need

23. Assume that you are preparing a report evaluating the work of a clerk who was transferred to your unit from another unit in the agency about a year ago.
Of the following, the method that would probably be MOST helpful to you in making this evaluation is to
    A. consult the evaluations this employee received from his former supervisors
    B. observe this employee at his work for a week shortly before you prepare the report
    C. examine the employee's production records and compare them with the standards set for the position
    D. obtain tactfully from his fellow employees their frank opinions of his work

23.____

24. Of the following, the CHIEF value of a flow of work chart to the management of an organization is its usefulness in
    A. locating the causes of delay in carrying out an operation
    B. training new employees in the performance of their duties
    C. determining the effectiveness of the employees in the organization
    D. determining the accuracy of its organization chart

24.____

25. Assume that a procedure for handling certain office forms has just been extensively revised. As supervisor of a small unit, you are to instruct your subordinates in the use of the new procedure, which is rather complicated.
Of the following, it would be LEAST helpful to your subordinates for you to
    A. compare the revised procedure with the one it has replaced
    B. state that you believe the revised procedure to be better than the one it has replaced
    C. tell them that they will probably find it difficult to learn the new procedure
    D. give only a general outline of the revised procedure at first and then follow with more detailed instructions

25.____

KEY (CORRECT ANSWERS)

1.	A		11.	B
2.	D		12.	B
3.	D		13.	D
4.	B		14.	A
5.	C		15.	B
6.	B		16.	B
7.	A		17.	C
8.	C		18.	B
9.	D		19.	C
10.	C		20.	B

21. A
22. B
23. C
24. A
25. C

TEST 3

DIRECTIONS: Each question or incomplete statement is followed by several suggested answers or completions. Select the one that BEST answers the question or completes the statement. *PRINT THE LETTER OF THE CORRECT ANSWER IN THE SPACE AT THE RIGHT.*

1. A methods improvement program might be called a war against habit. 1.____
   The MOST accurate implication of this statement is that
   A. routine handling of routine office assignments should be discouraged
   B. standardization of office procedures may encourage employees to form inefficient work habits
   C. employees tend to continue the use of existing procedures, even when such procedures are inefficient
   D. procedures should be changed consistently to prevent them from becoming habits

2. An office supervisor may give either a written or an oral order to his subordinates 2.____
   when making an assignment.
   Of the following, it would be MOST appropriate for a supervisor to issue an order in writing when
   A. a large number of two-page reports must be stapled together before the end of the day
   B. the assignment is to be completed within two hours after it is issued to his subordinates
   C. his subordinates have completed an identical assignment the day before
   D. several entries must be made on a form at varying intervals of time by different clerks

3. A supervisor should always remember that the instruction or training of new 3.____
   employees is most effective if it is given when and where it is needed.
   On the basis of this quotation, it is MOST appropriate to conclude that
   A. the new employee should be trained to handle any aspect of his work at the time he starts his job
   B. the new employee should be given the training essential to get him started and additional training when he requires it
   C. an employee who has received excessive training will be just as ineffective as one who has received inadequate training
   D. a new employee is trained most effectively by his own supervisor

4. A supervisor may make assignments to his subordinates in the form of a 4.____
   command, a request, or a call for volunteers.
   It is LEAST desirable for a supervisor to make an assignment in the form of a command when
   A. a serious emergency has risen
   B. an employee objects to carrying out an assignment
   C. the assignment must be completed immediately
   D. the assignment is an unpleasant one

5. For an office supervisor to confer periodically with his subordinates in order to anticipate job problems which are likely to arise is desirable MAINLY because
   A. there will be fewer problems for which hasty decisions will have to be made
   B. some problems which are anticipated may not arise
   C. his subordinates will learn to refer the problems arising in the unit to him
   D. constant anticipation of future problems tends to raise additional problems

6. As the supervisor of a staff of clerical employees performing various types of work, you are responsible for the accuracy and efficiency with which their work is performed.
   Of the following actions you may take to insure the accuracy of their work, the MOST practical one is for you to
   A. review each operation completed by a staff member before permitting the employee to proceed to the next operation
   B. keep a record of every error made by an employee and use this record to determine whether a careless employee should be transferred or discharged
   C. assign work in such a way that every operation is performed independently by two employees
   D. determine what errors are likely to occur and set up safeguards to prevent the occurrence of these errors

7. One of your subordinates has violated a staff regulation by failing to inform you that he will be absent on a certain day.
   Of the following, the MOST appropriate action for you to take FIRST is to
   A. discuss this matter with your immediate superior
   B. find out the reason for his failure to obey this staff regulation
   C. determine what disciplinary action other supervisors have taken in similar cases
   D. take no action if his absence did not interfere with the work of the unit; reprimand him if it did

8. A newly appointed clerk is assigned to a unit of an agency at a time when the supervisor of the unit is very busy and has little time to devote to instructing the new employee in the work he is to perform.
   Of the following, the MOST appropriate method of training this employee is for the supervisor to
   A. instruct the new employee to observe several experienced clerks at work and question them regarding any aspect of the work he does not understand
   B. delegate the job of training this employee to an employee in the unit who is qualified to instruct him
   C. assign the new employee a simple task and inform him that more complex and varied duties will be given him when the supervisor is less busy
   D. have the employee spend his time reading the agency's annual reports and the laws, rules, and regulations governing its work

9. The channels of communication between the management of a bureau and its employees not only should be kept open and working, but they should also be two-way channels.
Of the following, the MOST effective method for a supervisor to use to carry out this recommendation is to
    A. arrange periodic staff meetings and individual conferences to discuss problems and procedures with his subordinates
    B. change subordinates' assignments regularly so that they will be able to see how their work is related to the objectives of the bureau
    C. issue regular instructions, both written and oral, which clearly show each subordinate's assignments
    D. encourage his subordinates to discuss personal problems with him

10. Work measurement is an essential control tool to an office supervisor.
Of the following, the LEAST important reason for using work measurement as a control tool is that work measurement
    A. may indicate training needs of his subordinates
    B. simplifies the procedures used by the supervisor's subordinates in carrying out their assignments
    C. can indicate whether the supervisor is employing more subordinates than he really needs
    D. is a basis for determining which of the supervisor's subordinates are his most efficient

11. Internal management reporting in agencies is becoming more statistical in nature. Statistics have thus become a major tool in management supervision in agencies.
Before deciding to adopt statistical reporting as a management tool, the management of an agency should FIRST determine whether the
    A. employees of the agency understand the need for, and the use of, statistics in reporting
    B. supervisory staff in the agency is capable of putting reports into statistical form
    C. major activities of the agency can be reported statistically
    D. present achievements of the agency can be compared statistically with those of previous years

12. When assigning work, which of the following criteria would be BEST for a supervisor to use?
    A. Allow each employee to select the tasks he or she does best
    B. Assign all unimportant work to the slower employees
    C. Assign the more tiring tasks to the newer employees
    D. Assign tasks based on the abilities of employees

13. You have been supervising ten people for sixteen months. During that time, your employees have never reported any problems to you.
It is LIKELY that
    A. you are doing such a good job there is no room for improvement

B. since your staff is small, the chances of problems arising are smaller than in a larger unit
C. for some reason your staff is reluctant to discuss problems with you
D. your employees are very competent and are handling all of the problems well by themselves

14. Your supervisor informs you that three of your fifteen employees have complained to her about your inconsistent methods of supervision.
You should
   A. offer to attend a supervisory training program
   B. first ask her if it is proper for her to allow these employees to go over your head
   C. ask her what specific acts have been considered inconsistent
   D. explain that you have purposely been inconsistent because of the needs of these three employees

15. On short notice, a supervisor must ask her staff to work overtime.
Of the following, it would be BEST to
   A. explain they would be doing her a personal favor which she would appreciate a great deal
   B. explain why it is necessary
   C. reassure them that they can take the time off in the near future
   D. remind them that working overtime occasionally is part of the job requirement

16. One of your employees has begun reporting to work late on the average of twice a week.
You should
   A. send a memo to everyone in your unit, stressing that lateness cannot be tolerated
   B. privately discuss the matter with the employee to determine if there are any unusual circumstances causing the behavior
   C. bring the issue up at the next staff meeting, without singling out any employee
   D. ask one of your employees to discuss the matter with the individual

17. One of your employees submitted an application for acceptance into a career development workshop two months ago and has heard nothing. The individual tells you that when one of her co-workers submitted an application, he received a reply a week later.
Which is the BEST response for you to make?
   A. This is obviously a case of discrimination. I'll bring it to the Affirmative Action officer immediately.
   B. Next time you submit a request for something of this nature, let me know and I will write a cover letter that will carry more weight.
   C. Perhaps it was an oversight. Why don't you call the organization and ask why you've heard nothing?
   D. it looks like you won't be accepted this year. Be sure to try again next year.

18. In order to meet deadlines, a supervisor should
    A. schedule the work and keep informed of its progress
    B. delegate work
    C. hire temporary personnel
    D. know the capabilities of his or her most reliable employees

19. Your supervisor has given instructions to your employees in your absence that differ from those you had given them.
    You should
    A. have your employees follow your instructions
    B. have your employees follow your supervisor's instructions
    C. discuss the matter with your supervisor
    D. discuss the matter with your employees and find out which method they think is best

20. You have found it necessary to return an assignment completed by one of your employees so that several changes can be made. The employee objects to making these changes.
    The MOST appropriate action for you to take FIRST is to
    A. inform the employee that he or she is free to object to your supervisor
    B. ask if the employee has carefully read your proposed changes
    C. calmly state that your decision is final, and further discussion will most likely be useless
    D. allow the employee to present his or her objections against making the changes

21. Among the problems that confront a new supervisor in relation to her or his employees, the one which requires the MOST unusual degree of skill and diplomacy is
    A. changing established ideas
    B. calling attention to mistakes
    C. gaining the respect of employees
    D. training new employees

22. Of the following, the BEST indication of high morale in a supervisor's unit would be the
    A. unit never has to work overtime
    B. supervisor often enjoys staying late to plan work for the following day
    C. unit gives expensive birthday presents to each other
    D. employees are willing to give first priority to attaining group objectives, subordinating personal desires they may have

23. In the satisfactory handling of an employee's complaint which is fancied rather than real, the complaint should be considered
    A. not very important since it has no basis in fact
    B. as important as a grievance grounded in fact
    C. an attempt by the employee to create trouble
    D. an indication of a psychological problem on the part of the employee

24. You are attempting to teach a new employee in your unit how to change a typewriter ribbon. The employee is having a great deal of difficulty changing the ribbon, even though you have always found it simple to do.
Before you spend more time instructing the individual, you should
   A. ask if the employee working nearest would take responsibility for changing the ribbon in the future
   B. tell the employee that you never found this difficult and ask what he or she finds difficult about it
   C. review each of the steps you have already explained and determine whether the individual understands them
   D. tell the employee that you will continue after lunch because you are getting irritable

25. One of your workers has relatives who raise chickens. One day, you mention in casual conversation that you bought some eggs of poor quality at the grocery store. The following Monday, the worker places a box of fresh eggs on your desk. You thank him and offer to pay, but he refuses. On several occasions thereafter, he brings in additional eggs but still refuses to take payment. He is obviously proud of these products and seems to take great pleasure in sharing them with you. However, you begin to hear rumors that the other workers believe that you and the worker are very friendly and that he is receiving special privileges from you.
You should
   A. explain the situation to the worker, pointing out that he is being hurt by the conditions because of the feelings of others
   B. ignore the situation since the worker is merely being friendly and is actually receiving no favors in return
   C. supervise this worker more carefully than the others to insure that he will not take advantage of the situation
   D. refuse all gifts from the worker thereafter without further explanation

KEY (CORRECT ANSWERS)

1.	C	11.	C
2.	D	12.	D
3.	B	13.	C
4.	D	14.	C
5.	A	15.	B
6.	D	16.	B
7.	B	17.	C
8.	B	18.	A
9.	A	19.	C
10.	B	20.	D

21. A
22. D
23. B
24. C
25. A

TEST 4

DIRECTIONS: Each question or incomplete statement is followed by several suggested answers or completions. Select the one that BEST answers the question or completes the statement. *PRINT THE LETTER OF THE CORRECT ANSWER IN THE SPACE AT THE RIGHT.*

1. Lax supervision has been blamed largely on the unwillingness of supervisors to supervise their employees.
   The CHIEF reason for this unwillingness to supervise is based MAINLY on the supervisors'
   A. failure to accept modern concepts of proper supervision
   B. doubt of their ability to keep pace with modern techniques and developments in supervision
   C. fear of complaints from employees and the supervisors' wish to avoid unpleasantness
   D. inability to adhere to the same high standards of performance which are required of employees

   1.____

2. The appraisal of employees and their performance is an integral part of the supervisor's job. There is wide agreement that several basic principles must be taken into account by supervisors involved in the appraisal process in order to perform this function correctly.
   The one of the statements below that LEAST represents a basic principle of the appraisal process is:
   A. Appraisals should be based more on performance of definite tasks than on personality considerations.
   B. Appraisal of long-range potential should rely heavily on subjective judgment of that potential.
   C. Appraisal involves the use of value judgments by the supervisor and does, therefore, require reference to pre-established standards.
   D. Appraisal should aim at emphasizing employees' strengths rather than weaknesses.

   2.____

3. Although accuracy and speed are both important in the performance of work, accuracy should be considered more important MAINLY because
   A. most supervisors insist on accurate work
   B. much time is lost in correcting errors
   C. a rapid rate of work cannot be maintained for any length of time
   D. speedy workers are often inaccurate

   3.____

4. If an employee has done a complicated task well, his or her supervisor should
   A. tell the employee that he or she has done a good job
   B. call a staff meeting to see if anyone has suggestions for improving future performance of the task
   C. avoid commending the employee as performing competently is what they are paid to do
   D. confide in the employee that he or she is the best worker in your unit

   4.____

2 (#4)

5. You are a newly appointed supervisor in a large office. It had been the practice in that office for the employees to take an unauthorized coffee break at 10:00 A.M. You have been successful in stopping this practice, and for one week no one had gone out for coffee at 10:00 A.M. One day, a stenographer comes over to you at 10:15 A.M., appearing to be ill. She states that she doesn't feel well and that she would like to go out for a cup of tea. She asks your permission to leave the office for a few minutes.
You should
   A. telephone and have a cup of tea delivered to her
   B. permit her to go out
   C. refuse her permission, explaining that you don't wish to set a bad example
   D. tell her she can leave for an early lunch

5.____

6. One of the employees you supervise has just put up a small poster in her work area that two of your eight employees find obscene and distasteful. While you don't like the poster either, it doesn't upset you. The two employees already have complained to you about the poster.
Of the following, you should
   A. have the two employees talk to the individual and explain why they are offended
   B. privately explain to the individual that her poster is causing some problems and seek her cooperation in removing it
   C. do nothing as the employee has the right to express her feelings
   D. compromise and allow her to display the poster half of the time

6.____

7. One of the most effective ways to build a sense of employee pride, teamwork, and motivation is for the supervisor to seek advice, suggestions, and information from employees concerning ways in which work should be solved. Many experiments in group decision-making have indicated that work groups can help the supervisor in improving decision-making. Where employees feel that they are really part of a team and that they have a significant influence on the decisions that are made, they are more likely to accept the decisions and to seek new solutions to future difficult problems.
According to the above passage, a supervisor should
   A. almost always follow the advice of his or her employees in handling difficult problems
   B. always seek advice from employees when handling difficult problems
   C. choices A and D, but not B
   D. look to employees for assistance in decision-making

7.____

8. You have just had a private discussion with the employee with the poster in Question 6 above. You have explained that her poster is causing some problems, and have asked for her cooperation in removing it. She has politely refused to do so, saying, "looking at it cheers her up, and she's been depressed lately."
You should
   A. wait a day or two to see if the incident blows over before deciding whether to take any further action

8.____

185

B. call in the two disgruntled employees within the hour and let them know they'll have to live with the poster as you are not going to act as a censor in the office
C. check agency policies to see if it is legal to have posters down as it is interfering with the work of the unit

9. An employee reprimanded for poor performance tells her supervisor that her recent behavior has been due to a serious family problem. The supervisor suggests several programs which may be able to help her.
The action of the supervisor was
   A. *inappropriate*; the supervisor should not involve herself in the personal affairs of her subordinates
   B. *appropriate*; personal problems frequently affect job performance
   C. *inappropriate*; the employee may consider the supervisor responsible for the subsequent action of the social agencies
   D. *appropriate*; the discussion with the supervisor will in itself tend to solve the problem

10. Your supervisor informs you that the employee turnover rate in your office is well above the norm and must be reduced.
Which one of the following initial steps would be LEAST appropriate in attempting to overcome this problem?
   A. Decide to be more lenient about the performance standards and about employee requests for time off, so that your office will gain a reputation as a good place to work.
   B. Discuss the problem with a few of your employees whose judgment you trust to see if they can provide insight into the underlying causes of the problem.
   C. Review the records of employees who have left during the past year to see if they can shed some light on the underlying causes of the problem.
   D. Carefully review your training procedures to see if they can be improved

11. The management principle that each employee should be under the direct control of one immediate supervisor at any one time is known as the principle of
   A. chain of command   B. span of control
   C. unity of command   D. homogeneous assignment

12. The employees of a unit have been wasteful in the use of office supplies.
Of the following, the MOST desirable action for the supervisor to take to reduce this waste is to
   A. determine the average quantity of supplies used daily by each employee
   B. find out which employees have been most wasteful and reprimand those employees
   C. discuss this matter at a conference with the staff, pointing out the necessity for, and methods of, eliminating waste
   D. issue supplies for an assignment at the time the assignment is made and limit the quantity to the amount needed for that assignment only

13. You supervise nineteen employees in a unit which is located directly across from the commissioner's office. One of your new employees has a habit of *showing off* whenever the commissioner is nearby. You have just heard other employees laughing about this behavior among themselves. You like the new employee and would like the employee to be accepted by the others.
    Of the following, you should
    A. discuss the situation with two of the older employees and seek their cooperation in being a little more tolerant
    B. talk with the new employee and gently explain the situation
    C. discuss the situation with your most trusted employees and ask them to talk to the others
    D. do nothing

14. One of your employees comes to you and complains of sexual harassment by your supervisor. The employee has frequently complained about minor issues in the six months she's been there. You have known your supervisor for thirteen years and respect him a great deal. You have known your supervisor for thirteen years and respect him a great deal.
    Of the following, you should
    A. firmly let the employee know what a serious allegation she is bringing against your supervisor
    B. let the employee know you will take her concerns seriously
    C. call your supervisor and give him a chance to prepare a defense
    D. inform the employee that she had better have concrete proof for a charge of this nature

15. The one of the following which is usually the POOREST reason for transferring an employee is to
    A. grant a doctor's request that the employee work nearer to his or her home
    B. take care of changes in workload
    C. relieve the monotony of work assignments

16. You find that you have unjustly reprimanded one of your subordinates. You should
    A. ignore the matter, but be more careful in the future
    B. readily admit your mistake to the employee
    C. admit your mistake at your next staff meeting so that your employees will know how fair you are
    D. admit your mistake, but blame the misunderstanding on your supervisor

17. An experienced, self-confident employee carelessly omitted an essential operation on a job assigned to her. As a result, the completion of an important urgent report was delayed for several hours. A few days later, a relatively inexperienced, sensitive co-worker made a similar careless mistake with similar negative results. The supervisor of the two employees was more gentle in reprimanding the latter than the former employee.

The supervisor's action in administering reprimands of unequal severity to these two subordinates was
- A. *not appropriate*, because fairness requires that subordinates responsible for like mistakes receive reprimands of like severity
- B. *appropriate*, because supervisors should consider the temperament of subordinates when reprimanding them
- C. *appropriate*, because subordinates who accept greater responsibilities must likewise accept the consequent greater penalties for their mistakes
- D. *not appropriate*, because more experienced employees benefit less, in general, from reprimands than less experienced employees

18. You have just overheard a tense discussion in the cafeteria between two of your best employees. One of them has owed the other $40 for several months and has not paid it back or even mentioned the debt. The employees do not realize that you have heard them.
    During that week, you should
    - A. not discuss the matter with either of them
    - B. discuss the matter with both of them, as the conflict may adversely affect their job performance
    - C. discuss the matter with the one who has not paid back the money
    - D. put a clever but meaningful cartoon up on your wall about the importance of paying back debts to friends

19. You have been supervising twenty employees for three months. You suspect that one of your employees, who has worked in the unit longer than anyone else, has perfected the art of looking busy. You wish to find out how much work she is really accomplishing.
    Of the following, it would be LEAST appropriate to
    - A. have a frank discussion with the employee about her performance
    - B. set specific time limits on when you would like to get work back from her
    - C. try to observe her more carefully while she is working
    - D. be more careful when monitoring her work output

20. The supervisor of a central files bureau which has fifty employees customarily spends a considerable portion of time in spot-checking the files, reviewing material being transferred from active to inactive files, and similar activities. From the viewpoint of the department management, the MOST pertinent evaluation which can be made on the basis of this information is that the
    - A. supervisor is conscientious and hardworking
    - B. bureau may need additional staff
    - C. supervisor has not made a sufficient delegation of authority and responsibility
    - D. bureau needs an in-service training course as the work of its employees requires an abnormal amount of review

21. You have just been appointed as supervisor of ten employees. The supervisor you are replacing demanded that her subordinate accept their assignments without question. She refused to allow them to exercise initiative in carrying out assignments and maintained a constant check on their work performance.

The MOST appropriate policy for you to adopt would be to
- A. gradually remove the controls you consider too strict and provide opportunities for your staff to participate in formulating work plans and procedures
- B. continue her rigid policies, as the employees are used to this
- C. discontinue all strict controls immediately and give the employees complete freedom in carrying out their assignments
- D. ask your employees what method of supervision they would prefer

22. In any agency, the top administrative officials are concerned largely with the work of overall creative planning with respect to the anticipated progress of the agency. The first-line supervisors, on the other hand, are concerned largely with the control of current action for the execution of current jobs.
On the basis of this quotation, a first-line supervisor would be CHIEFLY responsible for
    - A. increasing or decreasing the responsibilities of his or her unit to reflect changes in the policies of the agency
    - B. modifying the work assignments of his or her present staff to handle a seasonal variation in the activities of the unit
    - C. revising the procedure that is used for transmitting instructions from the head of the agency to the unit heads
    - D. raising and lowering the production goals of his or her unit as often as necessary to adjust them to the abilities of employees

23. As a supervisor, you may find it necessary to consult with your superior before taking action on some matters.
Of the following, the action for which it is MOST important that you obtain the prior approval of your superior is one that involves
    - A. assuming additional functions for your unit
    - B. rotating assignments among your staff members
    - C. initiating regular meetings of your staff
    - D. assigning certain members of your staff to work overtime on an emergency job

24. Suppose that a clerk who is employed in a unit under your supervision performs his work quickly but carelessly. He is about to be transferred to another unit in your department. The chief of this other unit asks you for your opinion of this employee's work habits. The chief of this other unit asks you for your opinion of this employee's work habits.
Of the following, the MOST appropriate reply for you to make is to
    - A. point out this employee's good qualities only since he may correct his bad qualities after his transfer is effected
    - B. say nothing good or bad about this employee, thus permitting him to start his new assignment with a clean slate
    - C. inform the unit chief that this clerk performed his work speedily but was careless
    - D. emphasize his employee's good points and minimize his bad points

25. Of the following, the action that is likely to contribute MOST to the prestige of a supervisor is for him to
    A. expect al his subordinates to perform with equal efficiency any tasks assigned to them
    B. observe the same rules of conduct that he expects his subordinates to observe
    C. seek their advice on his personal problems and offer them his advice on their personal problems
    D. be always frank and outspoken to his subordinates in pointing out their faults

25.____

KEY (CORRECT ANSWERS)

1.	C		11.	C
2.	B		12.	C
3.	B		13.	D
4.	A		14.	B
5.	B		15.	D
6.	B		16.	B
7.	D		17.	B
8.	A		18.	A
9.	B		19.	A
10.	A		20.	C

21. A
22. B
23. A
24. C
25. C

PHILOSOPHY, PRINCIPLES, PRACTICES, AND TECHNICS OF SUPERVISION, ADMINISTRATION, MANAGEMENT, AND ORGANIZATION

TABLE OF CONTENTS

	Page
MEANING OF SUPERVISION	1
THE OLD AND THE NEW SUPERVISION	1
THE EIGHT (8) BASIC PRINCIPLES OF THE NEW SUPERVISION	1
I. Principle of Responsibility	1
II. Principle of Authority	2
III. Principle of Self-Growth	2
IV. Principle of Individual Worth	2
V. Principle of Creative Leadership	2
VI. Principle of Success and Failure	2
VII. Principle of Science	3
VIII. Principle of Cooperation	3
WHAT IS ADMINISTRATION?	3
I. Practices Commonly Classed as "Supervisory"	3
II. Practices Commonly Classed as "Administrative"	3
III. Practices Commonly Classed as Both "Supervisory" and "Administrative"	4
RESPONSIBILITIES OF THE SUPERVISOR	4
COMPETENCIES OF THE SUPERVISOR	4
THE PROFESSIONAL SUPERVISOR-EMPLOYEE RELATIONSHIP	4
MINI-TEXT IN SUPERVISION, ADMINISTRATION, MANAGEMENT, AND ORGANIZATION	5
I. Brief Highlights	5
A. Levels of Management	6
B. What the Supervisor Must Learn	6
C. A Definition of Supervision	6
D. Elements of the Team Concept	6
E. Principles of Organization	6
F. The Four Important Parts of Every Job	7
G. Principles of Delegation	7
H. Principles of Effective Communications	7
I. Principles of Work Improvement	7
J. Areas of Job Improvement	7
K. Seven Key Points in Making Improvements	8

	L.	Corrective Techniques for Job Improvement	8
	M.	A Planning Checklist	8
	N.	Five Characteristics of Good Directions	9
	O.	Types of Directions	9
	P.	Controls	9
	Q.	Orienting the New Employee	9
	R.	Checklist for Orienting New Employees	9
	S.	Principles of Learning	10
	T.	Causes of Poor Performance	10
	U.	Four Major Steps in On-the-Job Instructions	10
	V.	Employees Want Five Things	10
	W.	Some Don'ts in Regard to Praise	11
	X.	How to Gain Your Workers' Confidence	11
	Y.	Sources of Employee Problems	11
	Z.	The Supervisor's Key to Discipline	11
	AA.	Five Important Processes of Management	12
	BB.	When the Supervisor Fails to Plan	12
	CC.	Fourteen General Principles of Management	12
	DD.	Change	12
II.	Brief Topical Summaries		13
	A.	Who/What is the Supervisor?	13
	B.	The Sociology of Work	13
	C.	Principles and Practices of Supervision	14
	D.	Dynamic Leadership	14
	E.	Processes for Solving Problems	15
	F.	Training for Results	15
	G.	Health, Safety, and Accident Prevention	16
	H.	Equal Employment Opportunity	16
	I.	Improving Communications	16
	J.	Self-Development	17
	K.	Teaching and Training	17
		1. The Teaching Process	17
		a. Preparation	17
		b. Presentation	18
		c. Summary	18
		d. Application	18
		e. Evaluation	18
		2. Teaching Methods	18
		a. Lecture	18
		b. Discussion	18
		c. Demonstration	19
		d. Performance	19
		e. Which Method to Use	19

PHILOSOPHY, PRINCIPLES, PRACTICES, AND TECHNICS
OF
SUPERVISION, ADMINISTRATION, MANAGEMENT, AND ORGANIZATION

MEANING OF SUPERVISION

The extension of the democratic philosophy has been accompanied by an extension in the scope of supervision. Modern leaders and supervisors no longer think of supervision in the narrow sense of being confined chiefly to visiting employees, supplying materials, or rating the staff. They regard supervision as being intimately related to all the concerned agencies of society, they speak of the supervisor's function in terms of "growth," rather than the "improvement" of employees.

This modern concept of supervision may be defined as follows: Supervision is leadership and the development of leadership within groups which are cooperatively engaged in inspection, research, training, guidance, and evaluation.

THE OLD AND THE NEW SUPERVISION

TRADITIONAL
1. Inspection
2. Focused on the employee
3. Visitation
4. Random and haphazard
5. Imposed and authoritarian
6. One person usually

MODERN
1. Study and analysis
2. Focused on aims, materials, methods, supervisors, employees, environment
3. Demonstrations, intervisitation, workshops, directed reading, bulletins, etc.
4. Definitely organized and planned (scientific)
5. Cooperative and democratic
6. Many persons involved (creative)

THE EIGHT (8) BASIC PRINCIPLES OF THE NEW SUPERVISION

I. Principle of Responsibility
   Authority to act and responsibility for acting must be joined.
   A. If you give responsibility, give authority.
   B. Define employee duties clearly.
   C. Protect employees from criticism by others.
   D. Recognize the rights as well as obligations of employees.
   E. Achieve the aims of a democratic society insofar as it is possible within the area of your work.
   F. Establish a situation favorable to training and learning.
   G. Accept ultimate responsibility for everything done in your section, unit, office, division, department.
   H. Good administration and good supervision are inseparable.

II. Principle of Authority
   The success of the supervisor is measured by the extent to which the power of authority is not used.
   A. Exercise simplicity and informality in supervision
   B. Use the simplest machinery of supervision
   C. If it is good for the organization as a whole, it is probably justified.
   D. Seldom be arbitrary or authoritative.
   E. Do not base your work on the power of position or of personality.
   F. Permit and encourage the free expression of opinions.

III. Principle of Self-Growth
   The success of the supervisor is measured by the extent to which, and the speed with which, he is no longer needed.
   A. Base criticism on principles, not on specifics.
   B. Point out higher activities to employees.
   C. Train for self-thinking by employees to meet new situations.
   D. Stimulate initiative, self-reliance, and individual responsibility
   E. Concentrate on stimulating the growth of employees rather than on removing defects.

IV. Principle of Individual Worth
   Respect for the individual is a paramount consideration in supervision.
   A. Be human and sympathetic in dealing with employees.
   B. Don't nag about things to be done.
   C. Recognize the individual differences among employees and seek opportunities to permit best expression of each personality.

V. Principle of Creative Leadership
   The best supervision is that which is not apparent to the employee.
   A. Stimulate, don't drive employees to creative action.
   B. Emphasize doing good things.
   C. Encourage employees to do what they do best.
   D. Do not be too greatly concerned with details of subject or method.
   E. Do not be concerned exclusively with immediate problems and activities.
   F. Reveal higher activities and make them both desired and maximally possible.
   G. Determine procedures in the light of each situation but see that these are derived from a sound basic philosophy.
   H. Aid, inspire, and lead so as to liberate the creative spirit latent in all good employees.

VI. Principle of Success and Failure
   There are no unsuccessful employees, only unsuccessful supervisors who have failed to give proper leadership.
   A. Adapt suggestions to the capacities, attitudes, and prejudices of employees.
   B. Be gradual, be progressive, be persistent.
   C. Help the employee find the general principle; have the employee apply his own problem to the general principle.
   D. Give adequate appreciation for good work and honest effort.
   E. Anticipate employee difficulties and help to prevent them.
   F. Encourage employees to do the desirable things they will do anyway.
   G. Judge your supervision by the results it secures.

VII. Principle of Science
Successful supervision is scientific, objective, and experimental. It is based on facts, not on prejudices.
   A. Be cumulative in results.
   B. Never divorce your suggestions from the goals of training.
   C. Don't be impatient of results.
   D. Keep all matters on a professional, not a personal, level.
   E. Do not be concerned exclusively with immediate problems and activities.
   F. Use objective means of determining achievement and rating where possible.

VIII. Principle of Cooperation
Supervision is a cooperative enterprise between supervisor and employee.
   A. Begin with conditions as they are.
   B. Ask opinions of all involved when formulating policies.
   C. Organization is as good as its weakest link.
   D. Let employees help to determine policies and department programs.
   E. Be approachable and accessible—physically and mentally.
   F. Develop pleasant social relationships.

WHAT IS ADMINISTRATION

Administration is concerned with providing the environment, the material facilities, and the operational procedures that will promote the maximum growth and development of supervisors and employees. (Organization is an aspect and a concomitant of administration.)

There is no sharp line of demarcation between supervision and administration; these functions are intimately interrelated and, often, overlapping. They are complementary activities.

I. Practices Commonly Classed as "Supervisory"
   A. Conducting employees' conferences
   B. Visiting sections, units, offices, divisions, departments
   C. Arranging for demonstrations
   D. Examining plans
   E. Suggesting professional reading
   F. Interpreting bulletins
   G. Recommending in-service training courses
   H. Encouraging experimentation
   I. Appraising employee morale
   J. Providing for intervisitation

II. Practices Commonly Classified as "Administrative"
   A. Management of the office
   B. Arrangement of schedules for extra duties
   C. Assignment of rooms or areas
   D. Distribution of supplies
   E. Keeping records and reports
   F. Care of audio-visual materials
   G. Keeping inventory records
   H. Checking record cards and books

I. Programming special activities
   J. Checking on the attendance and punctuality of employees

III. Practices Commonly Classified as Both "Supervisory" and "Administrative"
   A. Program construction
   B. Testing or evaluating outcomes
   C. Personnel accounting
   D. Ordering instructional materials

RESPONSIBILITIES OF THE SUPERVISOR

A person employed in a supervisory capacity must constantly be able to improve his own efficiency and ability. He represent the employer to the employees and only continuous self-examination can make him a capable supervisor.

Leadership and training are the supervisor's responsibility. An efficient working unit is one in which the employees work with the supervisor. It is his job to bring out the best in his employees. He must always be relaxed, courteous, and calm in his association with his employees. Their feelings are important, and a harsh attitude does not develop the most efficient employees.

COMPETENCES OF THE SUPERVISOR

   I. Complete knowledge of the duties and responsibilities of his position.
   II. To be able to organize a job, plan ahead, and carry through.
   III. To have self-confidence and initiative.
   IV. To be able to handle the unexpected situation and make quick decisions.
   V. To be able to properly train subordinates in the positions they are best suited for.
   VI. To be able to keep good human relations among his subordinates.
   VII. To be able to keep good human relations between his subordinates and himself and to earn their respect and trust.

THE PROFESSIONAL SUPERVISOR-EMPLOYEE RELATIONSHIP

There are two kinds of efficiency: one kind is only apparent and is produced in organizations through the exercise of mere discipline; this is but a simulation of the second, or true, efficiency which springs from spontaneous cooperation. If you are a manager, no matter how great or small your responsibility, it is your job, in the final analysis, to create and develop this involuntary cooperation among the people whom you supervise. For, no matter how powerful a combination of money, machines, and materials a company may have, this is a dead and sterile thing without a team of willing, thinking, and articulate people to guide it.

The following 21 points are presented as indicative of the exemplary basic relationship that should exist between supervisor and employee:

1. Each person wants to be liked and respected by his fellow employee and wants to be treated with consideration and respect by his superior.
2. The most competent employee will make an error. However, in a unit where good relations exist between the supervisor and his employees, tenseness and fear do not exist. Thus, errors are not hidden or covered up, and the efficiency of a unit is not impaired.

3. Subordinates resent rules, regulations, or orders that are unreasonable or unexplained.
4. Subordinates are quick to resent unfairness, harshness, injustices, and favoritism.
5. An employee will accept responsibility if he knows that he will be complimented for a job well done, and not too harshly chastised for failure; that his supervisor will check the cause of the failure, and, if it was the supervisor's fault, he will assume the blame therefore. If it was the employee's fault, his supervisor will explain the correct method or means of handling the responsibility.
6. An employee wants to receive credit for a suggestion he has made, that is used. If a suggestion cannot be used, the employee is entitled to an explanation. The supervisor should not say "no" and close the subject.
7. Fear and worry slow up a worker's ability. Poor working environment can impair his physical and mental health. A good supervisor avoids forceful methods, threats, and arguments to get a job done.
8. A forceful supervisor is able to train his employees individually and as a team, and is able to motivate them in the proper channels.
9. A mature supervisor is able to properly evaluate his subordinates and to keep them happy and satisfied.
10. A sensitive supervisor will never patronize his subordinates.
11. A worthy supervisor will respect his employees' confidences.
12. Definite and clear-cut responsibilities should be assigned to each executive.
13. Responsibility should always be coupled with corresponding authority.
14. No change should be made in the scope or responsibilities of a position without a definite understanding to that effect on the part of all persons concerned.
15. No executive or employee, occupying a single position in the organization, should be subject to definite orders from more than one source.
16. Orders should never be given to subordinates over the head of a responsible executive. Rather than do this, the officer in question should be supplanted.
17. Criticisms of subordinates should, whoever possible, be made privately, and in no case should a subordinate be criticized in the presence of executives or employees of equal or lower rank.
18. No dispute or difference between executives or employees as to authority or responsibilities should be considered too trivial for prompt and careful adjudication.
19. Promotions, wage changes, and disciplinary action should always be approved by the executive immediately superior to the one directly responsible.
20. No executive or employee should ever be required, or expected, to be at the same time an assistant to, and critic of, another.
21. Any executive whose work is subject to regular inspection should, wherever practicable, be given the assistance and facilities necessary to enable him to maintain an independent check of the quality of his work.

MINI-TEXT IN SUPERVISION, ADMINISTRATION, MANAGEMENT, AND ORGANIZATION

I. Brief Highlights

Listed concisely and sequentially are major headings and important data in the field for quick recall and review.

A. Levels of Management
Any organization of some size has several levels of management. In terms of a ladder, the levels are:

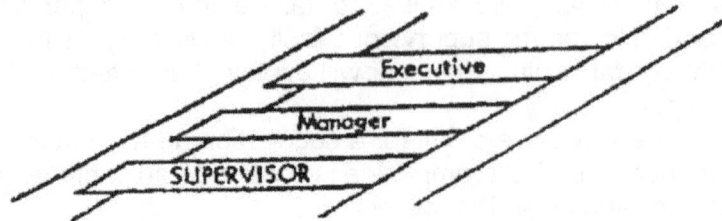

The first level is very important because it is the beginning point of management leadership.

B. What the Supervisor Must Learn
A supervisor must learn to:
1. Deal with people and their differences
2. Get the job done through people
3. Recognize the problems when they exist
4. Overcome obstacles to good performance
5. Evaluate the performance of people
6. Check his own performance in terms of accomplishment

C. A Definition of Supervisor
The term supervisor means any individual having authority, in the interests of the employer, to hire, transfer, suspend, lay-off, recall, promote, discharge, assign, reward, or discipline other employees or responsibility to direct them, or to adjust their grievances, or effectively to recommend such action, if, in connection with the foregoing, exercise of such authority is not of a merely routine or clerical nature but requires the use of independent judgment.

D. Elements of the Team Concept
What is involved in teamwork? The component parts are:
1. Members
2. A leader
3. Goals
4. Plans
5. Cooperation
6. Spirit

E. Principles of Organization
1. A team member must know what his job is.
2. Be sure that the nature and scope of a job are understood.
3. Authority and responsibility should be carefully spelled out.
4. A supervisor should be permitted to make the maximum number of decisions affecting his employees.
5. Employees should report to only one supervisor.
6. A supervisor should direct only as many employees as he can handle effectively.
7. An organization plan should be flexible.

8. Inspection and performance of work should be separate.
9. Organizational problems should receive immediate attention.
10. Assign work in line with ability and experience.

F. The Four Important Parts of Every Job
1. Inherent in every job is the *accountability* for results.
2. A second set of factors in every job is *responsibilities*.
3. Along with duties and responsibilities one must have the *authority* to act within certain limits without obtaining permission to proceed.
4. No job exists in a vacuum. The supervisor is surrounded by key *relationships*.

G. Principles of Delegation
Where work is delegated for the first time, the supervisor should think in terms of these questions:
1. Who is best qualified to do this?
2. Can an employee improve his abilities by doing this?
3. How long should an employee spend on this?
4. Are there any special problems for which he will need guidance?
5. How broad a delegation can I make?

H. Principles of Effective Communications
1. Determine the media.
2. To whom directed?
3. Identification and source authority.
4. Is communication understood?

I. Principles of Work Improvement
1. Most people usually do only the work which is assigned to them.
2. Workers are likely to fit assigned work into the time available to perform it.
3. A good workload usually stimulates output.
4. People usually do their best work when they know that results will be reviewed or inspected.
5. Employees usually feel that someone else is responsible for conditions of work, workplace layout, job methods, type of tools/equipment, and other such factors.
6. Employees are usually defensive about their job security.
7. Employees have natural resistance to change.
8. Employees can support or destroy a supervisor.
9. A supervisor usually earns the respect of his people through his personal example of diligence and efficiency.

J. Areas of Job Improvement
The areas of job improvement are quite numerous, but the most common ones which a supervisor can identify and utilize are:
1. Departmental layout
2. Flow of work
3. Workplace layout
4. Utilization of manpower
5. Work methods
6. Materials handling

7. Utilization
8. Motion economy

K. Seven Key Points in Making Improvements
1. Select the job to be improved
2. Study how it is being done now
3. Question the present method
4. Determine actions to be taken
5. Chart proposed method
6. Get approval and apply
7. Solicit worker participation

L. Corrective Techniques of Job Improvement
Specific Problems
1. Size of workload
2. Inability to meet schedules
3. Strain and fatigue
4. Improper use of men and skills
5. Waste, poor quality, unsafe conditions
6. Bottleneck conditions that hinder output
7. Poor utilization of equipment and machine
8. Efficiency and productivity of labor

General Improvement
1. Departmental layout
2. Flow of work
3. Work plan layout
4. Utilization of manpower
5. Work methods
6. Materials handling
7. Utilization of equipment
8. Motion economy

Corrective Techniques
1. Study with scale model
2. Flow chart study
3. Motion analysis
4. Comparison of units produced to standard allowance
5. Methods analysis
6. Flow chart and equipment study
7. Down time vs. running time
8. Motion analysis

M. A Planning Checklist
1. Objectives
2. Controls
3. Delegations
4. Communications
5. Resources
6. Manpower

7. Equipment
8. Supplies and materials
9. Utilization of time
10. Safety
11. Money
12. Work
13. Timing of improvements

N. Five Characteristics of Good Directions
In order to get results, directions must be:
1. Possible of accomplishment
2. Agreeable with worker interests
3. Related to mission
4. Planned and complete
5. Unmistakably clear

O. Types of Directions
1. Demands or direct orders
2. Requests
3. Suggestion or implication
4. volunteering

P. Controls
A typical listing of the overall areas in which the supervisor should establish controls might be:
1. Manpower
2. Materials
3. Quality of work
4. Quantity of work
5. Time
6. Space
7. Money
8. Methods

Q. Orienting the New Employee
1. Prepare for him
2. Welcome the new employee
3. Orientation for the job
4. Follow-up

R. Checklist for Orienting New Employees   Yes   No
1. Do you appreciate the feelings of new employees
   when they first report for work?   ___   ___
2. Are you aware of the fact that the new employee must
   make a big adjustment to his job?   ___   ___
3. Have you given him good reasons for liking the job and
   the organization?   ___   ___
4. Have you prepared for his first day on the job? ___   ___
5. Did you welcome him cordially and make him feel needed? ___ ___

		Yes	No

6. Did you establish rapport with him so that he feels free to talk and discuss matters with you? ___ ___
7. Did you explain his job to him and his relationship to you? ___ ___
8. Does he know that his work will be evaluated periodically on a basis that is fair and objective? ___ ___
9. Did you introduce him to his fellow workers in such a way that they are likely to accept him? ___ ___
10. Does he know what employee benefits he will receive? ___ ___
11. Does he understand the importance of being on the job and what to do if he must leave his duty station? ___ ___
12. Has he been impressed with the importance of accident prevention and safe practice? ___ ___
13. Does he generally know his way around the department? ___ ___
14. Is he under the guidance of a sponsor who will teach the right way of doing things? ___ ___
15. Do you plan to follow-up so that he will continue to adjust successfully to his job? ___ ___

S. Principles of Learning
 1. Motivation
 2. Demonstration or explanation
 3. Practice

T. Causes of Poor Performance
 1. Improper training for job
 2. Wrong tools
 3. Inadequate directions
 4. Lack of supervisory follow-up
 5. Poor communications
 6. Lack of standards of performance
 7. Wrong work habits
 8. Low morale
 9. Other

U. Four Major Steps in On-The-Job Instruction
 1. Prepare the worker
 2. Present the operation
 3. Tryout performance
 4. Follow-up

V. Employees Want Five Things
 1. Security
 2. Opportunity
 3. Recognition
 4. Inclusion
 5. Expression

W. Some Don'ts in Regard to Praise
1. Don't praise a person for something he hasn't done.
2. Don't praise a person unless you can be sincere.
3. Don't be sparing in praise just because your superior withholds it from you.
4. Don't let too much time elapse between good performance and recognition of it

X. How to Gain Your Workers' Confidence
Methods of developing confidence include such things as:
1. Knowing the interests, habits, hobbies of employees
2. Admitting your own inadequacies
3. Sharing and telling of confidence in others
4. Supporting people when they are in trouble
5. Delegating matters that can be well handled
6. Being frank and straightforward about problems and working conditions
7. Encouraging others to bring their problems to you
8. Taking action on problems which impede worker progress

Y. Sources of Employee Problems
On-the-job causes might be such things as:
1. A feeling that favoritism is exercised in assignments
2. Assignment of overtime
3. An undue amount of supervision
4. Changing methods or systems
5. Stealing of ideas or trade secrets
6. Lack of interest in job
7. Threat of reduction in force
8. Ignorance or lack of communications
9. Poor equipment
10. Lack of knowing how supervisor feels toward employee
11. Shift assignments

Off-the-job problems might have to do with:
1. Health
2. Finances
3. Housing
4. Family

Z. The Supervisor's Key to Discipline
There are several key points about discipline which the supervisor should keep in mind:
1. Job discipline is one of the disciplines of life and is directed by the supervisor.
2. It is more important to correct an employee fault than to fix blame for it.
3. Employee performance is affected by problems both on the job and off.
4. Sudden or abrupt changes in behavior can be indications of important employee problems.
5. Problems should be dealt with as soon as possible after they are identified.
6. The attitude of the supervisor may have more to do with solving problems than the techniques of problem solving.
7. Correction of employee behavior should be resorted to only after the supervisor is sure that training or counseling will not be helpful.

8. Be sure to document your disciplinary actions.
9. Make sure that you are disciplining on the basis of facts rather than personal feelings.
10. Take each disciplinary step in order, being careful not to make snap judgments, or decisions based on impatience.

AA. Five Important Processes of Management
1. Planning
2. Organizing
3. Scheduling
4. Controlling
5. Motivating

BB. When the Supervisor Fails to Plan
1. Supervisor creates impression of not knowing his job
2. May lead to excessive overtime
3. Job runs itself—supervisor lacks control
4. Deadlines and appointments missed
5. Parts of the work go undone
6. Work interrupted by emergencies
7. Sets a bad example
8. Uneven workload creates peaks and valleys
9. Too much time on minor details at expense of more important tasks

CC. Fourteen General Principles of Management
1. Division of work
2. Authority and responsibility
3. Discipline
4. Unity of command
5. Unity of direction
6. Subordination of individual interest to general interest
7. Remuneration of personnel
8. Centralization
9. Scalar chain
10. Order
11. Equity
12. Stability of tenure of personnel
13. Initiative
14. Esprit de corps

DD. Change

Bringing about change is perhaps attempted more often, and yet less well understood, than anything else the supervisor does. How do people generally react to change? (People tend to resist change that is imposed upon them by other individuals or circumstances.

Change is characteristic of every situation. It is a part of every real endeavor where the efforts of people are concerned.

1. Why do people resist change?
   People may resist change because of:
   a. Fear of the unknown
   b. Implied criticism
   c. Unpleasant experiences in the past
   d. Fear of loss of status
   e. Threat to the ego
   f. Fear of loss of economic stability

2. How can we best overcome the resistance to change?
   In initiating change, take these steps:
   a. Get ready to sell
   b. Identify sources of help
   c. Anticipate objections
   d. Sell benefits
   e. Listen in depth
   f. Follow up

II. Brief Topical Summaries

   A. Who/What is the Supervisor?
      1. The supervisor is often called the "highest level employee and the lowest level manager."
      2. A supervisor is a member of both management and the work group. He acts as a bridge between the two.
      3. Most problems in supervision are in the area of human relations, or people problems.
      4. Employees expect: Respect, opportunity to learn and to advance, and a sense of belonging, and so forth.
      5. Supervisors are responsible for directing people and organizing work. Planning is of paramount importance.
      6. A position description is a set of duties and responsibilities inherent to a given position.
      7. It is important to keep the position description up-to-date and to provide each employee with his own copy.

   B. The Sociology of Work
      1. People are alike in many ways; however, each individual is unique.
      2. The supervisor is challenged in getting to know employee differences. Acquiring skills in evaluating individuals is an asset.
      3. Maintaining meaningful working relationships in the organization is of great importance.
      4. The supervisor has an obligation to help individuals to develop to their fullest potential.
      5. Job rotation on a planned basis helps to build versatility and to maintain interest and enthusiasm in work groups.
      6. Cross training (job rotation) provides backup skills.

7. The supervisor can help reduce tension by maintaining a sense of humor, providing guidance to employees, and by making reasonable and timely decisions. Employees respond favorably to working under reasonably predictable circumstances.
8. Change is characteristic of all managerial behavior. The supervisor must adjust to changes in procedures, new methods, technological changes, and to a number of new and sometimes challenging situations.
9. To overcome the natural tendency for people to resist change, the supervisor should become more skillful in initiating change.

C. Principles and Practices of Supervision
1. Employees should be required to answer to only one superior.
2. A supervisor can effectively direct only a limited number of employees, depending upon the complexity, variety, and proximity of the jobs involved.
3. The organizational chart presents the organization in graphic form. It reflects lines of authority and responsibility as well as interrelationships of units within the organization.
4. Distribution of work can be improved through an analysis using the "Work Distribution Chart."
5. The "Work Distribution Chart" reflects the division of work within a unit in understandable form.
6. When related tasks are given to an employee, he has a better chance of increasing his skills through training.
7. The individual who is given the responsibility for tasks must also be given the appropriate authority to insure adequate results.
8. The supervisor should delegate repetitive, routine work. Preparation of recurring reports, maintaining leave and attendance records are some examples.
9. Good discipline is essential to good task performance. Discipline is reflected in the actions of employees on the job in the absence of supervision.
10. Disciplinary action may have to be taken when the positive aspects of discipline have failed. Reprimand, warning, and suspension are examples of disciplinary action.
11. If a situation calls for a reprimand, be sure it is deserved and remember it is to be done in private.

D. Dynamic Leadership
1. A style is a personal method or manner of exerting influence.
2. Authoritarian leaders often see themselves as the source of power and authority.
3. The democratic leader often perceives the group as the source of authority and power.
4. Supervisors tend to do better when using the pattern of leadership that is most natural for them.
5. Social scientists suggest that the effective supervisor use the leadership style that best fits the problem or circumstances involved.
6. All four styles—telling, selling, consulting, joining—have their place. Using one does not preclude using the other at another time.

7. The theory X point of view assumes that the average person dislikes work, will avoid it whenever possible, and must be coerced to achieve organizational objectives.
8. The theory Y point of view assumes that the average person considers work to be a natural as play, and, when the individual is committed, he requires little supervision or direction to accomplish desired objectives.
9. The leader's basic assumptions concerning human behavior and human nature affect his actions, decisions, and other managerial practices.
10. Dissatisfaction among employees is often present, but difficult to isolate. The supervisor should seek to weaken dissatisfaction by keeping promises, being sincere and considerate, keeping employees informed, and so forth.
11. Constructive suggestions should be encouraged during the natural progress of the work.

E. Processes for Solving Problems
1. People find their daily tasks more meaningful and satisfying when they can improve them.
2. The causes of problems, or the key factors, are often hidden in the background. Ability to solve problems often involves the ability to isolate them from their backgrounds. There is some substance to the cliché that some persons "can't see the forest for the trees."
3. New procedures are often developed from old ones. Problems should be broken down into manageable parts. New ideas can be adapted from old one.
4. People think differently in problem-solving situations. Using a logical, patterned approach is often useful. One approach found to be useful includes these steps:
   a. Define the problem
   b. Establish objectives
   c. Get the facts
   d. Weigh and decide
   e. Take action
   f. Evaluate action

F. Training for Results
1. Participants respond best when they feel training is important to them.
2. The supervisor has responsibility for the training and development of those who report to him.
3. When training is delegated to others, great care must be exercised to insure the trainer has knowledge, aptitude, and interest for his work as a trainer.
4. Training (learning) of some type goes on continually. The most successful supervisor makes certain the learning contributes in a productive manner to operational goals.
5. New employees are particularly susceptible to training. Older employees facing new job situations require specific training, as well as having need for development and growth opportunities.
6. Training needs require continuous monitoring.
7. The training officer of an agency is a professional with a responsibility to assist supervisors in solving training problems.

8. Many of the self-development steps important to the supervisor's own growth are equally important to the development of peers and subordinates. Knowledge of these is important when the supervisor consults with others on development and growth opportunities.

G. Health, Safety, and Accident Prevention
1. Management-minded supervisors take appropriate measures to assist employees in maintaining health and in assuring safe practices in the work environment.
2. Effective safety training and practices help to avoid injury and accidents.
3. Safety should be a management goal. All infractions of safety which are observed should be corrected without exception.
4. Employees' safety attitude, training and instruction, provision of safe tools and equipment, supervision, and leadership are considered highly important factors which contribute to safety and which can be influenced directly by supervisors.
5. When accidents do occur, they should be investigated promptly for very important reasons, including the fact that information which is gained can be used to prevent accidents in the future.

H. Equal Employment Opportunity
1. The supervisor should endeavor to treat all employees fairly, without regard to religion, race, sex, or national origin.
2. Groups tend to reflect the attitude of the leader. Prejudice can be detected even in very subtle form. Supervisors must strive to create a feeling of mutual respect and confidence in every employee.
3. Complete utilization of all human resources is a national goal. Equitable consideration should be accorded women in the work force, minority-group members, the physically and mentally handicapped, and the older employee. The important question is: "Who can do the job?"
4. Training opportunities, recognition for performance, overtime assignments, promotional opportunities, and all other personnel actions are to be handled on an equitable basis.

I. Improving Communications
1. Communications is achieving understanding between the sender and the receiver of a message. It also means sharing information—the creation of understanding.
2. Communication is basic to all human activity. Words are means of conveying meanings; however, real meanings are in people.
3. There are very practical differences in the effectiveness of one-way, impersonal, and two-way communications. Words spoken face-to-face are better understood. Telephone conversations are effective, but lack the rapport of person-to-person exchanges. The whole person communicates.
4. Cooperation and communication in an organization go hand in hand. When there is a mutual respect between people, spelling out rules and procedures for communicating is unnecessary.
5. There are several barriers to effective communications. These include failure to listen with respect and understanding, lack of skill in feedback, and misinterpreting the meanings of words used by the speaker. It is also common

practice to listen to what we want to hear, and tune out things we do not want to hear.
6. Communication is management's chief problem. The supervisor should accept the challenge to communicate more effectively and to improve interagency and intra-agency communications.
7. The supervisor may often plan for and conduct meetings. The planning phase is critical and may determine the success or the failure of a meeting.
8. Speaking before groups usually requires extra effort. Stage fright may never disappear completely, but it can be controlled.

J. Self-Development
1. Every employee is responsible for his own self-development.
2. Toastmaster and toastmistress clubs offer opportunities to improve skills in oral communications.
3. Planning for one's own self-development is of vital importance. Supervisors know their own strengths and limitations better than anyone else.
4. Many opportunities are open to aid the supervisor in his developmental efforts, including job assignments; training opportunities, both governmental and non-governmental—to include universities and professional conferences and seminars.
5. Programmed instruction offers a means of studying at one's own rate.
6. Where difficulties may arise from a supervisor's being away from his work for training, he may participate in televised home study or correspondence courses to meet his self-development needs.

K. Teaching and Training
1. The Teaching Process
Teaching is encouraging and guiding the learning activities of students toward established goals. In most cases this process consists of five steps: preparation, presentation, summarization, evaluation, and application.

   a. Preparation
   Preparation is two-fold in nature; that of the supervisor and the employee. Preparation by the supervisor is absolutely essential to success. He must know what, when, where, how, and whom he will teach. Some of the factors that should be considered are:
   1) The objectives
   2) The materials needed
   3) The methods to be used
   4) Employee participation
   5) Employee interest
   6) Training aids
   7) Evaluation
   8) Summarization

   Employee preparation consists in preparing the employee to receive the material. Probably the most important single factor in the preparation of the employee is arousing and maintaining his interest. He must know the objectives of the training, why he is there, how the material can be used, and its importance to him.

b. Presentation
In presentation, have a carefully designed plan and follow it. The plan should be accurate and complete, yet flexible enough to meet situations as they arise. The method of presentation will be determined by the particular situation and objectives.

c. Summary
A summary should be made at the end of every training unit and program. In addition, there may be internal summaries depending on the nature of the material being taught. The important thing is that the trainee must always be able to understand how each part of the new material relates to the whole.

d. Application
The supervisor must arrange work so the employee will be given a chance to apply new knowledge or skills while the material is still clear in his mind and interest is high. The trainee does not really know whether he has learned the material until he has been given a chance to apply it. If the material is not applied, it loses most of its value.

e. Evaluation
The purpose of all training is to promote learning. To determine whether the training has been a success or failure, the supervisor must evaluate this learning.
In the broadest sense, evaluation includes all the devices, methods, skills, and techniques used by the supervisor to keep himself and the employees informed as to their progress toward the objectives they are pursuing. The extent to which the employee has mastered the knowledge, skills, and abilities, or changed his attitudes, as determined by the program objectives, is the extent to which instruction has succeeded or failed.
Evaluation should not be confined to the end of the lesson, day, or program but should be used continuously. We shall note later the way this relates to the rest of the teaching process.

2. Teaching Methods
A teaching method is a pattern of identifiable student and instructor activity used in presenting training material.
All supervisors are faced with the problem of deciding which method should be used at a given time.

a. Lecture
The lecture is direct oral presentation of material by the supervisor. The present trend is to place less emphasis on the trainer's activity and more on that of the trainee.

b. Discussion
Teaching by discussion or conference involves using questions and other techniques to arouse interest and focus attention upon certain areas, and by doing so creating a learning situation. This can be one of the most

valuable methods because it gives the employees an opportunity to express their ideas and pool their knowledge.

c. Demonstration
The demonstration is used to teach how something works or how to do something. It can be used to show a principle or what the results of a series of actions will be. A well-staged demonstration is particularly effective because it shows proper methods of performance in a realistic manner.

d. Performance
Performance is one of the most fundamental of all learning techniques or teaching methods. The trainee may be able to tell how a specific operation should be performed but he cannot be sure he knows how to perform the operation until he has done so.
As with all methods, there are certain advantages and disadvantages to each method.

e. Which Method to Use
Moreover, there are other methods and techniques of teaching. It is difficult to use any method without other methods entering into it. In any learning situation, a combination of methods is usually more effective than any one method alone.

Finally, evaluation must be integrated into the other aspects of the teaching-learning process.

It must be used in the motivation of the trainees; it must be used to assist in developing understanding during the training; and it must be related to employee application of the results of training.

This is distinctly the role of the supervisor.

BASIC FUNDAMENTALS OF BOOKKEEPING

CONTENTS

		Page
I.	INTRODUCTION	1
II.	REQUIREMENTS OF A GOOD RECORD SYSTEM	1
III.	IMPORTANT BOOKKEEPING RECORDS	2
	A. Bookkeeping Books	2
	B. Financial Reports	2
	C. The Balance Sheet	3
	1. Assets	3
	a. Current Assets	4
	b. Fixed Assets	4
	c. Other Assets	5
	2. Liabilities	5
	a. Current Liabilities	5
	b. Long-Term Liabilities	6
	D. The Income Statement	6
	1. Sales	7
	2. Cost of Goods Sold	7
	3. Gross Margin	7
	4. Net Profit	8
IV.	OTHER RECORDS	9
	A. Daily Summary of Sales and Cash Receipts	9
	R. Petty Cash and Charge Funds	10
	C. Record of Cash Disbursement	11
	D. Accounts Receivable Records	12
	E. Property Records and Depreciation	12
	F. Schedule of Insurance Coverage	13
V.	CONCLUSION	13

BASIC FUNDAMENTALS OF BOOKKEEPING

I. INTRODUCTION

Why keep records? If you are a typical small-business man, your answer to this question is probably, "Because the Government requires it!" And if the question comes in the middle of a busy day, you may add a few heartfelt words about the amount of time you have to spend on records--just for the Government.

Is it "just for the Government," though? True, regulations of various governmental agencies have greatly increased the record-keeping requirements of business. But this may be a good thing for the small-business man, overburdened though he is.

Many small-business managers don't recognize their bookkeeping records for what they can really do. Their attitudes concerning these records are typified by one businessman who said, "Records only tell you what you have done in the past. It's too late to do anything about the past; I need to know what is going to happen in the future. "However, the past can tell us much about what may happen in the future; and, certainly we can profit in the future from knowledge of our past mistakes.

These same managers may recognize that records are necessary in filing their tax returns, or that a banker requires financial information before he will lend money, but often their appreciation of their bookkeeping systems ends at this point. However, there are many ways in which the use of such information can help an owner manage his business more easily and profitably.

The small-businessman is confronted with an endless array of problems and decisions every day. Sound decisions require an informed manager; and many management problems can be solved with the aid of the right bookkeeping information.

II. REQUIREMENTS OF A GOOD RECORD SYSTEM

Of course, to get information that is really valuable to you--to get the right information--requires a good bookkeeping system. What are the characteristics of a good system? You want one that is simple and easy to understand, reliable, accurate, consistent, and one that will get the information to you promptly.

A simple, well-organized system of records, regularly kept up, can actually be a timesaver--by bringing order out of disorder. Furthermore, competition is very strong in today's business areas. A businessman needs to know almost on a day-to-day basis where his business stands profit wise, which lines of merchandise or services are the most or the least profitable, what his working-capital needs are, and many other details. He can get this information with reasonable certainty only if he has a good recordkeeping system—one that gives him all the information he needs.

In setting up a recordkeeping system that is tailored to your business, you will probably need the professional help of a competent accountant. And you may want to retain the services of an accountant or bookkeeper to maintain these records. But it is your job to learn to interpret this information and to use it effectively.

One of the reasons that many managers have misgivings about keeping records is that they don't understand them or know how they can be used. The owner or manager of a small business may be an expert in his line of business; however, he generally does not have a background in keeping records. So he is usually confused. What we will try to do in this discussion is to highlight the "why and what of bookkeeping." In so-doing, we aim to eliminate that confusion.

III. IMPORTANT BOOKKEEPING RECORDS

Today's managers should be familiar with the following bookkeeping records:

- Journal
- Ledgers
- Balance sheet
- Income statement
- Funds flow statement

We will discuss each of them in turn. In addition, a brief discussion of other supporting records will be made.

A. Bookkeeping Books

The journal, which accountants call "the book of original entry," is a chronological record of all business transactions engaged in by the firm. It is simply a financial diary. The ledgers, or "books of account," are more specialized records used to classify the journal entries according to like elements. For example, there would be a separate ledger account for cash entries, another for all sales, and still others for items such as accounts receivable, inventory, and loans. All transactions are first entered in the journal, and then posted in the appropriate ledger. The journal and ledgers are of minor importance to the manager in making decisions, but they play a vital role for the accountant or bookkeeper because the more important accounting statements such as the balance sheet and the income statement are derived from the journal and ledger entries.

B. Financial Reports

The two principal financial reports in most businesses are the balance sheet and the income statement. Up to about 25 or 30 years ago, the balance sheet was generally considered to be the most important financial statement. Until that time, it was generally used only as a basis for the extension of credit and bank loans, and very little thought was given to the information it offered that might be important in „the operation and management of the business. Starting about 30 years ago, emphasis has gradually shifted to the income statement. Today the balance sheet and income statements are of equal importance, both to the accountant in financial reporting and to the manager faced with a multitude of administrative problems.

Essentially, the balance sheet shows what a business has, what it owes, and the investment of the owners in the business. It can be likened to a snapshot, showing the financial condition of the business *at a certain point in time*. The income statement, on the other hand, is a summary of business operations for a certain period--usually between two balance sheet dates. The income statement can be compared to a moving picture; it indicates the activity of a business *over a certain period of time*. In very general terms, the balance sheet tells you where you are, and the income statement tells you how you got there since the last time you had a balance sheet prepared.

Both the balance sheet and income statement can be long and complicated documents. Both accountants and management need some device that can highlight the critical financial information contained in these complex documents. Certain standard ratios or relationships between items on the financial statements have been developed that allow the interested parties to quickly determine important characteristics of the firm's activities. There are many relationships that might be important in a specific business that would not be as significant in another.

Other devices of the bookkeeper, such as funds flow statements, daily summaries of sales and cash receipts, the checkbook, account receivable records, property depreciation records, and insurance scheduling have also been found useful to management.

C. The Balance Sheet

As stated earlier, the balance sheet represents what a business has, what it owes, and the investment of the owners. The things of value that the business has or owns are called *assets*. The claims of creditors against these assets are called liabilities. The value of the assets over and above the *liabilities* can be justifiably called the owner's claim. This amount is usually called the owner's equity (or net worth).

This brings us to the *dual-aspect concept* of bookkeeping. The balance sheet is set up to portray two aspects of each entry or event recorded on it. For each thing of value, or asset, there is a claim against that asset. The recognition of this concept leads to the balance sheet formula: ASSETS = LIABILITIES + OWNER'S EQUITY. Let's take an example to clarify this concept. Suppose Joe Smith decides to start a business. He has $2,000 cash in the bank. He got this sum by investing $1,000 of his own money and by borrowing $1,000 from the bank. If he were to draw up a balance sheet at this time, he would have assets of $2 000 cash balanced against a liability claim of $1,000 and an owner's claim of $1,000. Using the balance sheet formula: $2,000 = $1,000 + $1,000. This formula means there will always be a balance between assets and claims against them. The balance sheet *always* balances unless there has been a clerical error.

The balance sheet is usually, constructed in a two-column format. The assets appear in the left hand column and the claims against the assets (the liabilities and owner's equity) are in the right hand column. Other formats are sometimes used; but, in any case, the balance sheet is-an itemized or detailed account of the basic formula: as sets = liabilities + owner's equity.

1. Assets

I have been speaking of assets belonging to the business. Of course, the business does not legally own anything unless it is organized as a corporation. But regardless of whether the business is organized as a proprietorship, a partnership, or a corporation, all business bookkeeping should be reckoned and accounted apart from the accounting of the personal funds and assets of, its owners.

Assets are typically classified into three categories:

- Current assets
- Fixed assets
- Other assets

a. Current Assets

For bookkeeping purposes, the term "current assets" is used to designate cash and other assets which can be converted to cash during the normal operating cycle of the business (usually one year). The distinction between current assets and noncurrent assets is important since lenders and others pay much attention to the total amount of current assets. The size of current assets has a significant relationship to the stability of the business because it represents, to some degree, the amount of cash that might be raised quickly to meet current obligations. Here are some of the major current asset items.

Cash consists of funds that are immediately available to use without restrictions. These funds are usually in the form of checking-account deposits in banks, cash-register money, and petty cash. Cash should be large enough to meet obligations that are immediately due.

Accounts, receivable are Arricnint8 'Owed to the company by its customers as a result of sales. Essentially, these accounts are the result of granting credit to customers. They may take the form of charge accounts where no interest or service charge is made, or they may be of an interest-bearing nature. In either case they are a drain on working capital. The more that is outstanding on accounts receivable, the less money that is available to meet current needs. The trick with accounts receivable is to keep them small enough so as not to endanger working capital, but large enough to keep from losing sales to credit-minded customers.

Inventory is defined as those items which are held for sale in the ordinary course of business, or which are to be consumed in the production of goods and services that are to be sold. Since accountants are conservative by nature, they include in inventory only items that are salable, and these items are valued at cost or market value, whichever is lower? Control of inventory and inventory expenses is one of management's most important jobs-particularly for retailers-- and good bookkeeping records in this area are particularly useful.

Prepaid expenses represent assets, paid for in advance, but whose usefulness will usually expire in a short time. A good example of this is prepaid insurance. A business pays for insurance protection in advance--usually three to five years in advance. The right to this protection is a thing of value--an asset--and the unused portion can be refunded or converted to cash.

b. Fixed Assets

"Fixed assets" are items owned by the business that have relatively long life. These assets are used in the production or sale of other goods and services. If they were held for resale, they would be classified as inventory, even though they might be long-lived assets.

Normally these assets are composed of land, buildings, and equipment. Some companies lump their fixed assets into one entry on their balance sheets, but you gain more information and can exercise more control over these assets if they are listed separately on the balance sheet. You may even want to list various types of equipment separately.

There is one other aspect of fixed-asset bookkeeping that we should discuss--and this is depreciation. Generally fixed assets-with the exception of land-depreciate, or decrease in value with the passing of time. That is, a building or piece of equipment that is five years old is not worth as much as it was when it was new. For a balance sheet to show the true value of these assets, it must reflect this loss in value. For both tax and other accounting purposes, the businessman is allowed to deduct this loss in value each year over the useful life of the assets, until, over a period of time, he has deducted the total cost of the asset. There are several accepted ways to calculate how much of an asset's value can be deducted for depreciation in a given year. Depreciation is allowed as an expense item on the income statement, and we will discuss this fact later.

c. Other Assets

"Other assets" is a miscellaneous category. It accounts for any investments of the firm in securities, such as stock in other private companies or government bonds. It also includes intangible assets such as goodwill, patents, and franchise costs. Items in the "other-assets" category have a longer life than current-asset items.

2. Liabilities

"Liabilities" are the amounts of money owed by the business to people other than the owners. They are claims against the company's total assets, although they are not claims against any specific asset, except in the cases of some mortgages and equipment liens. Essentially, liabilities are divided into two classes:

Current liabilities

Long-term Liabilities

a. Current Liabilities

The term "current liabilities" is used to describe those claims of outsiders on the business that will fall, due within one year. Here are some of the more important current-liabilities entries on the balance sheet:

Accounts payable represent the amounts owed to vendors, wholesalers, and other suppliers from whom the business has bought items on account. This includes any items of inventory, supply, or capital equipment which have been purchased on credit and for which payment is expected in less than one year. For example, a retail butcher purchased 500 pounds of meat for $250, a quantity of fish that cost $50, and a new air-conditioning unit for his store for $450. He bought all of these items on 60-day terms. His accounts payable were increased by $750. Of course, at the same time his inventory increased by $300 and his fixed assets rose by $450. If he had paid cash for these items, his accounts payable would not have been affected, but his cash account would have decreased by $750, thus keeping the accounting equation in balance.

Short-term loans, which are sometimes called notes payable, are loans from individuals, banks, or other lending institutions which fall due within a year. Also included in this category is the portion of any long-term debt that will come due within a year.

Accrued expenses are obligations which the company has incurred, but for which there has been no formal bill or invoice as yet. An example of this is accrued taxes. The owner knows the business has the obligation to pay taxes; and they are accruing or accumulating each day. The fact that the taxes do not have to be paid until a later date does not diminish the obligation. Another example of accrued expenses is wages. Although wages are paid weekly or monthly, they are being earned hourly or daily and constitute a valid claim against the company. An accurate balance sheet will reflect these obligations.

b. Long-Term Liabilities

Claims of outsiders on the business that do not come due within one year are called "long-term liabilities" or, simply, "other liabilities." Included in this category are bonded indebtedness, mortgages, and long-term loans from individuals, banks, and others from whom the business may borrow money, such as the SBA. As was stated before, any part of a long-term debt that falls due within one year from the date of the balance sheet would be recorded as part of the current liabilities of the business.

Owner's Equity

The owner's equity section of the balance sheet is located on the right-hand side underneath the listing of the liabilities. It shows the claims of the owners on the company. Essentially, this is a balancing figure--that is, the owners get what's left of the assets after the liability claims have been recognized. This is an obvious definition, if you will remember the balance sheet formula. Transposing the formula as we learned it a few minutes ago, it becomes Assets - Liabilities = Owner's Equity. In the case where the business is a sole proprietorship, it is customary to show owner's equity as one entry with no distinction being made between the owner's initial investment and the accumulated retained earnings of the business. However, in the case of an incorporated business, there are entries for stockholders' claims as well as for earnings that have been accumulated and retained in the business. Of course, if the business has been consistently operating at a loss, the proprietor's claim may be less than his initial investment. And, in the case of a corporation, the balancing account could be operating deficit rather than retained earnings.

If we put together the entries we have been talking about, we have a complete balance sheet. There is a lot of information in this statement. It tells you just what you have and where it is. It also tells you what you owe. You need this information to help you decide what actions you should take in running your business. If you need to borrow money, the banker or anyone else from whom you borrow will want to look at your balance sheet.

D. THE INCOME STATEMENT

In recent years the income statement has become as important as the balance sheet as a financial and management record. It is also called the profit and loss statement, or simply the P and L statement. This financial record summarizes the activities of the company over a period of time, listing those that can be expressed in dollars. That is, it reports the revenues of the company and the expenses incurred in obtaining the revenues, and it shows the profit or loss resulting from these activities. The income statement complements the balance sheet. While balance sheet analysis shows the change in position of the company at the end of accounting periods, the income statement shows how the change took place during the accounting period. Both reports 'are necessary for a full understanding of the operation of the business.

The income statement for particular company should be tailored to fit the activities of that company, and there is no rigid format that must be followed in constructing this report. But the following categories are found in most income statements.

1. Sales

The major activity of most businesses is the sales of products and services, and the bulk of revenue comes from sales. In recording sales, the figure used is net sales-that is, sales after discounts, allowances, and returned goods have been accounted for.

2. Cost of Goods Sold

Another important item, in calculating profit or loss, is the cost of the goods that the company has sold. This item is difficult to calculate accurately. Since the goods sold come from inventory, and since the company may have bought parts of its inventory at several prices, it is hard to determine exactly what is the cost of the particular part of the inventory that was sold. In large companies, and particularly in companies using cost accounting, there are some rather complicated methods of determining "cost of goods sold, " but they are beyond the scope of this presentation. However, there is a simple, generally accepted way of calculating cost of goods sold. In this method you simply add the net amount of purchases during the accounting period to your beginning inventory, and subtract from this your ending inventory. The result can be considered cost-of-goods sold.

3. Gross Margin

The difference between sales and cost of goods sold is called the "gross margin" or gross profit. This item is often expressed as a percentage of sales, as well as in dollar figures. The percentage gross margin is a very significant figure because it indicates what the average markup is on the merchandise sold. So, if a manager knows his expenses as a percentage of sales, he can calculate the mark up necessary to obtain the gross margin he needs for a profitable operation. It is surprising how many small-business men do not know what basis to use in setting markups. In fact, with the various, allowances, discounts, and markdowns that a business may offer, many managers do not know what their markup actually is. The gross margin calculation on the income statement can help the manager with this problem.

There are other costs of running a business besides the cost of the goods sold. When you use the simple method of determining costs of goods sold, these costs are called "expenses."

For example, here are some typical expenses: salaries and wages, utilities, depreciation, interest, administrative expenses, supplies, bad debts, advertising, and taxes--Federal, State, and local. These are typical expenses, but there are many other kinds of expenses that may be experienced by other businesses. For example, we have shown in the Blank Company's balance sheet that he owns his own land and building--with a mortgage, of course. These accounts for part of his depreciation and interest expenses, but for a company that rents its quarters, rent would appear as the expense item. Other common expenses are traveling expense, commissions, and advertising.

Most of these expense items are self-explanatory, but there are a few that merit further comment. For one thing, the salary or draw of the owner should be recorded among the expenses--either as a part of salaries and wages or as part of administrative expenses. To exclude the owner's compensation from expenses distorts the actual profitability of the business. And, if the company is incorporated, it would reduce the allowable tax deductions of the business. Of course, for tax purposes, the owner's salary or draw in a proprietorship or partnership is considered as part of the net profit.

We discussed depreciation when we examined the balance sheet, and we mentioned that it was an item of expense. Although no money is actually paid out for depreciation, it is a real expense because it represents reduction in the value of the assets.

The most important thing about expenses is to be sure to include all of the expenses that the business incurs. This not only helps the owner get a more accurate picture of his operation but it allows him to take full advantage of the tax deductions that legitimate expenses offer.

4. Net Profit

In a typical company when expenses are subtracted from gross margin, the remainder is profit. However, if the business receives revenue from sources other than sales, such as rents, dividends on securities held by the company, or interest on money loaned by the company, it is added to profit at this point. For bookkeeping purposes, the resulting profit is labeled "profit before taxes." This is the figure from which Federal income taxes are figured. If the business is a proprietorship, the profit is taxed as part of the owner's income. If the business is a corporation, the profits may be taxed on the basis of the corporate income tax schedule. When income taxes have been accounted for, the resultant entry is called "net profit after taxes," or simply "net profit." This is usually the final entry on the income statement.

Another financial record which managers can use to advantage is the funds flow statement. This statement is also called statement of sources and uses of funds and sometimes the "where got--where gone" statement. Whatever you call it, a record of sources and uses of past funds is useful to the manager. He can use it to evaluate past performance, and as a guide in determining future uses and sources of money.

When we speak of "funds" we do not necessarily mean actual "dollars" or "cash." Although accounting records are all written in monetary terms, they do not always involve an exchange of money. Many times in business transactions, it is credit rather than dollars that changes hands. Therefore, when we speak of funds flow, we are speaking of exchanges of *economic values* rather than merely the physical flow of dollars.

Basically, funds are used to: increase assets and reduce liabilities. They are also sometimes used to reduce owner's equity. An example of this would be the use of company funds to buy up outstanding stock or to buy out a partner. Where do funds come from? The three basic sources of funds are a reduction in assets, increases in liabilities, and increased owner's equity. All balance sheet items can be affected by the obtaining and spending of company fund's.

To examine the construction and use of a funds flow statement, let's take another look at the Blank Company. Here we show comparative balance sheets for two one-year periods. For the sake of simplicity, we have included only selected items from the balance sheets for analysis. Notice that the company gained funds by:

reducing cash $300,

increasing accounts payable $400,

putting $500 more owner's equity in the business, and

plowing back $800 of the profit into the business.

These funds were used to:

increase accounts receivable $300,
increase inventory $200,

buy $500 worth of equipment, and

pay off $1,000 worth of long-term debt.

This funds flow statement has indicated to Mr. Blank where he has gotten his funds and how he has spent them. He can analyze these figures in the light of his plans and objectives and take appropriate action.

For example, if Mr. Blank wants to answer the question "Should I buy new capital equipment?" a look at his funds flow statement would show him his previous sources of funds, and it would give him a clue as to whether he could obtain funds for any new equipment.

I V. OTHER RECORDS

Up to this point, we have been talking about the basic types of bookkeeping records. In addition, we have discussed the two basic financial statements of a business: the balance sheet and the profit and loss statement. Now let us give our attention briefly to some other records which are very helpful to running a business successfully.

One element that appears on the balance sheet which I believe we can agree is important is cash. Because it is the lifeblood of all business, cash should be controlled and safe-guarded at all times. The daily summary of sales and cash receipts and the checkbook are used by many manager s of small businesses to help provide that control.

A. Daily Summary of Sales and Cash. Receipts

Not all businesses summarize their daily transactions. However, a daily summary of sales and cash receipts is a very useful tool for checking how your business is doing on a day-to-day basis. At the close of each day's business, the actual cash on hand is counted and "balanced" against the total of the receipts recorded for the day. This balancing is done by means of the Daily Summary of Sales and Cash Receipts. This is a recording of every cash 'receipt and every charge sale, whether you use a cash register or sales checks or both. If you have more than one cash register, a daily summary should be prepared for each; the individual cash-register summaries can then be combined into one overall summary for convenience in handling.

In the daily summary form used for purposes of illustration, (see Handout), the first section, "Cash Receipts," records the total of all cash taken in during the day from whatever source. This is the cash that must be accounted for over and above, the amount in the change and/ or petty cash funds. We shall touch upon these two funds later. The three components of cash receipts are (1) cash sales, (2) collections on accounts, and (3) miscellaneous receipts.

The daily total of cash sales is obtained from a cash-register tape reading or, if no cash register is used, by totaling the cash-sales checks.

For collections on accounts, an individual record of each customer payment on account should be kept, whether or not these collections are rung up on a cash register. The amount to be entered on the daily summary is obtained by totaling these individual records.

Miscellaneous receipts are daily cash transactions that cannot be classified as sales or collections. They might include refunds from suppliers for overpayment, advertising rebates or allowances, . collections of rent from sub-leases or concessions, etc. Like collections on account, a sales check or memo should be made out each time such cash is taken in.

The total of daily cash receipts to be accounted for on the daily summary is obtained by adding cash sales, collections on account, and miscellaneous receipts.

The second section, "Cash on Hand," of a daily summary is a count of the cash actually on hand plus the cash that is represented by petty cash slips. The daily summary provides for counts of your total coins, bills, and checks as well as the amount expended for petty cash. The latter is determined by adding the amounts on the individual petty cash slips. By totaling all four of these counts, you obtain the total cash accounted for. To determine the amount of your daily cash deposit, you deduct from the "total cash accounted for" the total of the petty cash and change funds.

Cash to be deposited on the daily summary should always equal the total receipts to be accounted for minus the fixed amount of your petty cash and change funds. If it does not, all the work in preparing the daily summary should be carefully checked. Obviously, an error in giving change, in ringing up a sale, or neglecting to do so, will result in a cash shortage or overage. The daily summary provides spaces for such errors so that the proper entries can be made in your bookkeeping records. The last section of your daily summary, "Sales," records the total daily sales broken down into (1) cash sales and (2) charge sales.

As soon as possible after the daily summary has been completed, all cash for deposit should be taken to the bank. A duplicate deposit slip, stamped by the bank, should be kept with the daily summary as evidence that the deposit was made.

B. Petty Cash and Charge Funds

The record of, daily, sales and cash. Receipts which we have just described. is designed. on the assumption that a petty cash fund and a change cash fund, or a combination change and petty cash fund, are used. All businesses, small and large, have day-to-day expenses that are so small they do not warrant the drawing of a check. Good management practice calls for careful control of such expenses. The petty cash fund provides such control. It is a sum of money which is obtained by drawing a check to provide several days, a week's, or a month's need of cash for small purchases. The type of business will determine the amount of the petty cash fund.

Each time a payment is made from the petty cash, a slip should be made out. If an invoice or receipt is available, it should be attached to the petty-cash slip. The slips and the money ordinarily, but not necessarily, are kept separate from other currency in your cash till, drawer, or register. At all times, the total of unspent petty cash and petty cash slips should equal the fixed amount of the fund. When the total of the slips approaches the fixed amount of the petty cash fund, a check is drawn for the total amount of the slips. The money from this check is used to bring the fund back to its fixed amount.

In addition to a petty cash fund, some businesses that receive cash in over-the-counter transactions have a change fund. The amount needed for making change varies with the size and type of business, and, in some cases, with the days of the week. Control of the money in your change fund will be made-easier, however, if you set a fixed amount large enough to meet all the ordinary change-making needs of your business. Each day, when the day's receipts are balanced and prepared for a bank deposit, you will retain bills and coins totaling the fixed amount of the fund for use the following day. Since you had that amount on hand before you made the day's first sale, the entire amount of the day's receipts will still be available for your bank deposit.

In some cases, the petty cash fund is kept in a petty cash box or safe, apart from the change fund. However, the same fund can serve for both petty cash and change. For example, if you decide that you need $50 for making change and $25 for petty cash, one $75 fund can be used. Whenever, in balancing the day's operations, you see that the petty cash slips total more than $25, you can write a petty cash check for the amount of the slips.

C. Record of Cash Disbursement

To safeguard your cash, it is recommended that all receipts be deposited in a bank account and that all disbursements, except those made from the petty cash fund, are made by drawing a check on that account. Your bank account should be used exclusively for business transactions. If your business is typical, you will have to write checks for merchandise purchases, employee's salaries, rent, utilities, payroll taxes, petty cash, and various other expenses. Your check stubs will serve as a record of cash disbursements.

The checkbook stub should contain all the details of the disbursement including the date, payee, amount and purpose of the payment. In addition, a running balance of the amount you have in your bank account should be maintained by subtracting the amount of each check from the existing balance after the previous check was drawn. If the checks of your checkbook are prenumbered, it is important to mark plainly in the stub when a check is voided for one reason or another.

Each check should have some sort of written document to support it--an invoice, petty-cash voucher, payroll summary and so on. Supporting documents should be approved by you or someone you have authorized before a check is drawn. They should be marked paid and filed after the check is drawn.

Periodically, your bank will send you a statement of your account and return cancelled checks for which money has been withdrawn from your account. It is important that you reconcile your records with those of the bank. This means that the balances in your checkbook and on the bank statement should agree. Uncashed checks must be deducted from your checkbook balance and deposits not recorded on the bank statement must be added to its balance in order to get both balances to agree.

D . Accounts Receivable Records

If you extend credit to your customers, you must keep an accurate account of your credit sales not only in total as you have done on the daily summary but also by the amount that each individual customer owes you. Moreover, you must be systematic about billings and collections. This is important. It results in better relations with your charge customers and in fewer losses from bad debts.

The simplest method of handling accounts receivable--other than just keeping a file of sales-slip carbons--is to have an account sheet for each credit customer. Charge sales and payments on charge sales are posted to each customer sheet. Monthly billing to each of your charge customers should be made from their individual account sheets.

At least two or three times a year, your accounts receivable should be aged. You do this by posting each customer's account and his unpaid charges in columns according to age. These columns are labeled: not due; 1 to 30 days past due; 31 to 60 days past due; 61 to 90 days past due; etc. This analysis will indicate those customers who are not complying with your credit terms.

E . Property Records and Depreciation

In every type of business, it is necessary to purchase property and equipment from time to time. This property usually will last for several years, so it would be unrealistic to show the total amount of the purchase as an expense in any one year. Therefore, when this property is set up in the books as an asset, records must be kept to decrease its value over its life. This decrease is known as depreciation. I have mentioned this before during this talk. The amount of the decrease in value in one year, that is, the depreciation, is charged as an expense for the year.

I am talking about this expense, particularly, because no cash is paid out for it. It is a non-cash, not-out-of-pocket expense. You don't have to hand over actual money at the end of the month.

Records should be kept of this because, otherwise, there is a danger that this expense will be overlooked. Yet it is impossible to figure true profit or loss without considering it. When you deduct the depreciation expense from your firm's income, you reduce your tax liabilities. When you put this depreciation expense into a depreciation allowance account, you are keeping score on your "debt" to depreciation.

In a barber shop, to take a simple example, depreciation of its chairs, dryers, and clippers at the end of the year amounts to $136. You deduct this $136 from the shop's income, in this case, to pay the debt credited to your depreciation allowance account. Since this equipment has the same depreciation value each year, the depreciation allowance account at the end of 3 years will show that a total of $408 worth of equipment has been used up. The books of the barbershop therefore show an expense of $408 which actually has not been spent. It is in the business to replace the depreciated equipment. If replacement will not take place in the immediate future, the money can be used in inventory, or in some other way to generate more sales or profits.

How you handle this money depends on many things. You can set it aside at a low interest rate and have that much less operating money. Or you can put it to work in your business where it will help to keep your finances healthy.

Remember, however, that you must be prepared financially when it is time to buy replacement equipment. A depreciation allowance account on your books can help to keep you aware of this. It helps you keep score on how much depreciation or replacement money you are using in your business.

Keeping score with a depreciation allowance account helps you to know when you need to convert some of your assets into replacement cash. If, for example, you know on January 1 that Your delivery truck will be totally depreciated by June 30, you can review the situation objectively. You can decide whether you ought to use the truck longer or replace it. If you decide to replace it, then you can plan to accumulate the cash, and time the purchase in order to make the best deal.

F. Schedule of Insurance Coverage

The schedule of insurance coverage is prepared to indicate the type of coverage and the amount presently in force. This schedule should list all the insurance carried by your business-- fire and extended coverage, theft, liability, life, business interruption and so forth.

This schedule should be prepared to present the following: name of insurance company, annual premium, expiration date, type of coverage, amount of coverage, asset insured, and estimated current value of asset insured.

An analysis of this schedule should indicate the adequacy of insurance coverage.
A review of this schedule with your insurance agent is suggested.

V. CONCLUSION

During the brief time allotted to this subject of the basic fundamentals of bookkeeping, we have just scratched its surface. What we have tried to do is to inform you, as small-business managers, of the importance of good records. We have described the components of the important records that you must have if you are going to manage your business efficiently and profitably. In addition, we have brought to your attention some of the subsidiary records that will aid you in managing your business.

There are other records such as breakeven charts, budgets, cost accounting systems, to mention a few, which can also benefit the progressive manager. However, we do not have the time even to give you the highlights of those management tools. Your accountant can assist you in learning to understand and use them. Moreover, he can help you to develop and use the records we have discussed. For further information about them, you also can read the publications of the Small Business Administration, some of which are available to you free of charge.

By reading and using the accounting advice available to you, you can make sure that you have the right records to improve your managing skill and thereby increase your profits.

www.ingramcontent.com/pod-product-compliance
Lightning Source LLC
Chambersburg PA
CBHW082034300426
44117CB00015B/2473